T0282751

WOMEN'S STUDIES QUARTERLY

VOLUME 51   NUMBERS 3 & 4   FALL/WINTER 2023

An educational project of the Feminist Press at the City University of New York, the College of Staten Island, City University of New York, and Queens College, City University of New York, with support from the Center for the Study of Women and Society and the Center for the Humanities at the Graduate Center, City University of New York

EDITORS
Shereen Inayatulla, York College, City University of New York
Andie Silva, York College, City University of New York

EDITORIAL DIRECTORS
Dána-Ain Davis and Kendra Sullivan

GUEST EDITORS
Red Washburn, Queens College and the Graduate Center, City University of New York
JV Fuqua, Queens College, City University of New York

POETRY EDITORS
Cheryl Clarke
JP Howard
Julie R. Enszer

CREATIVE PROSE EDITORS
Keisha-Gaye Anderson
Lauren Cherelle
Vi Khi Nao

VISUAL ARTS EDITOR
Maya von Ziegesar

EDITORIAL ASSISTANTS
Googie Karrass
Maya von Ziegesar

EDITORIAL INTERN
Angela Boscarino

SOCIAL MEDIA & EVENTS MANAGER
Juwon Jun

EDITORS EMERITAE
Brianne Waychoff 2020–2022 ▪ Natalie Havlin 2017–2020
Jillian M. Báez 2017–2020 ▪ Matt Brim 2014–2017 ▪ Cynthia Chris 2014–2017
Amy Herzog 2011–2014 ▪ Joe Rollins 2011–2014 ▪ Victoria Pitts-Taylor 2008–2011
Talia Schaffer 2008–2011 ▪ Cindi Katz 2004–2008 ▪ Nancy K. Miller 2004–2008
Diane Hope 2000–2004 ▪ Janet Zandy 1995–2000 ▪ Nancy Porter 1982–1992
Florence Howe 1972–1982; 1993–1994

The Feminist Press at the City University of New York

EXECUTIVE DIRECTOR & PUBLISHER
Margot Atwell

EDITORIAL DIRECTOR
Lauren Rosemary Hook

ART DIRECTOR
Drew Stevens

DEVELOPMENT COORDINATOR & PRODUCTION EDITOR
Rachel Page

WSQ: Women's Studies Quarterly, a peer-reviewed, theme-based journal, is published by the Feminist Press at the City University of New York.

COVER ART
Self-portrait by Brianne Waychoff

WEBSITE
feministpress.org/wsq
womensstudiesquarterly.com

EDITORIAL CORRESPONDENCE
WSQ: Women's Studies Quarterly, The Feminist Press at the City University of New York, The Graduate Center, 365 Fifth Avenue, Suite 5406, New York, NY 10016; wsqeditorial@gmail.com and wsqeditors@gmail.com.

PRINT SUBSCRIPTIONS
Subscribers in the United States: Individuals—$60 for 1 year; $150 for 3 years. Institutions—$85 for 1 year; $225 for 3 years. Subscribers outside the United States: Add $40 per year for delivery. To subscribe or change an address, contact *WSQ* Customer Service, The Feminist Press at the City University of New York, The Graduate Center, 365 Fifth Avenue, Suite 5406, New York, NY 10016; 212-817-7915; info@feministpress.org.

FORTHCOMING ISSUES
WSQ Pandemonium, Tracey Jean Boisseau, Purdue University, Adrianna L. Ernstberger, Marian University
WSQ Unbearable Being(s), Debarati Biswas, New York City College of Technology, Laura Westengard, New York City College of Technology

RIGHTS & PERMISSIONS
Fred Courtright, The Permissions Company, 570-839-7477; permdude@eclipse.net.

SUBMISSION INFORMATION
For the most up-to-date guidelines, calls for papers, and information concerning forthcoming issues, write to wsqeditors@gmail.com or visit feministpress.org/wsq or womensstudiesquarterly.com.

ADVERTISING
For information on display-ad sizes, rates, exchanges, and schedules, please write to *WSQ* Marketing, The Feminist Press at the City University of New York, The Graduate Center, 365 Fifth Avenue, Suite 5406, New York, NY 10016; 212-817-7918; sales@feministpress.org.

ELECTRONIC ACCESS AND SUBSCRIPTIONS
Access to electronic databases containing backlist issues of *WSQ* may be purchased through JSTOR at www.jstor.org. Access to electronic databases containing current issues of *WSQ* may be purchased through Project MUSE at muse.jhu.edu, muse@muse.jhu.edu; and ProQuest at www.il.proquest.com, info@il.proquest.com. Individual electronic subscriptions for *WSQ* may also be purchased through Project MUSE.

ISSN: 0732-1562   ISBN: 978-1-55861-184-9 $25.00

L. Ayu Saraswati, University of Hawaiʻi
Gunja SenGupta, Brooklyn College
Barbara Shaw, Allegheny College
Lili Shi, Kingsborough Community College
Robyn Spencer, Lehman College
Saadia Toor, College of Staten Island
Laura Westengard, New York City College of Technology, CUNY
Kimberly Williams, Mount Royal University
Kimberly Williams Brown, Vassar College

Contents

6 Contents

Dedication to Brianne Waychoff

Brianne always showed up. They supported me as a colleague when I took my first adjunct position at Bronx Community College. They invited me to present alongside them on a panel about feminist activism when I was just starting out in graduate school. They cosplayed Billy Hoyle (from *White Men Can't Jump*) at a Halloween party I threw in the Bronx. Brianne was a genuine spirit who cared about building community, laughing, and making a path for others along the way. Thank you, Brianne, for being a friend, mentor, and a kick-ass Billy Hoyle! Rest easy.

Editors' Note

Shereen Inayatulla and Andie Silva

We are delighted to witness the publication of this special issue, *Nonbinary*, at the beginning of our term as *WSQ* general editors. The urgency and timeliness of this issue cannot be overstated. We are living in a moment of deep polarization, distrust, and grief; every day we experience deliberate attacks and laws against trans, nonbinary, and LGBTQIA+ communities, and must re-energize our fight against oppression by building coalitions. At the same time, we observe a flourishing of identities and the rise of generations committed to self-expression beyond binaries. This special issue emerges from these material conditions and offers paths to engage with, apply, and celebrate nonbinary plurality without reifying a monolithic experience limited to one single concern.

We want to thank all of the contributors whose capacious definitions of and approaches to nonbinary experiences showcase the intellectual, educational, artistic, and personal benefits to thinking and thriving outside rigid binary structures. As the contributions in this volume attest, nonbinary thinking can invite us to not only challenge polarization but also find moments of community and make space for hope and joy. Nonbinary perspectives encourage us to push back against an either/or framework; against borders used to police land, bodies, and scholarly disciplines; and against settler-colonial violences that impose a false sense of normativity that is weaponized to uphold dominant power structures. As Marquis Bey brilliantly explores in this issue's Alerts and Provocations section, nonbinary is also *not neutral*: nonbinary resists pressures to choose between oppressive modes of being and refuses the imposition of gender as a static category that must shape one's life.

WSQ: Women's Studies Quarterly 51: 3 & 4 (Fall/Winter 2023) © 2023 by Shereen Inayatulla and Andie Silva.

It is thrilling to observe how the pieces included in this special issue, chosen long before our term began, connect with our vision as coeditors: to amplify the work of practitioners at the helm of gender justice movements and centralize those who are queer, trans, nonbinary, disabled, Black, Indigenous, and people of color. The contributions here exemplify the ways scholarship can embrace multiplicity and reject historically sanctioned divisions between so-called academic and popular genres, conventions, or forms of expression. The deliberate mingling of articles, art, poetry, presentations, and the like offers a richer, more layered conversation.

A million thanks to the guest editors of *Nonbinary*, Red Washburn and JV Fuqua, for their care and dedication in ushering this issue into existence. Their efforts in preparing and editing this issue are immeasurable. Profound gratitude to the team of creative editors, whose attentiveness to the poetry, prose, and visual art bring depth and dimensionality to this issue. We are grateful to the Feminist Press for oversight on the production and distribution of this journal, especially editorial director Lauren Rosemary Hook, executive director Margot Atwell, and production editor Rachel Page. Although our paths crossed only briefly, we thank outgoing assistant editor Nick Whitney and wish Nick the best in an exciting career opportunity ahead. We are looking forward to working with the *WSQ* editorial board to continue this journal's legacy and gather new perspectives that can enrich future issues.

As new members of the *WSQ* editorial team, we are brimming with gratitude for Red Washburn's guidance through our onboarding process. Red and Brianne's editorial vision, labor, and leadership have left a transformational imprint upon *WSQ*—one that we humbly endeavor to sustain during our term as coeditors. To stay connected with Red's work and learn more about Red's books, *Irish Women's Prison Writing: Mother Ireland's Rebels, 1960–2010s* and the forthcoming *Nonbinary: Tr@ns-Forming Gender and Genre in Nonbin@ry Literature, Performance, and Visual Art*, we encourage *WSQ* readers to visit www.redwashburn.com.

We are indebted to the *WSQ* editorial assistants, Maya von Ziegesar and Googie Karrass, for their labor, support, and tireless patience as we navigate the day-to-day intricacies of our new roles. We wish Googie the best as she moves on from her term at *WSQ* to focus on her dissertation, and we extend a warm welcome to our new editorial assistant, Jah Elyse Sayers. It is an honor to be surrounded by such a brilliant and knowledgeable team of collaborators. We would also like to thank editorial directors

Kendra Sullivan (Center for the Humanities) and Dána-Ain Davis (Center for the Study of Women and Society), who have not only welcomed us with kindness and enthusiasm but are expertly familiarizing us with the many institutional collaborations that make *WSQ* possible. Lastly, we are moved by the support from our home institution, York College, CUNY. We owe so much to our amazing students, who inspire us to accept new challenges and continue the struggle to end oppressions of all kinds.

Andie Silva
Associate Professor of English
York College
City University of New York

Shereen Inayatulla
Professor of English
York College
City University of New York

Introduction

Red Washburn and JV Fuqua

This special issue of *WSQ, Nonbinary,* reflects upon the work that the concept "nonbinary" does in terms of unsettling the codes of gender, sexuality, race, and other categories of being and knowing. For this issue, we understand nonbinary to serve as a direct challenge to the tenacity of binary logics, ethics, and orientations. We also acknowledge that we have made a choice in using the word "nonbinary" that is only a gesture at the breaking of binaries that utilize other words and languages. Nonbinary is a moving thing, and the word may become outdated in the near future, as queer language is wont to do. Not only located, but perhaps most recognizably found, in discussions of gender and sexuality, nonbinary must be thought in relation to deep conceptions of identity and belonging across the spectrum of power and difference. Feminist theory has long focused upon the problematic aspects of binary thinking in relation to the dyads of nature/ culture, sex/gender, biology/culture, human/nonhuman, or the individual/collective. Currently, in the wake of the COVID-19 pandemic, we see the consequences of nonbinary thinking as it relates to fact/fiction and schisms in public discourse and everyday life. Nonbinary directs attention to the power and the precarious ways of being, knowing, and doing that fall outside such normatively derived epistemological, structuring pairs.

In 2008, *WSQ* published *Trans-,* its first issue devoted to the subject of "transing" (Stryker, Currah, and Moore 2008), from gender to the human/ nonhuman divide, region, power, and racialized identities. During the following twelve years, the popular media landscape has hosted a veritable explosion of images and narratives of nonbinary ways of being. From performer Billy Porter to writer, artist, and activist Alok Vaid-Menon, *Queer Eye's* Jonathan Van Ness, and *Billions* actor Asia Kate Dillon, nonbinariness

WSQ: Women's Studies Quarterly 51: 3 & 4 (Fall/Winter 2023) © 2023 by Red Washburn and JV Fuqua.
All rights reserved.

has circulated through popular culture and podcasts with surprising speed. However, in feminist, critical race, postcolonial, and queer theory, nonbinary continues to receive, in the best cases, merely an inclusive nod in discussions of trans- or, in the worst cases, disregard. This is not to say that in all trans- work, nonbinary must be parsed. It is, rather, to acknowledge that nonbinary needs to be considered for its relationality to trans- as well as for its differences from, and challenges to, that concept, along with intersecting identities of race, class, sexuality, ethnicity, ability, age, religion, et cetera. We, as guest editors, ask how it is the case that nonbinary representations and narratives circulate through culture, why it is the case that nonbinariness and its intersections with other identities continue to be overlooked in relation to feminist theory and critical race, ethnic, postcolonial, disability, and LGBTQIA+ studies—specifically, trans studies—and how we can resist binary ideologies and practices to reposition nonbinary as the intentional practice of freedom. In other words, where is the "NB" in the alphabet of identities? Nonbinary, in short, might be a way to enact, finally, feminist life—life unbeholden to normative, circumscriptive impositions that stem, in no small part, from heteropatriarchy.

Red Washburn
Overview
Nonbinary is a site of possibility. It is a citation that is political. How can we imagine trans identities, creative views, and transdisciplines? What kind of intellectual and social worlds do we want to create? How can we be free in them? It is life-affirming to know who you are, how to express it, and what you study. This issue, *Nonbinary*, explores these themes and dreams. It asks us to think about a world with gender expansion, self-determination, and cultural wondering. It begs us to disrupt binary thought and practice issuing from structural inequality, such as racism, classism, sexism, cissexism, ethnocentrism, colonialism, ableism, ageism, speciesism, and capitalism. It insists we critique binaries and borders, using the body and bodies as a politics of location. It emphasizes that man/woman, white/black, first world/third world, and us-versus-them logic is illogical and problematic as well as deeply unjust and inhumane. It tells us to challenge it all and leaves us without a white-supremacist and colonial map. It guides us through ethnic studies, indigenous studies, critical race studies, feminist studies, trans studies, postcolonial studies, and disability studies. It invites us to grapple with

questions to which we will never know the answers, though we will live, grow, and love hard and happily in unknown conceptual galaxies. As we destabilize, we heal. As we deconstruct, we make new. As we decolonize, we free our minds. We will be free, and we will work towards being free in the sun, in the woods, at the beach, in our communities of dissent, in our own families, in our rituals, in our marches, at our potlucks, at our libraries, at our universities, in our bathrooms, in our bedrooms, in our sanctuaries, in our own names, in our own bodies, in our own spaces, and in our own places across the spectrum of difference. Nonbinary is an intellectual intervention into creative invention of words, images, and productions as essential, exciting, and euphoric. It is the blessing of the tower card, not reversed, dancing in the rumble and shifting into no destinations, the cosmos of gender trouble and troubling. Nonbinary is a state of joy without adherence to the state, and it shows us that we can get to not-there and that we are not-here yet, as Muñoz's *Cruising Utopia* has demonstrated. We already have been not-there, not-done that. Nonbinary has promised, keeps promising, and the future is nonbinary.

Questions

In this issue, we explore a number of concepts and questions. How might nonbinary be theorized and historicized? How do texts and performances of nonbinariness challenge and reconfigure transness? How do untranslatable states of nonbinary open up possibilities in trans studies? In what ways can gender outlaws and outlaw genres coexist together? How can we talk about the connections between borders, binaries, and bodies? How can nonnormativity, unbelongingness, and unassimilation be forms of freedom under state-sanctioned colonialism, racism, ethnocentrism, sexism, and cissexism? How do we envision gender self-determinations and genre reimaginations as part of a radical conversation? How do we discuss unpersonhood/dehumanization, uncertainty/precarity, dislocation/displacement, rejection/ejection, and homelessness/exile as binary problems? What does it mean to be at home in one's body and in society without binary logic and laws? How are binaries part of a white-supremacist and colonial project? What is your nonbinary vision for a utopia or a world without carceral systems as well as systems of white supremacy, cissexist patriarchy, colonialism, and capitalism? We asked our contributors to reflect on these questions, and we are still reflecting on them ourselves. We also welcome our readers to linger over these questions while encountering the journal's offerings. We all will keep asking more questions in our questioning of gender, and that process, like gender itself, will not have an end.

Process

Our process editing this issue has been as nonlinear as gender itself. As two white trans, nonbinary, masculine-of-center, and queer professors, we have contributed from this position, and yet we have remained deeply committed to representation of difference in this issue. We have also written this introduction without our dear friend and brilliant colleague Dr. Brianne Waychoff, a coeditor of this issue from the start who passed away in July 2022 of 9/11-related kidney cancer. I wrote it in a time of substantial grief, without my mom, Colleen Washburn, my uncle, Glenn McGuire, my cat, Volt, and my dog, Ziggy; and JV, without their friends, their cat, Raymond, and their German shepherd, Sylvie. Overall, it has been a truly apocalyptic time of grief, never post-COVID. It is a time of four hundred–plus anti-trans laws. It is an anti-trans, an anti-Black, anti-Latinx, anti-Asian, anti-Indigenous, and anti-Arab moment, anti-immigrant, anti-crip, anti-abortion, and anti-just-all-around. However, grief has spaciousness for happiness, neutrality, and other affective realms, too, and by the time we finished this issue, we were in and out of many of them, just as all the political categories of gender exist outside of, and perhaps in tension with, the relentless binaries of man and woman. Indeed, grief is a queer process that calls forth a great rupture between the beloved and the lost, between presence and absence, and between the living and the dead. Nonetheless, as a cleaving process, it makes space whether or not that space is desired. Our process has led us to critical discovery, intellectual bliss, and creative freedom as we lift. We hope the scholars, the artists, and the activists in this issue do the same or not-same for you all. Our process is a process, never done, an idea is just the start of ideas, an identity intersects with identities, and spaces sit on other spaces—the Other's spaces—and nonbinary gender is not a negative, just using language genderqueerly. We went in as somebody and something and as not somebody and something, and we left as somebody and something else, and yet not somebody and something else. Transition is not a destination, and the work continues on and beyond, including beyond this issue and us.

Selections

This issue, *Nonbinary*, features diverse forms of work. The scholarly articles pull together numerous concepts and explorations. J. Logan Smilges and

Joy Ellison discuss the importance of disability in connection to gender and other intersecting identities, with the former focusing on neurodivergence and the latter on praxis, particularly in the photography of Leslie Feinberg. Building off the work of Marquis Bey, Kadji Amin, and other key scholars in the burgeoning field of nonbinary studies, Smilges's attention on the intersections of trans and nonbinary studies is essential. Ellison's analysis of Feinberg's photos is a wonderful honoring of hir work, and I was happy to include it alongside Minnie Bruce Pratt's and Leslie Feinberg's classic works. I was especially grateful to collaborate with and feature Minnie Bruce Pratt's work, as she died while this issue was in production. Like Ellison, Beshouy Botros also uses portraits in their essay, addressing depictions of transfemininity in Egypt. Lena Mattheis, Chris Straayer, Gizem Senturk, and Susan Stryker explore various forms of culture in their essays as well. Lena Mattheis writes about language in the literature of Aphra Behn and Margaret Cavendish, Chris Straayer writes about gender nonconformity in the visual art of Kris Grey, Gizem Senturk writes about ecology and the television program *Deep Space Nine*, and Susan Stryker writes about the musician Ornette Coleman and the civil rights lawyer and activist Pauli Murray. Taken together, these essays discuss art, culture, and social change in meaningful ways. In particular, as a humanities and transdisciplinary scholar and writer as well as someone currently writing my own academic project about nonbinary literature, performance, and art, we find the essays by Chris Straayer, Susan Stryker, and Gizem Senturk intellectually and creatively rich in their discussions of cultural work. I am very excited about the aesthetic representations of nonbinary life. I love how these scholars use cultural works as portals to critical inquiry and forms of dissent, and I found their insights fascinating. However, like Gizem Senturk, I also was overjoyed that we could include Tebi Ardiles, Paulina Bravo, Fabián Fernández, and Corina González-Weil, for their essay on biology education in Chile is critical. In addition, I was delighted to feature work that is transnational and postcolonial in scope. Omi Salas-SantaCruz's essay addresses the politics of refusal and erasure in nonbinary epistemologies, focusing on "trans* Latinidades" by using classic Latinx feminist and queer theory à la Anzaldúa, et cetera. Denis Boyacı and Aslıhan Öğün Boyacıoğlu's essay critiques "gender critical" ideology in Turkey during this moment of political urgency for trans people. Lou Rich's essay looks at gendered sanctions in Greco-Roman antiquity and ancient China. Raagini Bora's essay examines "Desi genderqueerness," highlighting Hijras and Kothis in India. These essays demonstrate nonbinary work throughout the world in interesting and captivating ways. Lastly, C. Libby's article unpacks nonbinary saints, offering refreshing insights into saints like Liberata. We close the scholarly portion with a brilliant and thoughtful Alerts and Provocations section by Marquis Bey, calling us to think through Black nonbinary identities in relation to coalitional drives. I am elated that we could include wonderful prose by Mattilda Bernstein Sycamore, Dána-Ain Davis, and Audacia Ray, poetry by Kay Ulanday Barrett and Ximena Keogh Serrano, and visual art by Salgu Wissmath, Adrians Black Varella, Maya von Ziegesar, Linc Ross, Abby C. Emerson, Kyra Gregory, Elvis Bakaitis, and Brianne Waychoff. Overall, I am pleased and honored to include this important work in *WSQ's Nonbinary*.

JV Fuqua

We wrote this introduction as a frame that holds the journal's assembled thoughts. Each journal issue, no matter the topic, represents an assembly of difference, of diverse meditations upon an articulated theme. During the time that this journal issue was conceived and the time of its publication, the political and cultural landscape for nonbinary lives has become increasingly hostile and violent. This context for the publication of the journal has featured organized neo-Nazi attacks on Drag Story Hour events, the banning of public drag performances, legislation specifically targeting trans, nonbinary, and gender nonconforming individuals across multiple Republican-led states, and the dismantling of LGBTQIA+ and anti-racist curricula at public schools and universities across the nation. It is to this unsettling and uncertain time that *Nonbinary* speaks, through diverse scholarly articles, poetry, prose, and art. Though the current days may be foreboding, we, as editors, believe that this collection of nonbinary expression is an act of resistance as well as a source of hope and possibility.

Indeed, as we configured our ideas in this introduction that is its own exercise in invoking other possible ways and worlds, Florida protofascist governor Ron DeSantis signed into law five different, yet equally horrifying, bills targeting the transgender community. For example, House Bill 1521, "Facility Requirements Based on Sex," restricts transgender people from using bathrooms that correspond to their gender identity, even if that gender identity is legally verified by officially state-authorized and updated gender markers on driver's licenses and the like. According to this law, effective July 1, 2023, if a cisgender person observes a transgender individual in that same public accommodation space, employees can expel the transgender person. Further, the transgender person could face up to one year in jail on "criminal trespass" charges (Reed 2023). Even if gender markers and other official documents correctly denote that person's *legal* identity, this classification is superseded by the Florida law HB 1521 indicating that sex is determined "by the person's sex chromosomes, naturally occurring sex hormones, and internal and external genitalia present at birth." These laws are of course unfolding against the backdrop of DeSantis's continued attacks on all educational, including higher educational, diversity, equity, and inclusion programs—most notable would be his firing of administrators and faculty at the New College of Florida (Wallace-Wells 2023). In addition to these policies, some states, such as Texas, have already implemented practices that remove trans children from their families of origin (Klosterboer 2023).

While this journal issue responds creatively and presciently to the current flurry of anti-trans/anti-nonbinary legislation and trans- and queerphobic, racist, misogynistic violence against minoritized communities and individuals, several of our collected texts seem particularly rich in their responses to some of the most dangerous consequences of binary epistemologies. Of our collected articles, two works speak directly to the previously described legislative dangers for nonbinary and trans individuals as well as the full-on dismantling of public education that is perceived as straying from "conventional" understandings of science and the liberal arts. For example, in "Nature Is Nonbinary: Gender and Sexuality in Biology Education in Chile" by Tebi Ardiles, Paulina Bravo, Fabián Fernández, and Corina González-Weil, the authors describe the heteronormativity of biology and science education at the primary, secondary, and higher educational levels. Through their collaborative development of what they call "fleta pedagogy" (queer pedagogy), hegemonic science and biology curricula are revised to emphasize the multiplicitous features inherent in the natural world and indeed in the human one as well. The authors describe their pedagogical "big idea" or intervention in this way:

> In nature, sexual behaviors are not presented in a binary, dichotomous, or absolute way. Yet, there is a gradient of possibilities that generates diversity and contributes to the survival of the species. Human sexuality is not exempt from such diversity, which is translated into intertwined sociocultural, affective, psychological, value, and political dimensions that, alongside shaping the sexuality of a subject, interact with each other. As a result, sexuality cannot be restricted to merely a reproductive function or a binary.

Striving to intervene in several different university classroom contexts, including bachelor's- and master's-level courses, the authors describe the challenges and possibilities of such an approach informed by nonbinary, trans, and queer theories. Given the politicized constraints that the far right have been implementing in the U.S. with regard to university and public school education, their work allows readers to understand how these events move across national borders and ideologies.

Furthering the discussion of the rise of anti-trans and anti-LGBTQ state-organized policies, Denis E. Boyacı and Aslıhan Öğün Boyacıoğlu's "Tracing 'Gender Critical' Ideology in Turkey: A Study of the Feminist Movement on Sex/Gender in Relation to Trans and Queer Inclusivity" reveals a familiar yet culturally specific iteration of transphobia and trans-misogyny propagated by second-wave feminists in Turkey. One of the perhaps surprising developments in various national movements regarding LGBTQIA+ and nonbinary rights has been the apparently unlikely alliance between trans-exclusionary radical feminists (TERFs) and far-right organizations. These alliances are made all the more unsettling and dangerous, it seems to us, when they are also connected to and integrated with authoritarian or authoritarian-leaning governments such as that of Tayyip Erdoğan in the case of Turkey or the previous Trump administration, as well as current U.S. political laws and policies at the level of Republican-led states. These essays stand out for their discussion of these critical themes.

Conclusion
At various points throughout this introduction, we have spoken about our deceased friend and colleague, Dr. Brianne Waychoff. We would like to invoke them once more as we gratefully acknowledge just how animating and inspiring our personal and professional time with Brianne has been. Indeed, Brianne's self-portrait, taken as they were struggling with their illness, wraps around these texts; their image—the fractured self-portrait—stares back at the reader, back at the beholder of their face. If the reader holds the journal, they see Brianne first. Brianne's spirit of generosity, solidarity, and tireless collaboration points inward to the contents of this *Nonbinary* journal issue while it also beckons us outward like an incantation. In these disheartening and demoralizing times, such inspiration is no small thing. Abjection and despair seem to greet us each day as queer outlaws; we try simply to live with dignity and respect. Doing this work without Brianne has

been hard. Often, JV has looked out at the trees, shaken a fist, and hollered that Brianne missed out on the editing labor! Red also searched for connection to Brianne in dreams, texts, and emails, wishing their words and wisdom were centered in this issue. At times, and given the rise in violence against queers, trans people, and BIPOC in this nation, all the mundane hatred and bigotry, we editors often wondered about the entire journal endeavor—what is one more academic journal in the face of all this nonsense? Brianne might point out the significance of seemingly small gestures, as they do in the brief pages of their *Ben & Brianne @ Home* COVID zine. They might emphasize that the act of calling for and gathering these nonbinary voices into conversation with each other is undoubtedly a feminist act. It is a political act, a form of resistance to general fuckery. We choose to speculate about a better now and a better not-yet. Within collaboration, within solidarity with others—in scholarly articles, prose, photography, illustration, and poetry—these works embolden us to keep on keeping on, as *Women's Studies Quarterly* has persevered for more than fifty years.

Thank-Yous

We want to acknowledge the *WSQ* community for making this issue happen. First and foremost, we want to thank Dr. Brianne Waychoff for their brilliance and support. We dedicate this issue to Breezo. We want to thank Dr. Dána-Ain Davis at the Center for the Study of Women and Society and Kendra Sullivan at the Center for Humanities for their vision and work. We also want to extend a hearty thank-you to the editorial assistants, especially Googie Karrass and Maya von Ziegesar, both of whom worked tirelessly on communicating with the scholars, writers, and artists to make this issue happen. We want to thank all the scholars, writers, and artists who contributed to this issue. We love their work, and we are happy to celebrate it in this issue. We also want to thank the Feminist Press leadership for all their help with scheduling, copyediting, and distributing our issues, especially to editorial director Lauren Rosemary Hook, former assistant editor Nick Whitney, and Rachel Page. We want to thank the new general editors, Dr. Shereen Inayatulla and Dr. Andie Silva, for their support. Thank you to the poetry, prose, and art editors as well as the editorial board. We want to thank our loved ones, including pets. In particular, Red wants to thank their wife, Audacia Ray, and pets, Lux, Banshee, and Zalie. Last but not least, we want to thank each other for all of our work and commitment to this issue during a very difficult time.

Red Washburn (they/he) is professor of English and director of Women's and Gender Studies at Queens College. They are affiliate faculty in Women's and Gender Studies at the Graduate Center. Red's articles appear in *Journal for the Study of Radicalism*, *Women's Studies: An Interdisciplinary Journal*, and *Journal of Lesbian Studies*. Their essays are in several anthologies, including *Theory and Praxis: Women's and Gender Studies at Community Colleges*, *Introduction to Women's, Gender & Sexuality Studies: Interdisciplinary and Intersectional Approaches*, and *Trans Bodies, Trans Selves: A Resource for the Transgender Community*. They are the coeditor of Sinister Wisdom's *Dump Trump: Legacies of Resistance*, *45 Years: A Tribute to Lesbian Herstory Archives*, and *Trans/Feminisms*. Finishing Line Press published their poetry collections *Crestview Tree Woman* and *Birch Philosopher X*. They received an ACLS/Mellon fellowship for their next project, *Nonbinary: Tr@ns-Forming Gender and Genre in Nonbin@ry Literature, Performance, and Visual Art*. They can be reached at Red.Washburn@qc.cuny.edu.

JV Fuqua grew up in Texas. Fuqua has a PhD in cultural and critical studies from the University of Pittsburgh and is an associate professor of media history and theory in the Department of Media Studies at Queens College. Fuqua was the director of the Women and Gender Studies Program at Queens College from 2017–2023. Fuqua was Provost Diversity Fellow at Queens College for AY 22/23. Their articles have been published in journals such as *Cultural Studies*, *Journal of Television and New Media*, and the *European Journal of American Culture*. Other writings have appeared in anthologies and in digital sources such as *In Media Res*. Their first monograph, *Prescription TV: Therapeutic Discourse in the Hospital and at Home*, was published in 2012 by Duke University Press. Fuqua is an internationally recognized scholar who has served on the board of the international feminist media collective "Console-ing Passions" and is currently a member of the editorial board of *WSQ*. They can be reached at JV.Fuqua@qc.cuny.edu.

Works Cited

Klosterboer, Brian. 2023. "Texas' Attempt to Tear Parents and Trans Youth Apart, One Year Later." *ACLU: News and Commentary*, February 23, 2023. Accessed May 20, 2023. https://www.aclu.org/news/lgbtq-rights/texas-attempt-to-tear-parents-and-trans-youth-apart-one-year-later.

Reed, Erin. 2023. "Florida's Trans Bathroom Ban Signed: Arrests to Follow Regardless of Legal Gender Status." *Erin in the Morning*, May 17, 2023. Accessed May 18, 2023. https://www.erininthemorning.com/p/floridas-trans-bathroom-ban-signed.

Stryker, Susan, Paisley Currah, and Lisa Jean Moore. 2008. "Introduction: Trans-, Trans, or Transgender?" *Women's Studies Quarterly* 36 (3/4): 11–22. http://www.jstor.org/stable/27649781.

Wallace-Wells, Benjamin. 2023. "What Is Ron DeSantis Doing to Florida's Public Liberal-Arts College?" *New Yorker*, February 22, 2023. Accessed May 20, 2023. https://www.newyorker.com/news/the-political-scene/what-is-ron-desantis-doing-to-floridas-public-liberal-arts-college.

Self-Portrait with Mom Fixing My Hair

Linc Ross

In the early '90s I played a lot with drag and photography as a way to explore my feelings about my own gender. We had words like "androgynous," "tomboy," and "soft-butch." Currently, identifying as nonbinary seems much more accurate as I don't identify as male and I also don't identify as female. My explorations were more psychological and when I played with drag in relationship to another person it got really interesting. My mom is probably the person in the world who I most formed my gender identity in relationship to. She lives now with advanced dementia and continues to be nonjudgmental, embracing me for all of who I am.

Linc Ross has worked in China, Kyrgyzstan, Azerbaijan, Europe, and North Africa, and their work has been exhibited internationally in museums and galleries. Ross has been a grantee of the Trust for Mutual Understanding and Asian Cultural Council; an artist-in-residence at The View Art Gallery, Gansu, the Watermill Center, New York, and CICRP in Marseilles, France; a Fellow of the Bronx Museum AIM Program; and a recipient of the Hayward Prize through the American Austrian Foundation. Ross has also taught at Parsons School of Design, Columbia University, and at the Harvey Milk School, where they developed a photography and video program for LGBTQ youth. Ross holds an MFA from Columbia University and a BA from Sarah Lawrence College. Ross can be reached at studiolisaross@gmail.com or www.studiolisaross.com.

WSQ: Women's Studies Quarterly 51: 3 & 4 (Fall/Winter 2023) © 2023 by Linc Ross. All rights reserved.

Linc Ross. *Self-Portrait with Mom Fixing My Hair*, 1992. Silver gelatin print.

PART I. ARTICLES

Seasons of Nonbinary and Neurodivergence; or, So What If We're All X?

J. Logan Smilges

Abstract: The category of nonbinary has entered a new season. No longer emergent but maturing, it is facing new, pressing questions about what the term means, who it is for, in what ways it can be mobilized toward specific political agendas, and how it facilitates or impedes forms of community. In this essay, I unpack the anxieties that some trans and nonbinary people have expressed toward these questions and that are sometimes invoked to cast doubt on the politics or ethics of *nonbinary*. Rather than accept or reject these anxieties at face value, I re-story them to honor their sources while yet insisting on a path forward for *nonbinary*, a path that depends not on how we define it but on how we occupy it. By allegorizing the anxieties in nonbinary and neurodivergent communities, I propose that the language of *access needs* and *disability impacts* may provide models for negotiating accountability and care in pursuit of trans justice. Keywords: nonbinary; neurodivergence; identity; accountability; community

There is anxiety in the air. The odor of restlessness wafts under our noses. As the spring of our emergence comes to an end, summer arrives for us nonbinary people. It's a long, hot season. What once felt fresh and open to possibility is settling into something more durable. The bud of our identity has blossomed, and now it longs for direction. When to spread its petals wide, when to curl up into itself, how to feed, and where to fall? Nonbinary people are adjusting ourselves to the demands of a new season. No longer an uncommon identity that skirts clear definitions in the shadows, *nonbinary* is in direct sun as well as the *Merriam-Webster* dictionary, the Canadian census, and Target's Pride Collection. Whatever our queer intentions with the term may have been, the category of nonbinary is undergoing a process

WSQ: Women's Studies Quarterly 51: 3 & 4 (Fall/Winter 2023) © 2023 by J. Logan Smilges. All rights reserved.

of domestication into the liberal rhetoric of diversity. *Nonbinary* means something now, even if that meaning is contested.

Over the past couple of years, I have grown fond of thinking with seasons. What began as an autistic perseveration on why flowers make me cry has evolved into an affection for seasonality, as both a literal cycle of life and a figurative method for charting the temporalities of feeling I share with others. I have begun to ask myself not only what I am feeling but also why I am feeling that way *right now*. A seasonal framework constellates my feelings with others as we experience the world changing together. Even if the forces guiding another person's feelings remain unnamed, I allow myself the affective intuition to observe their season and to note the ways our seasons overlap and diverge. By attending to why I feel something *right now*, I am dipping into what Amy Gaeta calls "crip autotheory," whereby I relinquish the able-normative desire to stake universal claims that stand the test of time, in favor of a disabled knowledge that embraces "passivity and partiality" (2023, 9). I do not claim that my season feels the same as anyone else's, but I do believe that attending to the timeliness of one's own feelings can teach us how to attend to why others might be feeling a certain way right now, too.

The season facing many trans and nonbinary people right now is saturated by legislative and administrative violence. The criminalization of trans medicine, the foreclosure of access to reproductive care, and the onslaught of public vitriol stoked by conservative politicians and gender-critical feminists alike are all shaping the season in which gender-minoritized people find themselves. It is a season, as Tourmaline, Eric A. Stanley, and Johanna Burton (2017) warn us, marked by the "trap door" of visibility. As if there were ever any doubt, representational politics are failing us. Our people have never been more "seen," nor have many of us ever been more scared.

Fear as such is an unruly affect. It can drive us forward into a new season, or it can park us into one that should have expired long ago. As I observe the fear that so many of my trans and nonbinary kin are experiencing, as I read their fear alongside my own, I find myself interested in the range of responses people have to it. Thinking with seasons helps me to notice patterns in the timing, in addition to the content, of people's fear. Among the patterns I have noticed is an uptick in the frequency with which trans and nonbinary people are sharing anxieties about the category of nonbinary: anxieties about what the term means, who it is for, in what ways it can be mobilized toward specific political agendas, and how it facilitates or impedes forms of community. To me, these anxieties are both indicative of a new season for *nonbinary*, one that treats it as no longer emergent but maturing and responsive to a wider season of escalated antitrans brutality and state-sponsored gender fascism.

I distinguish these anxieties from the ones spouted by those who wish trans and nonbinary people harm. I believe that there are good-faith expressions of fear that are substantively different from paternalistic admonitions of concern, such as those found in the rhetoric so often invoked to "protect" children from queer and trans adults. Some fear is intracommunity and comes from a place of deep care for our collective future. To feel anxiety about the language we use to describe ourselves, others, and our mutual relationships is not necessarily to reject that language, let alone the sincerity with which people use it. Instead, it is to embrace the discomfort and dissonance that haunt all identitarian subjects under liberalism. It is to acknowledge the blistering heat that threatens to choke us, so that just maybe we can work together to find the cool shadow of a tree to prolong our lives.

In what follows, I explore several well-circulated anxieties about *nonbinary* with the intention of offering a new narrative for what they might tell us about the possibilities engendered by the category's new season. While I acknowledge that these anxieties provide important insights into *nonbinary*'s season of maturation, I also push back against how they are sometimes instrumentalized to cast doubt on the viability of the category. From there, I follow my seasonal intuition to *neurodivergence*, another category about which some people have begun sharing anxieties as it, too, enters a season of heightened visibility. By allegorizing the anxieties in nonbinary and neurodivergent communities, I introduce several practices used by disabled people that may provide models for negotiating accountability and care in pursuit of trans justice. Far from rejecting the category, I propose that *nonbinary* is in an enviable, seasonal position for reimagining gender politics toward collective liberation.

A Season of Anxiety

Within just a few months of each other, Brock Colyar, a *New York* magazine features writer, and queer and trans studies scholar Kadji Amin both published essays speaking to their growing discomfort with the category of nonbinary. That their pieces are directed toward different audiences— one public, one academic—gestures toward the scope of the anxieties at hand. Colyar and Amin come from different intellectual spaces and different generations, and yet the affective tenor of their writing bears stark resemblance. In part, this resemblance emerges from the fact that both authors share a material investment in trans community. Colyar is nonbinary themself, and Amin publicly identifies as an "old fogie transsexual" (Gill-Peterson 2021). Whether occupying the category or living adjacent to it through another form of transition, Colyar and Amin maintain overlapping social space with nonbinary people. Admittedly, it's a relief to engage with the work of folks who share a common goal of improving the quality of trans lives. While I take issue with elements of Colyar's and Amin's arguments, I aim to practice a critical generosity that takes stock of the seasonal context surrounding the two writers as members of a shared community.

In "They, Then and Now," Colyar (2022) opines that they/them pronouns—the combination most readily associated with nonbinary identity—are no longer doing the political work that they used to. When Colyar first began identifying as nonbinary, they recall that "it felt sexy and radical," like a "punk provocation" and "political declaration." Claiming *nonbinary* enabled them to articulate a dissatisfaction with existing gender categories, and adopting neutral pronouns reinforced this articulation by requesting that others verbally acknowledge their identity's distance from the gender binary. Over time, however, Colyar has become disillusioned with their pronouns, which have come to feel like a waste of energy that belabors them with the responsibility of correcting others' misgendering, that provides nontrans people with the opportunity "to virtue-signal their wokeness," and that ultimately domesticates Colyar's gender nonconformance into something palatable for "a human-resources-approved corporate product." Colyar wonders in the essay what nonbinary identity and neutral pronouns do for them. As the article's subtitle asks, "Who is it serving?"

In "We Are All Nonbinary: A Brief History of Accidents," Amin takes a roundabout stab at Colyar's question, concluding that if nonbinary identity is serving anyone, it isn't gender-minoritized folks. To make his case, Amin outlines a genealogy for *nonbinary* that frames it as the inevitable result of liberalism's steady recuperation of gender and sexual difference into legible modes of subjectivity. Critiquing logics of divergence and binarism, Amin argues that nonbinary identity presupposes the existence of binary gender identity, which theoretically incorporates both cis and trans people who are entirely, and without exception, comfortable operating within the boundaries of a dyadic gender system. Binary gender, he suggests, is an illusion akin to heterosexuality or cisgender identity; *"no one is binary"* (114). The fictitiousness of binary gender is belied by what Amin considers *nonbinary*'s most concerning characteristic: that it lacks "positive social content" (116). Unlike homosexuality, which implies same-gender erotic intimacies, and transgender, which according to Amin connotes some form of social transition, *nonbinary* requires no evidence, except self-identification. So long as a person says they are nonbinary, they are nonbinary, regardless of how they present to the world. For Amin, the apparent substancelessness of nonbinary identity is evidence of the "binary Western thinking" that has produced it (116). Like Colyar, Amin is pessimistic about the political offerings of *nonbinary*, leading him to suggest that gender politics would be better off *"without* gender identity" at all (118). For both writers, *nonbinary* doesn't do—perhaps could never have done—what they wanted. Whether as a disappointment or a fulfillment of low expectations, *nonbinary*'s new season, for them, may be its last.

I, however, am not ready to give up hope on *nonbinary*, despite sharing some of Colyar's and Amin's anxieties. I believe there is a path forward for the category, a path that depends not on how we define it but on how we occupy it. Amin makes a strong case that gender politics should not be reducible to identity, so it follows that if we want *nonbinary* to retain its political potentialities and to remain motile for our reimaginings of gendered expression and embodiment, then we must be prepared to approach *nonbinary* as a *doing*, in addition to a *being*. To *do nonbinary* might include contextualizing gender identity as an individual experience made possible by social relations. To claim a gender identity is to enter a social terrain with others who share that identity, and if we want that social terrain to be more than merely shared rhetorical space, such that perhaps it may forge a channel to community, then we must treat one another as though we are already in community. To *do nonbinary* is not to perform a caricature of nonbinariness or to take on the aesthetic of thin, white androgyny. It is, to the contrary, to build and tend to networks of care across difference that acknowledge the circulation of power beyond the binaristic logics of gender identity.

Re-storying Anxiety

To explain what I mean by *doing nonbinary*, I want to reread Colyar's and Amin's essays, neither of which lands quite where I wish it would. In Colyar's case, I share their observation that the social significance of nonbinary identity is shifting. It makes sense that the more mainstream that nonbinary identity and they/them pronouns become, the less queer their flavors will be. I do not share Colyar's disappointment in this shift, though, because I never shared the expectation that it would be otherwise. In order to be disappointed by *nonbinary*'s liberal recuperation, one must have initially idealized claiming a gender identity as a stable political act. But this is not how identity nor politics function. Both are seasonal phenomena. Any identity's relation to politics is contingent on the conditions that surround it. No identity is guaranteed its radicality. No identity can secure the radicality of the people who deploy it. Identity may sometimes gesture toward a person's relation to power, but it is never more than shorthand.

It is worthwhile to note that Colyar explains their initial reason for adopting nonbinary identity as being "eager to join in on the hype." That "hype" could describe a gender identity should have foreshadowed for Colyar the category's eventual movement away from alterity. There is nothing wrong with claiming a gender identity because it seems chic, but chic and radical are generally incompatible if we are talking about anything other than surface-level aesthetics. Coming away from Colyar's piece, I am left alienated from the category we both inhabit. Colyar's entrance to nonbinary identity, as a style qua politics, along with the fear they bear toward its domestication, presents the category in a way that I have never experienced it.

For me, the category of nonbinary is a way to name the interanimation of my gender and disabilities. As a neurotrans person (Smilges 2023), my disabilities render it impossible for me to perform abled masculinity or femininity with any degree of consistency. My crip bodymind is actively ungendered in such a way that any claim I might make to "man" or "woman" would be illegible or at the very least unstable when measured up against a cisableist rubric. *Nonbinary* is thus less an identity I have chosen than a disaffiliatory position in which I am fixed. Though I have deep affection for nonbinary community and take pleasure in using they/them pronouns, I cannot ignore that my intimacy with *nonbinary* is predicated on violent estrangement. I never expected the identity to perform a politics of disavowal, because I was not given the choice to experience gender otherwise.

As is the case for Colyar and me, *nonbinary* does not mean the same thing to everyone, and the various meanings it holds are contoured by people's wider relations to power. As Aniruddha Dutta (2018) notes, gender is increasingly assumed to be an "individualized, interiorized" experience that is "not based on fulfilling external material criteria" (89). While there are good reasons for prioritizing self-determination over material criteria when it comes to gender, such as to protect trans people who may not pass as cisgender, it is also the case that an identity category with no material criteria is bound to include folks with multiple and perhaps even contradictory experiences of that category. In the context of nonbinary identity, what it means—what it *can* mean—depends on how each of us is situated along the lines of race, class, disability, and sexuality, in addition to expressions of cissexism and transmisogyny that operate beyond the rubric of identity.

For example, Marquis Bey (2020) proposes that they/them pronouns function for them as "a discursive nonbinariness begotten by blackness." *They* simultaneously invokes Black community and hails an alternative gendered subjectivity. The pronoun denotes multiple forms of plurality that gesture not toward a new gender identity but toward new gender socialities: "they ain't gotta be unknown to be *they*, and in the possibility of being *they* yet known, they become possible in another kind of way." On their faculty webpage (2022b), Bey further explains that their "tentative and always-in-process relationship to gender nonbinariness" is best understood as "an attempted unrelation to gender." For them, being nonbinary precludes proper subjectivity, since "to be a subject *is* to be within the binary" (2022a, 146). In lieu of adopting nonbinary identity as a form of renunciation, qua Colyar, or inheriting nonbinary affiliation through disability, such as I do, Bey maintains an adjacent position to the category through their affection for they/them pronouns as a site of Black possibility. For each of us, *nonbinary* signals something different, and these differentiated signals are tuned by the seasons that brought us to *nonbinary* in the first place. It reasons that if each of us has a unique path into/around/beside *nonbinary*, we are not likely sharing the same experience of it. Perhaps, contra Colyar, rather than asking *who* neutral pronouns and nonbinary identity are serving, we might instead ask, "*How* are they serving different needs for different people, and *what* differences does serving these different needs make for whom and when?" These questions additionally prove useful to me as a way of unpacking some of my discomfort with Amin's essay. While I share his critique of idealizing gender identity, I nevertheless disagree with the conclusion he draws about *nonbinary*'s political trajectory. In the final section of his article, Amin stakes two claims that are meant, as a subheading proposes, to throw "A Wrench in the Western Identity Machine" (2022, 116). Both of them require some careful reading.

First, Amin proposes that "the core binary that governs nonbinary thought . . . [is] that, foundational to Western thought, between the auto-logical sovereign individual and the unchosen genealogical bonds of the social" (2022, 116). Here, Amin argues that *nonbinary* epitomizes the danger of autological subjectivity; that is, if anyone can claim an identity for any reason, then that identity does not mean anything in particular. Amin draws his understanding of autology and genealogy from Elizabeth A. Povinelli (2006), who introduces the autological subject and genealogical society as two ways of staking liberal identity claims. The autological subject corre-sponds with those claims premised on "self-making, self-sovereignty, and the value of individual freedom" (4). The genealogical society, by contrast, concerns the "social constraints placed on the autological subject by vari-ous kinds of inheritances" (4), such as those social, cultural, and material factors that mitigate a person's capacity to indulge self-determination. Amin interprets the autological subject and genealogical society as opposing logics that form a new binary upon which nonbinary identity rests. *Nonbinary*, for him, is autological subjectivity sans genealogical society: an identity with no rules.

I would like to propose an alternative interpretation of Povinelli that situates autology and genealogy in an imbricated rather than opposing rela-tionship. In *The Empire of Love* (2006), Povinelli describes autology and genealogy as sharing a "strategic shape-shifting partnership" (14). Both discourses are vectors of liberalism that reshape the physical world and alter the physical body in an effort to shift focus away from "social status or the bare facts of the body" and toward the culturally assigned value of an iden-tity (5). Genealogy governs autology; it dictates the extent to which the autological subject may be autological. According to this reading, no binary between autology and genealogy exists, but rather there is a dynamic rela-tion that acclimatizes itself to the specific conditions surrounding a given subject. People cannot claim nonbinary identity (exercising their autolog-ical instinct) without also heralding genealogical law. Two people may use the same nomenclature to describe themselves, but the "economy of gene-alogy" within which that nomenclature is deployed does not guarantee an even distribution of power to all who deploy it (206). Two nonbinary people can both claim nonbinary identity, but their distinct genealogical inheritances might radically diversify their expressions of and attachments to nonbinariness.

This potential for radical diversification leads Amin to his second claim, that *nonbinary* "is not a true social category but rather a vast umbrella with no positive social content" (2022, 117). As Amin understands it, a gender category's social dimension is maintained through shared characteristics among its members. These characteristics are not necessarily inherited, but Amin nevertheless aligns them with genealogical society because they must be "based on presentation and behavior, not self-identification alone" (116). Since nonbinariness requires no such presentation or behavior beyond self-identification, Amin surmises that the category must be "devoid" of that which makes gender a social phenomenon (116).

In my experience, though, *nonbinary* is no more devoid of positive social content than it is reducible to Colyar's definition of it as "punk provocation." *Nonbinary* might be better understood as a relitigation of the social, a reworking of genealogical law that exposes both autology and genealogy as disciplinary mechanisms used to regulate the grammars by which we assess what we have in common, what we do not, and why it matters. I agree with Amin that the language of *nonbinary* is a disservice to people who find themselves thrust into a binarized gender identity by default. But the failure of language to adequately capture a liberal subject is a function of liberalism touching all autological subjects within a genealogical society. As Amin himself admits, *trans* raises similar linguistic problems through its relation to *cis*. *Homosexual*, also, invokes an artificial antithesis through *heterosexuality*. The linguistic problem facing *nonbinary* is not unique to *nonbinary*, even if the category's breadth makes the problem more visible.

That Amin perceives no positive social content in *nonbinary* is an indication not that the category is asocial or antisocial, but that it is pressing up against the borders of the social as we know it, fracturing the illusion that genealogical inheritances are any more suited to liberation than autological claims. *Nonbinary*'s apparent overindulgence of autology, its openness to individuals who seem to share nothing in common, is not a problem for gender politics but an opportunity to think expansively about the politics of gender. As Amin himself proposes in another essay, there is value in sitting with "the creative and resourceful ways" in which the language of nonbinary identity is reappropriated to describe a range of bodies with a range of relationships to gender and power (2023, 103). If anything, the problem facing *nonbinary* is not of social content but of social welfare, of accountability, of operating within a variegated social terrain that is not the same for all nonbinary people. The problem facing nonbinary community is how to be nonbinary in community—that is, how to share an identity with folks for whom that identity may mean something very different. What responsibilities do we have to one another, and how do we distribute these responsibilities with attention to our differences?

Allegorizing Anxiety

To get at these questions, I want to detour toward another (and for many of us, an overlapping) community that is experiencing its own season of exponential growth. Similar to nonbinariness, the language of neurodivergence is proliferating in ways that, just a decade ago, were nearly unthinkable. As part of the emerging "neurodiversity paradigm," *neurodivergence* has come to name anyone whose mind "functions in ways which divert significantly from the dominant societal standards of 'normal'" (Walker 2021, 34). Nick Walker explains that *neurodivergence* includes "genetic and innate" neurotypes, such as autism and ADHD, as well as neurotypes "produced by brain-altering experience," such as injury, trauma, or substance use (34). Because of the wide range of neurodivergences that exist, the glue holding the category together is found less in consistent similarities among neurodivergent people than in their collective departure from neurotypicality. "Neurotypical is the opposite of *neurodivergent*," says Walker. "Neurotypicality is the way-of-being from which neurodivergent people diverge" (36). Like the binaries structuring gender and sexuality, the binary between neurodivergence and neurotypicality ensures their mutual constitution. There is no *neurodivergence* without the figure of the neurotypical person.

However, in much the same way that binary gender is a normative ideal, rather than a common phenomenology, neurotypicality is also a figment of the neurodivergent imagination. The "neurotypical neurodivergent dichotomy," as Archie Brechin (2018) calls it, implies the existence of a neurotypical majority, despite that few people would describe their neurology as always in line with "dominant societal standards of 'normal'" (Walker 2021, 35). Neurotypicality is a mirage that does more to ensure the categorical coherence of *neurodivergence* than it does to accurately describe a population. Almost identical to *nonbinary*'s relationship to binary gender in this way, *neurodivergence* depends on a fragile juxtapositional logic. And this logic is nowhere more evident than in the celebrated role of self-diagnosis as an authorized mode of neurodivergent community membership. Self-diagnosis is an autological practice that requires no social or material evidence beyond a person's felt experience. M. Remi Yergeau explains that self-diagnosis "resists definition or containment, straddling and fucking common notions of identification and disability" (2018, 166). Self-diagnosis not only interrogates clinical authority but also insists on *neurodivergence*'s desirability—that it might be an identity people choose for themselves. Though there remain nonautological paths to it, such as through nonconsensual diagnosis, *neurodivergence* is increasingly self-determined, and the language of neurodivergence makes no distinction between neurominorities. *Neurodivergence*, no matter how you occupy it or how you arrive to it, is still *neurodivergence*.

Its autological dimension notwithstanding, *neurodivergence* remains tethered to genealogical society. The rise of autological claims has led to the formation of a community with multiple and at times conflicting relationships to ableism and to power more generally. There remain critical differences, for example, among those whose congenital neurodivergence has led to forced institutionalization, those whose neurodivergence is easily commodifiable and targeted by pharmaceutical companies, those whose acquired neurodivergence was generated by the trauma of state violence, and those whose neurodivergences span more than one of these categories. When we consider this variation, it becomes clear that, again like *nonbinary*, *neurodivergence* is home to people who sometimes share little in common.

Fortunately, neurodivergent community has developed several rhetorical strategies to negotiate power differentials among its members. While these strategies are imperfect, they motion toward the kind of extra-identitarian sociality made possible by identities, such as nonbinary and neurodivergent, whose capaciousness renders their social content unpredictable. This is a sociality maintained not through the liberal discourses of commonality but through the radical care made possible by accountability. The strategies to which I am alluding fall under the rubric of access. To talk about access is to talk about power, because access is demi-identitarian, floating in, out of, and around categories, blurring the edges of community membership.

Typically, access is addressed through the language of *access needs*, meaning adjustments that disabled people require in order to achieve full participation. Access needs can be informed by disability or neurodivergent identities, but they are not generalizable to everyone who occupies them. Access is contingent, depending on both the individual and their context. When a neurodivergent person is asked about their access needs, they are not being asked about their relationship to *neurodivergence*. They are instead being asked about the seasonality of ableism, about how their bodymind is interacting with power in a particular moment. The language of access needs enables neurodivergent communities to make legible the differences among community members without interrogating the authenticity of anyone's community membership. Everyone in the world could claim neurodivergence, and access needs would still differentiate each person's shifting relation to power.

Once people's access needs have been established, the conversation can move toward ensuring that access is provided and that access labor is distributed equitably. This is where the language of *disability impacts* becomes useful. I first learned the phrase from Jessica Horvath Williams, who originated the term in conversation with Angela M. Carter. To discuss disability impacts is to discuss symptomatology beyond the language of pathology. My disability impacts are how my disabilities impact me or how I experience my disabilities. The concept extends the language of access needs by not only attending to differences among people who share a disability identity but also creating an opportunity to talk about how each person can contribute to the community's collective needs. When asked about my own disability impacts, I can share my trouble with sensory integration and my fragile executive functioning. Once I've learned your disability impacts, we can negotiate how their (dis)alignment can be channeled toward a network of care that actively works toward the full participation of us both.

I am under no illusion that talking about access needs and disability impacts solves every problem that attends being in community with others. The language cannot guarantee that people are honest about their experience of neurodivergence or that they follow through on their commitments to facilitating others' access. The language also cannot guarantee a solution to access friction or when people's access needs rub up against each other in ways that make providing access mutually challenging. Discussing access needs and disability impacts is a rhetorical gesture toward the radical reflexivity that is required to ensure true accountability within a diverse community. Nevertheless, I want to observe this gesture with all the generosity I can muster, because, as Ada Hubrig reminds us, "we don't have the luxury to completely halt these practices to reflect on them" (2021, 218). We should be critical of them in a way that allows us to remain "in motion" (218), stumbling through this turbulent season, always doing our best to improve the imperfect tools at our imperfect disposal.

Alleviating Anxiety

It is with such urgent generosity that I offer up these neurodivergent strategies for nonbinary appropriation. I am thinking of access needs and disability
impacts as "possibility models" for both communities, where their purpose
is not to carve out a linear path for others to copy but to offer reassurance
that new ways of being and being together are realizable (Smythe 2022).
The strategies used to observe power differentials and adjudicate care labor
among neurodivergent and disabled people may also be useful to nonbinary
and trans folks—many of whom are neurodivergent—as they, too, seek to
be more accountable to one another.

Nonbinary people need not adopt wholesale the language of disability
impacts and access needs to find their structures useful. What would it mean
for nonbinary people to begin developing language that communicates our
individual relationships to cissexism and other forms of gendered power?
This language might speak to the material demands or social implications
of transition across its many iterations. What would happen if nonbinary
people were to be more forthcoming about how their nonbinariness affects
their daily lives? The effects may include experiences of dysphoria, the imbri-
cations of gender with other identities or axes of marginalization, or perhaps
the variable nature of nonbinariness across time and space. These questions
are not meant to encourage typologizing among nonbinary people; rather,
they are intended to nuance how nonbinary community addresses the
distribution of power within its own borders. Anyone (everyone!) can be
nonbinary so long as we are actively working to honor one another's differences more intentionally and to show up for one another more graciously.

It is hard for me sometimes to remember that the language I have made
into a home is not mine alone. All of us remain bound to identity, to finding a home in language, so it behooves us to invest our energy in learning
how to share our home with friends and strangers. In sharing a home, we
are not merely coexisting in the same space but also forging new kin. We
are surviving a season together; it is only together that any of us survive at
all. By surviving this season in *nonbinary*'s life cycle, we may usher in a new
season for trans liberation, one that leans into the immensity of identity in
order to more carefully situate each of ourselves within it. If we are careful—by which I mean honest with ourselves, attentive to others, unstinting
with our care, and patient through the heat—we can build accountability
into the bedrock of being and doing *nonbinary*. We, too, can model possibility for getting through the summer.

J. Logan Smilges is an assistant professor of English Language and Literatures at the University of British Columbia. They are the author of *Queer Silence: On Disability and Rhetorical Absence* (University of Minnesota Press, 2022) and *Crip Negativity* (University of Minnesota Press, 2023). They can be reached via email at logan.smilges@ubc.ca.

Works Cited

Amin, Kadji. 2022. "We Are All Nonbinary: A Brief History of Accidents." *Representations* 158 (1): 106–19.

———. 2023. "Taxonomically Queer? Sexology and New Queer, Trans, and Asexual Identities." *GLQ: A Journal of Lesbian and Gay Studies* 29 (1): 91–107.

Bey, Marquis. 2020. "How Ya Mama'n'em? Blackness, Nonbinariness, and Radical Subjectivity." *Peitho* 22 (4). https://cfshrc.org/article/how-ya-mamanem-blackness-nonbinariness-and-radical-subjectivity/.

———. 2022a. *Black Trans Feminism*. Durham, NC: Duke University Press.

———. 2022b. "Marquis Bey: About." Northwestern University. https://afam.northwestern.edu/people/faculty/marquis-bey.html. Accessed May 23, 2023.

Brechin, Archie. 2018. "Neurotypical Neurodivergent Dichotomy." Autism Society, May 1, 2018. https://www.autism-society.org/stories/neurotypical-neurodivergent-dichotomy/.

Colyar, Brock. 2022. "They, Then and Now: Asking for Pronouns Has Become a Social Standard. Who Is It Serving?" *The Cut*, June 22, 2022. https://www.thecut.com/article/brock-colyar-pronouns-nonbinary-essay.html.

Dutta, Aniruddha. 2018. "Allegories of Gender: Transgender Autology versus Transracialism." *Atlantis Journal* 39 (2): 86–98.

Gaeta, Amy. 2023. "Diagnostic Advertisements: The Phantom Disabilities Created by Social Media Surveillance." In "This Feature Has Been Disabled: Critical Intersections of Disability and Information Studies," special issue of *First Monday*. https://firstmonday.org/ojs/index.php/fm.

Gill-Peterson, Jules. 2021. "Two Transsexuals Talk Nonbinary." *Sad Brown Girl*, April 30, 2021. https://sadbrowngirl.substack.com/p/two-transsexuals-talk-nonbinary.

Hubrig, Ada. 2021. "Care Work, Queercrip Labor Politics, and Queer Generosities." *QED: A Journal in GLBTQ Worldmaking* 8 (3): 213–21.

Povinelli, Elizabeth A. 2006. *The Empire of Love: Toward a Theory of Intimacy, Genealogy, and Carnality*. Durham, NC: Duke University Press.

Smilges, J. Logan. 2023. "Neurotrans: Thorazine, HIV, and Marsha P." *Trans Studies Quarterly* 9 (4): 34–52.

Smythe, S. A. 2022. "Can I Get a Witness? Black Feminism, Trans Embodiment, and Thriving Past the Fault Lines of Care." *Palimpsest* 11 (1): 85–107.

Tourmaline, Eric A. Stanley, and Johanna Burton, eds. 2017. *Trap Door: Trans Cultural Production and the Politics of Visibility.* Cambridge, MA: MIT Press.

Walker, Nick. 2021. *Neuroqueer Heresies: Notes on the Neurodiversity Paradigm, Autistic Empowerment, and Postnormal Possibilities.* Fort Worth, TX: Autonomous Press.

Yergeau, M. Remi. 2018. *Authoring Autism: On Rhetoric and Neurological Queerness.* Durham, NC: Duke University Press.

Nonbinary Pronouns in Literary History: Queer(ing) Pronouns in the Works of Aphra Behn and Margaret Cavendish

Lena Mattheis

Abstract: This article seeks to explore how nonbinary, ambiguous, and gender-neutral pronouns are used for gender nonconforming characters in seventeenth-century British literature. Focusing on a particularly interesting time for gender nonconformity in British literature, the article traces queer pronoun use in three poems by Aphra Behn and in the prose narrative *Assaulted and Pursued Chastity* (1656) by Margaret Cavendish. While the history and grammaticality of singular they and other gender-neutral pronouns has been explored in several linguistic studies, the aesthetic dimension and historicity of gender-neutral language in literature is still frequently questioned. An examination of what is only a small sample of literary texts that consciously play with unstable pronouns, ambiguously gendered characters, and gender nonconforming language emphasizes the artistic and creative dimension of nonbinary and gender-neutral pronouns. The fact that we find ambivalent pronouns and gender nonconforming characters at the core of many plays, poems, and novels in literary history also shows that readers have been able to comprehend and empathize with queerly gendered characters and pronouns for centuries. **Keywords:** pronouns; singular they; trans; gender; literary history

There are many reasons why a literary studies approach that focuses on pronouns as elements of form can help us gain new perspectives on some of the current, frequently transphobic and racist, debates on gender-neutral language. First, despite supposed grammatical or aesthetic shortcomings, gender-neutral pronouns, including singular they, have been in use, in literary as well as quotidian discourse, for centuries. Through an exploration of queer(ed) pronoun use in seventeenth-century British literature, this essay seeks to show how nonbinary, gender-neutral, and ambiguous pronouns

WSQ: Women's Studies Quarterly 51: 3 & 4 (Fall/Winter 2023) © 2023 by Lena Mattheis. All rights reserved.

have not only functioned as practical linguistic means to refer to people of unknown genders but have been used to explicitly refer to people and characters that exist beyond the gender binary—whether that be trans, nonbinary, or gender nonconforming in a different way. While this will be the main aim of this essay, I also want to highlight how gender-neutral and ambiguous pronouns were (and are) used *because of*, not despite a lack of, their aesthetic effect in literature. Linguist Anna Livia, reflecting on her work in *Pronoun Envy* (2000), writes about the relevance of studying queer pronouns beyond linguistic corpora, "in the unspontaneous, carefully planned discourse of fiction. It reveals not what native speakers naturally do, but what they are able to understand and the inventions and models that influence their understanding" (2003, 157). Observing how gendered language was transed in literary history provides a fresh perspective on contemporary readers' ability to relate to gender nonconformity and queer language. Literary examples, then, show not only that queer use of pronouns has a long history and a creative quality but also, crucially, that readers have been able to grasp the concept of nonbinary pronoun use for centuries.

The use of gender nonconforming (GNC) pronouns in literature is inextricably linked with feminist and queer issues, trans perspectives, and, of course, with intersectional identities.[1] The seventeenth-century texts by British writers Aphra Behn and Margaret Cavendish that this essay will center on are protofeminist texts, written in contexts that did not consider gender, sex, and sexual orientation as distinct, or as identities per se. The GNC characters presented in these texts are therefore not neatly identifiable as queer, trans, or nonbinary. Indeed, trying to classify them as such would not only be anachronistic but would also reinforce a gender binary that has a comparatively much shorter and more geographically limited history than transness and gender fluidity (see Lugones 2010). At the same time, the fact that these characters and texts do not conform to the gendered expectations presented in their storyworlds is abundantly clear. I therefore take my cue from Kit Heyam's insightful and highly relevant history *Before We Were Trans* (2022), in which they approach subjects from history and literature with a compassionate as well as productive openness towards ambiguity. Heyam acknowledges that describing the way in which characters are read and presented as GNC with gender-neutral or ambiguous pronouns (among other formal devices) does not mean having to force these characters into a specific box; it allows us to open up boxes and possibilities where appropriate.

Perceptions of gender and gendered norms are always specific to spatio-temporal contexts and cultures. For this essay, I have selected three poems by Aphra Behn and a prose text by Margaret Cavendish, all of which use GNC pronouns in distinct ways. This is a conscious selection of rather well-known texts and authors, which aims to emphasize that GNC pronouns are neither obscure nor only found in a particular type of text or genre. Considering the shocking rise in transphobia in the current British cultural climate, a focus on the rich queer, trans, and nonbinary traditions of British literary history seems timely. The seventeenth century offers particularly interesting treatments of gender nonconformity in British literature. Despite the patriarchal restrictions that also weighed heavily on Behn and Cavendish, although the latter was very privileged from birth, there was room for gender nonconformity in art and in life. This openness to ambiguity was limited by a more forceful insistence on harmful gender binaries and antiqueer legislation in the eighteenth and nineteenth centuries (see for example Epstein 1990, Goldner 2011, or Martin 1998). In these turbulent times, caught between possibilities for gender transgressions and the impossibilities of being female* writers, Behn and Cavendish defied norms in their personal lives and their careers and breathed life into a plethora of characters that can easily be read as gender nonconforming and potentially trans or nonbinary.

A Note on Nonbinary and GNC Pronouns

Pronouns can be used queerly in many different ways: singular they as a gender-neutral pronoun and also as a pronoun used specifically to describe GNC and nonbinary people, neopronouns in fiction and in linguistic history, epicene pronouns from different languages (the neutral *on* in French or *hen* in Swedish, for example), the oblique stroke of the slash separating and connecting at the same time in *s/he*, the fusion of binarily gendered pronouns in *iel* (French) or *sier* (German), and even the *I* of a first-person narration can conceal or ambiguate gender. Plural forms can be employed queerly; a character can be described with several different pronouns, or simply with no pronouns at all. All of these strategies are used and have been used in literature and literary history. These pronouns reflect the diversity of language that nonbinary and GNC people might use to refer to themselves or to be referred to.

While neopronouns and mixed forms tend to be perceived as more cumbersome in general usage, many studies show that generic singular they is used with ease by Anglophone speakers and, contrary to popular belief, is perceived as grammatical by most (see Bradley, Schmid, and Lombardo 2019). By contrast, "the distinction between gender-neutral (silent on gender) vs. non-binary (referring to gender-nonconforming referents) pronouns is underexplored" (Bradley et al. 2019, 1) and although I am not a linguist, this is exactly what I want to engage with for my readings in this article. How are pronouns not simply generic or silent on the subject of gender but rather employed in a queer way to denote gender nonconformity in literature? This distinction is relevant in an immense variety of contexts, from human-computer interaction (Spiel, Keyes, and Barlas 2019) to psychology (Ansara and Hegarty 2012), education (McEntarfer and Iovannone 2022), and many other areas of life, art, and society. The aesthetic, narratological, and formal strategies literary texts employ to express GNC subjectivity in pronouns can be enlightening for all of them.

Ambiguity in Aphra Behn

Largely forgotten or dismissed for frank expressions of female* desire and norm-defying bodies until the mid-nineteenth century (see Martin 1998, 197, or Duyfhuizen 1991, 63–64), Aphra Behn's extensive oeuvre in poetry, drama, and prose was rediscovered by 1970s feminists and is of particular interest in queer studies for its sapphic content and gender-bending characters and storylines. Virginia Woolf's passionate endorsement of Behn's work in *A Room of One's Own* ([1928] 2014) is frequently referenced by both queer and feminist scholars. Although much of Behn's life remains a mystery, Behn likely had lovers of different genders and sexual orientations (see Todd 2017)—a fluidity that is reflected in the characters peopling the multifaceted sensual writing. Behn's poetry is probably most frequently cited when it comes to gender ambiguity—"the slippery nature of Behn's gender performances become most apparent under cover of poetry" (Martin 1998, 202)—although the experimental epistolary novel *Love-Letters between a Nobleman and His Sister* (1684–1687) clearly also defies gendered expectations on the level of both content and literary form, as do several of Behn's plays and the novel *Oroonoko; or, the Royal Slave* (1688).

The impressive volume and range of Behn's work makes choosing exemplary texts a challenge, but I find that the three poems "On a Juniper-Tree Cut Down to Make Busks" ([1684] 2013), "The Willing Mistress" ([1673] 2002), and "To the Fair Clarinda, Who Made Love to Me, Imagined More

Than Woman" ([1688] 2002) present particularly intriguing uses of queer pronouns. To begin with an interesting case of queer ecology, "On a Juniper-Tree" depicts a sensual love triangle between two human lovers and a tree. The poem begins by centering the nonhuman first-person speaker, who kindly lends shade to the lovers Philocles (he/him) and Chloris (she/her) and, enticed by their caresses, soon becomes actively involved in the sex act. The juniper tree is attributed with male and female characteristics, and it is the masculine human lover that interacts with its phallic root, creating possibilities for homosexual and bisexual readings: "The Shepherdess my Bark caressed, / Whilst he my Root (Love's Pillow) kissed" (lines 82–83). The tree's ambiguous gender and sexuality present a concept of gender nonconformity that was popular at the time: that of the hermaphrodite or the hermaphroditic body, which can connote what we would today refer to as homosexual desire; nonbinary, trans, or GNC gender performance; or intersex embodiment (see Frangos 2004). Through ambiguous language and a first-person point of view, the tree is able to inhabit "a perfectly chosen and perfectly indeterminate subject position that through hermaphroditic suggestion slips the bonds of our binary understanding and slides beneath our linguistic capabilities to a gender position that is radically indefinable" (Martin 1998, 203–4). The tree's pronoun use is queered through the literary and linguistic form of this subject position: the botanical being is not a passive "it" but an active "I" we can understand and empathise with. Though somewhat anthropomorphized, the tree remains flora and invites readers to experience the erotic encounter through a perspective that is beyond dimorphically gendered human bodies.

Behn's "The Willing Mistress," in a very different type of queering, shows how pronoun use can become queer when we consult the archives and compare different manifestations of a text throughout its publication history. Depicting another pastoral tryst with nonhuman co-conspirators, the more popular version of the poem begins: "Amyntas led me to a Grove, / Where all the Trees did shade us; / The Sun it self, though it had Strove, / It could not have betray'd us: / The place secur'd from humane Eyes" (lines 1–5), and then shows the two lovers' bodies embracing, again leaving room for ambiguity as to what exactly these bodies look like: "Which made me willing to receive / That which I dare not name" (lines 15–16). The unnaming of the body part renders the lover's embodiment potentially nonbinary or GNC.

This version of "The Willing Mistress" is included in Behn's play *The Dutch Lover* (1673), but a different version was published a year prior. As

Janet White writes in an impressive thesis on lesbian salience in Behn's work:

> Prior to inclusion in *Poems Upon Several Occasions*, "The Willing Mistress"
> is thought to have undergone several changes. While we might assume that
> the lovers in the play's [*The Dutch Lover*, 1673] version of the poem are
> heterosexual, a year earlier in 1672 "The Willing Mistress" was included in
> *The Covent Garden Drolery* entitled "Song." This earlier version of the poem
> begins "I led my Silvia to a Grove" and the first line of the third stanza reads
> "My greedy eyes" rather than "His charming Eyes." (White 2015)

Although this earlier version of the poem therefore lends itself to a sapphic
reading, the inverted point of view creates space for gender ambiguity. Does
a female speaker take on a masculine role here? Is the speaker now the
male seducer? Or is the "I" beyond gender, expressing the desire of a GNC
person? Interestingly, it is now no longer the receiving sexual partner that
refuses to name, to make unambiguous, the body parts involved, but the
active partner—"Which made her willing to receive; / That which I dare
not name" (Behn 2020, 447)—creating even more space to read the queer
pronoun use as referring to a person existing outside of physical, identity-
related, or relational binaries.

Behn's "To the Fair Clarinda," a love poem dedicated to a GNC addressee
(thou/thee/thy) by a first-person plural "we," is most frequently referenced
when it comes to Behn moving beyond the gender binary. Clarinda's beauty
is particularly intriguing because it transcends masculine and feminine:
"Fair lovely Maid, or if that Title be / Too weak, too Feminine for Nobler
thee, / Permit a Name that more Approaches Truth: / And let me call thee,
Lovely Charming Youth" (lines 1–4). The use of the second-person singular
pronoun "thou" is relevant here not because it was unusual but because of
its role in the history of singular they. As Dennis Baron reminds us, "you"
had been an exclusively plural pronoun "until the 1600s, when it slowly,
slowly starts pushing out *thou, thee, thy*, and *thine*, second-person singular
pronouns that English speakers had been using since the days of *Beowulf*"
(2020, 152)—making singular "you" a more recent addition to the world
of Anglophone pronouns than singular they, which, it is worth mentioning, "was common by the late 1300s" (153).[2] The form of address, however,
not only makes a case against claims that pronouns cannot shift in number
("thou" having been replaced by singular "you," previously only used as
plural), it also leaves the gender of both the speaker and the addressee
ambiguous. While this form of direct personal address with ungendered

first- and second-person pronouns is common in love poetry of the time, the poem overtly addresses this ambiguity and "seems explicitly concerned both with definitions—with 'naming' the gender of the beloved object—and with 'constraints,' both personal and social. The act of naming in line 4 renders Clarinda's gender indefinite: a 'maid' is clearly female, but a youth is more neutral—somehow 'in-between' a woman and a fully developed man" (Martin 1998, 204). The speaker also makes contradicting assumptions about the beloved's body—about whether or not "A Snake lies hid beneath the Fragrant Leaves" (line 17)[3]—but the desire and love remain, not despite but because of the nonconformity of the beloved's physical appearance and gender performance. The ending of the poem reminds us again of then-common ideas about "hermaphroditic" bodies and gender performances: "While we the noblest Passions do extend / The Love to *Hermes*, *Aphrodite* the Friend" (lines 22–23). Making the poem rather personal, Behn places the first name Aphra in between Hermes and Aphrodite and renders the relationship within the poem herm-*aphro*ditic. In Behn's time, the word "hermaphrodite" could indicate a third sex, an intersex body, but also a female body in masculine clothing or a gay man taking the receiving part of a sexual relationship. The term likely had many additional, more subtle connotations, which are more difficult to reconstruct. No matter which interpretation of "hermaphrodite" we choose to focus on, Behn's work is clearly marked by a continuous fascination not just with GNC characters but also with disabled and unusually formed bodies (see Mintz 2006).

Although Behn uses this openness to ambiguity to create complex and seductive GNC characters, it is important to note that the ambivalence of the GNC and female* characters also points to the misogynist, racist, and classist ideas that shaped the world around Behn. Even as a white English person who worked as a spy for Charles II and was paid (if poorly) for writing, Behn struggled to gain the same recognition as, for example, her contemporary, the Earl of Rochester. Instead, Behn's work was condemned and erased for breaking the rules of both Protestant and libertine literary conventions, in ways male contemporaries were celebrated for.

Mixed Pronouns in Margaret Cavendish

A common queer use of pronouns in theater and narrative prose presents itself in the instability of pronouns for characters who are cross-dressing or otherwise presenting as a different gender.[4] We find this strategy in parts of Aphra Behn's oeuvre but also in drama and prose written by Margaret Cavendish, Duchess of Newcastle, who was not only pioneering as a female author publishing under her own name but also produced a very early work of science fiction with *The Blazing World* (1666). As Sujata Iyengar points out, the "pronominal ambiguity" (2002, 657) in her writing was a common feature of early modern romance and Elizabethan and Jacobean theater dealing in gender transgressions. Writing about Cavendish's prose narrative *Assaulted and Pursued Chastity* (1656), Iyengar notes that Cavendish moves beyond this somewhat established pronoun switch in dramatic dialogue and "uses the male personal pronoun to refer to the cross-dressed Travellia, as if the heroine (like Virginia Woolf's Orlando) does indeed change sex for the duration of 'his' adventure" (657).[5] While I agree that Travellia does more than simply take on a (pronominal) disguise, in my reading, Travellia does not *change* sex but is and remains a GNC character throughout the entire narrative. Cavendish mixes differently gendered pronouns and descriptions not just until the end of the ("cross-dressed") adventure but until the end of the narrative. The mixing of pronouns however does indeed begin when Travellia is, as the name suggests, travelling and "the master walking upon the Deck, seeing a handsome youth stand there in Pages clothes, asked him who he was, and how he came there. Said she, I do suppose, you are bound for the Kingdom of Riches, where I desire to go" (Cavendish 2004, 61).

As suggested by the GNC attributes Travellia displays in this brief excerpt (being a "handsome youth" in "Pages clothes" on a male-connoted adventure), Cavendish's depictions of nonnormative gender go far beyond the slippage of pronouns. To give a brief summary of the rather complex plot of *Assaulted and Pursued Chastity*, the GNC protagonist, who we come to know as Travellia but who is also called Miseria prior to taking on a masculine appearance and as Affectionata later on,[6] is threatened with rape by a prince, whom Travellia, in self-defense, wounds with a pistol. Dressed in masculine clothing, Travellia travels to new shores and befriends the Queen of Amity, who is at war with the King of Amour for refusing to marry him. The value placed on female* friendship, or queer relationships with fluid boundaries, is underlined not just by the name of the queendom but also by the fact that the queen only agrees to wed the king and allows the suddenly docile prince to marry her intimate companion Travellia, on the condition that the relationship between the queen and Travellia remains close. The queen instructs the prince: "I will yield her to you, upon that condition you carry her not out of my kingdom; for since I cannot marry her, and so make her my husband, I will keep her if I can, and so make her my friend" (Cavendish 2004, 114). As we can see in this sapphic demand, not just the pronouns but also the gendered nouns are queered, as Travellia is both a "she" and a "husband" in this sentence.[7] In a compelling piece comparing the unruly erotic of Aphra Behn's GNC characters to the solution-oriented rebellion in Cavendish's romances,[8] Min notes that the homosocial and homoerotic relationships in *Assaulted and Pursued Chastity* allow the two main female* characters to step out of their assigned roles and social contracts and take on new power, names, and titles. Whether we read the relationship between Travellia and the queen—through an anachronistic contemporary lens— as a lesbian love story, as a relationship between a powerful woman and a trans* man, as a nonbinary sapphic affair (my favorite reading), or even as T4T, the ambiguous power dynamics and language create a fascinating openness that is only slightly narrowed by the utilitarian heterosexual marriages between king and queen and the prince and Travellia that bring a peaceful ending to the queer romantic adventure.

Underlining the importance of GNC ambiguity, of choosing not one but multiple possibilities, roles, and readings, Tien-yi Chao observes that "the mixed use of 'he' and 'she' highlights the heroine's gender as a fluid and complex identity, endorsing the Duchess's [Cavendish's] argument against fixed gender denotation in her prefaces" (Chao 2007, 92, quoted in Chao 2021). Cavendish even uses different pronouns and differently gendered descriptors within the same sentence, for example when Travellia's identity is questioned on a maritime journey:

> Asking him what he was; she answered him, that she was a gentleman's son, whom by the reason of civil wars, was carried out of his own country very young by his mother, and so related the truth of his being cast into that Kingdom, only she fained she was a youth, and had served a lady as her page; but desiring to return into his own Country, had mistaken and put himself into a wrong vessel. (Cavendish 2004, 61)

While one could argue that the first switch from "he" to "she" reflects a shifting focalization from the master of the ship who perceives Travellia as male to Travellia's own point of view, Travellia then fluidly moves back to mentioning "his own Country" in reported speech that would not necessitate the pronoun switch in the way a direct speech act may. Travellia thus clearly uses both sets of pronouns interchangeably, making Travellia's gender far more ambiguous than that of protagonists in other cross-dressing or disguise narratives that were popular at the time. The GNC or nonbinary gender expression in the narrative is clearly visible in the way Travellia presents through clothing and behavior, in the variously gendered contexts and roles in which Travellia feels comfortable, and in the way the narrative voice describes Travellia through queered pronouns.

Both Cavendish's and Behn's writing offer many other instances of queer pronoun use for GNC characters, and they are by no means the only authors playing with gender ambiguity and queer storylines on the page and on the stage. I highly recommend Emma Frankland's article "Trans Women on Stage," which explores, in particular, John Lyly's *Galatea* and the ways in which trans texts, readings, and performances can help combat erasure in history and in the present day. While previous scholarship has read Behn's and Cavendish's GNC characters and their pronouns as playfully stretching conceptions of gender but ultimately returning to a binarily gendered expression, I want to emphasize that what we see in these texts goes far beyond narratives of disguise and should be reconsidered as trans and nonbinary embodiment and language.

Orlando: A Conclusion

A queer intertextual path that has led many a reader to Aphra Behn's work is Behn's mention in Virginia Woolf's *A Room of One's Own* ([1928] 2014) as the author who has earned all women "the right to speak their minds" (79). In Woolf's mind, the importance of Behn's work could not be overstated. In the same chapter, Woolf also reflects on the magnificent scientist Cavendish would have made, though she is not very impressed with the Duchess's writing. Woolf, of course, has her own gender-bending protagonist with GNC pronouns: Orlando, who is modeled on her androgynous romantic partner and fellow writer, Vita Sackville-West. While Orlando begins the novel as a nobleman (he/him) and later becomes a woman (she/her), in the moment of transition, when the narrator reflects most genuinely on Orlando's gender, they are described with singular they:

> Orlando had become a woman—there is no denying it. But in every other respect, Orlando remained precisely as he had been. The change of sex, though it altered their future, did nothing whatever to alter their identity. Their faces remained, as their portraits prove, practically the same. His memory—but in the future we must, for convenience's sake, say "her" for "his," and "she" for "he"—her memory then, went back through all the

events of her past life without encountering any obstacles. (Woolf [1928] 2000, 98)

A brief metareflection reminds readers that we are still following the same character we got to know in the first ninety-eight pages of the novel, but that we should adapt our pronoun use to reflect the physical change they have undergone. This omniscient commentary also makes clear that the use of "she/her," which we are instructed to adopt in the future, is dictated solely by societal expectations and has nothing to do with the way in which Orlando sees or describes themselves, making "they/them" Orlando's most natural form of address.

Although pronouns are but a small part of the complexities that can arise in speaking and writing about gender nonconformity and nonbinary gender, they are still, almost a century after *Orlando*'s publication and roughly 350 years since Behn's and Cavendish's peak activity, a topic of contention. Literary history shows that queer(ed) pronouns can be affirming and empowering, whether that be through ambiguous pronouns, unstable pronouns, or plural, singular, first, second, or third person. Changing names and pronouns, mixing them, using singular they to refer to a generic or specific "they"—all of these strategies have been and are used successfully in much wider contexts than the few examples presented here reveal. This also shows that readers were able to understand and enjoy GNC language and relate to GNC characters for much longer than some of the critics of recent movements towards nonbinary and trans* inclusion would have us believe.

In their insightful book *Life Isn't Binary* (2019), Meg-John Barker and Alex Iantaffi write about the harmful binaries that are imposed on all aspects of life: from sexuality, relationships, and language, to bodies, emotions, and thinking. Throughout their engagement with these topics, they explain how external binaries force us to tell certain stories about ourselves and to tell them in a certain way—in order to be relatable, in order to not be harmed, in order to access healthcare . . . Barker and Iantaffi eloquently summarize: "We can see that gender is not inevitably binary when we look back through time and around the world today. When we do, we see many other ways of understanding gender" (2019, 55). I firmly believe that studying literary texts and their queer use of pronouns can not only provide a historical foundation for discussions of nonbinary identity, genderqueerness, and queer language but also allow us to open up harmful binary narratives in the past, present, and future of gender nonconformity.

The handwritten and leather-bound manuscript of *Orlando* that Woolf had sent to her beloved Vita reveals, in interlinear notations and corrections, the pronominal possibilities Woolf had considered for the titular character: mixing pronouns, sticking to one set, and changing the name Orlando to Orlanda (see Baron 2020, 124). The manuscript evidence showing these considerations reveals that something crucial is lost in Woolf's pronominal dilemma. The following sentence from the manuscript: "The sound of trumpets died away & Orlando stood for a moment *in all his/her beauty*, stark naked" (Baron 2020, 125; emphasis mine), becomes, in the final version of the book: "The sound of trumpets died away and Orlando stood stark naked" (Woolf [1928] 2000, 98). What we lose in editing, as well as in many debates about whether nonbinary and GNC pronouns are grammatically correct or aesthetically pleasing, is exactly what is lost here: all their nonbinary beauty.

Dr. Lena Mattheis is a lecturer in contemporary literature at the University of Surrey. Lena's research interests include queer and trans studies, literary urban studies, spoken word poetry, and mapping. To find out more about Lena's work in literary urban studies and mapping, please consult *Translocality in Contemporary City Novels* (Palgrave, 2021) or articles published in *Literary Geographies*, *Narrative*, and other peer-reviewed journals. Lena also hosts the Queer Lit podcast, which you can listen to on any podcasting platform. If you would like to talk about pronouns, queer writing, or maps, please get in touch: l.mattheis@surrey.ac.uk.

Notes

1. I find "gender nonconforming" to be the most appropriate term in this context, since I am looking at characters that defy gender norms of their cultural, temporal, spatial, and narrative contexts. Although many other terms could potentially apply to these characters, more specific terminology could easily limit a character instead of opening multiple possibilities, as I aim to do in my readings.

2. For a diachronic overview tracing the linguistic development of singular they, see Nabila, Setiawan, and Widyastuti (2021).

3. Duyfhuizen reads this image as a clitoral one that is rendered more powerful by an added phallic connotation.

4. It is important to note that the common gender transgressions in Elizabethan theater, both with regards to plots and to male-presenting actors playing female roles, form an important part of trans* history and will have likely provided spaces for queer, GNC, and trans* people to live more authentically (see Adams 2013 and Frankland 2019). The term "cross-

dressing" is therefore only applicable to some aspects of these gender transgressions, while others were in fact very likely the opposite of theatrical masquerade, allowing GNC and trans* people to present more authentically, albeit for a short time and in a restricted place.

5. Iyengar's insightful work also considers Cavendish's complicated and problematic views on the entanglements of race, class, and gender and the transgressions of genres in her mix of fiction and philosophical treaties.

6. Although the names are not overtly gendered, they "allegorize her travails" (Min 2020, 153): Travellia is "Miseria" while being sexually assaulted by the prince and "Affectionata" when enamoured with the queen, the telling names emphasizing the choice of homoerotic and homosocial bonds over heterosexual relationships. The etymology of the word "travel," at the root of "Travellia," can lead us to Old French, where *travailler* could mean "to toil" but also "to torture." In the Anglophone context, this meaning is softened to "to trouble" and, of course, to "taking on a (difficult) journey." Travellia is thus not simply "traveling" geographically but also "troubling" the gender binary by "traveling" between genders.

7. In *Female Husbands: A Trans History* (2020), Jen Manion writes specifically about people who were assigned female at birth but lived as men, with the same social roles and responsibilities as husbands, from roughly 1740 to 1840 in the U.K. and 1830 to 1910 in the U.S. Although the term "female husband" was popularized even later to describe this phenomenon (and of course Manion is looking at the histories of people in the world rather than characters in literature), I wonder whether being a female husband to the queen is what would have best suited Travellia.

8. I use the word "erotic" here in Audre Lorde's sense as well as more directly referring to sexual desire and eroticism.

Works Cited

Adams, Annalisa. 2013. "'His Play Shan't Ask Your Leave to Live': Following the Ghosts of Trans Embodiment in Restoration Drama." MA thesis, Georgetown University.

Ansara, Gavriel Y., and Peter Hegarty. 2012. "Cisgenderism in Psychology: Pathologising and Misgendering Children from 1999 to 2008." *Psychology & Sexuality* 3 (2): 137–60.

Barker, Meg-John, and Alex Iantaffi. 2019. *Life Isn't Binary: On Being Both, Beyond and In-between.* London: Jessica Kingsley Publishers.

Baron, Denis. 2020. *What's Your Pronoun? Beyond She and He.* New York: Liveright Publishing.

Behn, Aphra. (1673) 2002. "The Willing Mistress." *Poetry Archive*. Reprinted from *The Dutch Lover*. https://www.poetry-archive.com/b/the_willing_mistress.html. Accessed July 28, 2022.

———. (1684) 2013. "On a Juniper-Tree Cut Down to Make Busks." *Bartleby*. Reprinted from *Poetica Erotica: A Collection of Rare and Curious Amatory Verse*, ed. Thomas Robert Smith, 1921–22. New York: Boni and Liveright, https://www.bartleby.com/334/693.html. Accessed July 28, 2022.

———. (1684–1687). 2005. *Love-Letters between A Nobleman and His Sister*. Project Gutenberg. http://www.public-library.uk/pdfs/3/744.pdf.

———. (1688) 2014. *Oroonoko; or, The Royal Slave*. New York: Melville House.

———. (1688) 2002. "To the Fair Clarinda, Who Made Love to Me, Imagined More Than Woman." *Poetry Archive*. First published in *A Miscellany of New Poems by Several Hands*. https://www.poetry-archive.com/b/to_the_fair_clarinda.html. Accessed July 28, 2022.

———. 2020. "Song." In *The Broadview Anthology of Seventeenth-Century Verse*, ed. Alan Rudrum, Holly Faith Nelson, and Joseph Black, 447. Peterborough: Broadview Press.

Bradley, Evan D., Julia Salkind, Ally Moore, and Sofi Teitsort. 2019. "Singular 'They' and Novel Pronouns: Gender-Neutral, Nonbinary, or Both?" *Proceedings of the Linguistic Society of America* 4 (36): 1–7.

Bradley, Evan D., Maxwell Schmid, and Hannah Lombardo. 2019. "Personality, Prescriptivism, and Pronouns: Factors Influencing Grammaticality Judgments of Gender-Neutral Language." *English Today* 35 (4): 41–52.

Cavendish, Margaret. 2004. "Assaulted and Pursued Chastity." In *The Blazing World and Other Writings*, 45–118. London: Penguin Books.

Chao, Tien-yi. 2007. "The Construction of Transmutable Gender in Margaret Cavendish's Assaulted and Pursued Chastity." *In-between* 16 (1/2): 83–93.

———. 2021. "'Liberty Is Dangerous, Especially amongst the Effeminat Sex': Strategies for Single Women's Travel Safety in 'Assaulted and Pursued Chastity'(1656)." *English Studies* 102 (8): 1024–45.

Duyfhuizen, Bernard. 1991. "'That Which I Dare Not Name': Aphra Behn's 'The Willing Mistress.'" *ELH* 58 (1): 63–82.

Epstein, Julia. 1990. "Either/Or—Neither/Both: Sexual Ambiguity and the Ideology of Gender." *Genders*, no. 7: 99–142.

Frangos, Jennifer. 2004. "Aphra Behn's Cunning Stunts: 'To the Fair Clarinda.'" *The Eighteenth Century* 45 (1): 21–40.

Frankland, Emma. 2019. "Trans Women on Stage: Erasure, Resurgence and #notadebate." In *The Palgrave Handbook of the History of Women on Stage*, ed. Jan Sewell and Clare Smout, 775–805. Cham: Palgrave Macmillan.

Goldner, Virginia. 2011. "Trans: Gender in Free Fall." *Psychoanalytic Dialogues* 21 (2): 159–71.

Heyam, Kit. 2022. *Before We Were Trans: A New History of Gender*. London: Basic Books.

Iyengar, Sujata. 2002. "Royalist, Romancist, Racialist: Rank, Gender, and Race in the Science and Fiction of Margaret Cavendish." *ELH* 69 (3): 649–72.

Livia, Anna. 2000. *Pronoun Envy: Literary Uses of Linguistic Gender*. Oxford: Oxford University Press.

———. 2003. "'One Man in Two Is a Woman': Linguistic Approaches to Gender in Literary Texts." In *The Handbook of Language and Gender*, ed. Janet Holmes and Miriam Meyerhoff, 142–58. Melbourne: Blackwell Publishing.

Lugones, María. 2010. "Toward a Decolonial Feminism." *Hypatia* 25 (4): 742–59.

Manion, Jen. 2020. *Female Husbands: A Trans History*. Cambridge: Cambridge University Press.

Martin, Roberta C. 1998. "'Beauteous Wonder of a Different Kind': Aphra Behn's Destabilization of Sexual Categories." *College English* 61 (2): 192–210.

McEntarfer, Heather Killelea, and Jeffry Iovannone. 2022. "Faculty Perceptions of Chosen Name Policies and Non-binary Pronouns." *Teaching in Higher Education* 27 (5): 632–47.

Min, Eun Kyung. 2020. "Fictions of Obligation: Contract and Romance in Margaret Cavendish and Aphra Behn." *Eighteenth-Century Fiction* 32 (2): 245–69.

Mintz, Susannah B. 2006. "Freak Space: Aphra Behn's Strange Bodies." *Restoration: Studies in English Literary Culture, 1660–1700* 30 (2): 1–19.

Nabila, Izzatia, Slamet Setiawan, and Widyastuti. 2021. "To Disclose a Less Generic Pronoun: Addressing the Non-binary 'They'." *Lakon: Jurnal Kajian Sastra Dan Budaya* 10 (2): 84–93.

Spiel, Katta, Os Keyes, and Pinar Barlas. 2019. "Patching Gender: Non-binary Utopias in HCI." Paper presented at *CHI*, Glasgow, May 4–9: 1–11.

Todd, Janet. 2017. *Aphra Behn: A Secret Life*. Bloomsbury.

White, Jane. 2015. "Aphra Behn and the Poetics of Lesbian Salience in the Seventeenth Century." *Brightonline*, no. 1. Accessed July 28, 2022. https://blogs.brighton.ac.uk/brightonline/issue-1/words-indeed-can-no-more-show-5-aphra-behn-and-the-poetics-of-lesbian-salience-in-the-seventeenth-century/.

Woolf, Virginia. (1928) 2000. *Orlando*. London: Penguin Classics.

———. (1928) 2014. *A Room of One's Own*. London: Penguin Classics.

Nature Is Nonbinary: Gender and Sexuality in Biology Education in Chile

Tebi Ardiles, Paulina Bravo, Fabián Fernández,
and Corina González-Weil

Abstract: This article brings together four educators to collaboratively discuss how nonbinary representations and narratives circulate through education, especially in biology education in the context of Chile. This discussion is illustrated with an experience that began in August 2020 with a master's course and continued with the practice of teaching biology to students in a school science classroom and to teachers-to-be at the university, both with a focus on the natural, the human, and the nonbinary features of the nonhuman. Finally, the implications of these experiences for our practice and a broader context of teaching biology are discussed. **Keywords:** nonbinary; biology education; master's course; teaching biology; school science classroom

Context: Where We Started

According to the Spanish Royal Academy's dictionary, the third of four uses of the letter *o* is for disjunctive conjunction, which means it "denotes difference, separation or alternative between two or more people, things or ideas" (RAE 2021), exactly as the word "o" is used in its English form, "or." This disjunction is commonly used in everyday vocabulary to separate actions or objects into dichotomous categories, such as "Do you prefer tea or coffee?" In the following paragraphs, the necessary and innocuous use of the disjunctive conjunction will be overshadowed by its discursive dangers in topics related to sexuality, since the letter *o* in Spanish indicates binarism. As we see it, this linguistic binary use serves to classify people into hierarchical values, where those on the left side of the *o* are higher in status than the ones positioned on its right. This disjunction means not only separation but also

WSQ: Women's Studies Quarterly 51: 3 & 4 (Fall/Winter 2023) © 2023 by Tebi Ardiles, Paulina Bravo, Fabián Fernández, and Corina González-Weil. All rights reserved.

damage. In this way, being a man "o" a woman, straight "o" gay, cisgender "o" transgender acquires a historical and social burden marked by discrimination, exclusion, and more recently, shouting down voices.

According to the Organisation for Economic Cooperation and Development (2019, 1), 2.7 percent of the population of fifteen OECD member countries comprises LGBT people, equivalent to 515,000 inhabitants in Chile and 189,000,000 people worldwide. Data coming from the U.S. Centers for Disease Control and Prevention (CDC) show that 13.4 percent of American students recognize themselves as lesbian, gay, or bisexual, and another 5.1 percent declare to have some gender nonconformity (Jarpe-Ratner 2020). Despite these data, in seventy-two countries, being homosexual is considered a crime, and in many others, including Chile, there are still events of discrimination and violence against these communities. Research by MOVILH (2013; Spanish acronym for Movimiento de Integración y Liberación Homosexual) revealed that 68.2 percent of LGBT Chilean people had suffered some discrimination.

One critical feminist theory that attempts to bring the discrimination situation to the fore—not necessarily from a discursive perspective—is queer theory (Ardiles 2021). Queer theory, despite being difficult to define due to its ontological and epistemological nature (Snyder and Broadway 2004), is describable in three basic principles, namely (1) to deconstruct the social construction of identity, (2) to break binaries, and (3) to interrupt heteronormativity. Queer theory questions the normative processes that structure lives, actions, language, power, and knowledge, defining and categorizing processes, people, ideas, identities, and institutions. Thus, queer theory alters the normative processes; it challenges categorical thinking and specificity, aiming to break the binary, and examines how the social construction of sexuality is normalized. Heterosexuality is presented as the only way to be human (Butler 2006, 2007, 2019; Gunckel 2009; Varela 2020). It reveals how truths and selves, or *yoes*, are socially constructed.[1] It questions how and by whom identities are created and spaces are opened to reconstruct the self. As such, queer theory is more interested in what can be rather than what is (Gunckel 2009, 63). From an educational perspective, queer theory criticizes institutions of learning and processes of education as limiting possible identities, promoting binary constructions, and naturalizing heteronormativity. Queer theory provides a framework for examining schools, curricula, and pedagogy to find identities, bodies, and experiences that have been silenced, ignored, and made invisible, thereby providing a lens to understand how schools are reproducing the norms of culture. Science education serves as an exemplary site to apply queer theory and to question schools, identities, knowledge, teaching, and learning (Gunckel 2009).

Specifically in science education, queer theory exposes how science curricula are heteronormative, promote binaries, and reinforce the construction of limited identities by avoiding nonbinariness. Snyder and Broadway (2004) pointed out, for example, that high school biology textbooks construct sexuality in a strictly heteronormative way. None of the textbooks they examined discussed sexuality outside of the heterosexual realm. Likewise, none included a discussion of homosexuality or any other nonheterosexual orientation. At the same time, there were only brief references to AIDS risks and there was no discussion of human sexuality for a purpose beyond reproduction (Gunckel 2009). Furthermore, as Fifield and Letts (2014) stated, some scientific skills, such as classification—an essential skill in the scientific process—promote a view that all things and beings can be categorized, labeled, and organized into neat packages based on identifiable characteristics and relationships. Thus, students of all ages learn to use dichotomous keys based on binary descriptions to classify objects and organisms (Gunckel 2009). In Gunckel's words, classification processes naturalize "order," so anyone who does not fit is not considered "normal."

In response to the above, queering science education would mean questioning the binary constructions of gender and sexuality in human nature, disputing heteronormativity, and opening spaces for marginalized identities. This stance supposes teachers and students to adopt a critical lens toward scientific knowledge and its processes (Gunckel 2009). Queering science education requires science educators, researchers, teachers, and students to examine and dispute how science is (hetero)sexualized. In this vein, questioning the nature of science and scientific knowledge, towards interrupting heteronormative structures and opening spaces to explore new identities and possibilities, requires teachers to become more than transmitters of knowledge. In so doing, queer pedagogy could be considered a border pedagogy that challenges heteronormative borders (Gunckel 2009). In biology, for example, queer pedagogy could mean addressing misconceptions such as the notions that homosexuality does not occur in nature or that sex is only for reproduction (Gunckel 2009). This is not about sexualizing biology but instead interpreting how biology is already explicitly heteronormative. Queering biology by incorporating nonbinarism and genderqueer perspectives encourages all biology educators "to be interested in the complex relationships between the various ways in which sexualities are organised and in what knowledge is produced and represented" (Sumara and Davis 1999, 203).

In our research, we used the concept of *fleta pedagogy* when referring to queer pedagogy. In Spanish, synonymous with the English word "queer" are the words *weco, maricón,* or *fleto* as derogatory ways to refer not only to gay men but also to most people belonging to the LGBTQIA+ community. We realized that it therefore made less sense to use "queer," since our process is carried out between Chilean Spanish speakers. Therefore, we started by using the concept of fleta instead of queer, also aiming to resignify a derogative word, as "queer" has been. Other ways of naming queer theory in the Latinx context include *marica, bollera,* or even *cuir theory*; however, for this article, the word "fleta" will be used to refer to the principles of queerness in our context. In doing so, when we refer to the broader framework of queer theory and queer pedagogy, we will use the word "queer," while when we refer to the pedagogy and research made in Chile, we will use the word "fleta" (Ardiles 2021).

In Chile, science classrooms are hetero- and cisnormative. Sex education, which includes sexual orientation, gender, and sex, is taught in science classes, using a conservative approach. An analysis of the Chilean curriculum shows that only six learning objectives are related to human sexuality and gender identity and affect, and the first one is in sixth grade. Likewise, in the seventh and tenth grades, mention is made of issues raised by fleta theory, like sexual orientation, gender, and identity expression. However, these contents are utterly disjointed from other contents, and what is more, they are never related to the biological learning asked in this unit. The Chilean curriculum is entirely silent on intersexuality, neurophysiological evidence of sexual behavior, epigenetic characteristics of homosexuality, and alloparenting and homoparenting in human and nonhuman species, and it is even oblivious to the importance of cooperation as widely understood in evolutionary and ecological terms.

Given this backdrop, we have sought a way to include fleta pedagogy, fleta science, and fleta biology in Chilean science classrooms. We did it by considering the "Big Ideas on Science Education" framework (Harlen 2010). The term "big idea" was coined by a group of science educators, teachers, and scientists from seven different countries under the leadership of Wynne Harlen, who developed a set of crucial ideas to promote the understanding of the natural world. Their work aimed to address the problem of students' negative perceptions towards science by teaching them these key ideas (Harlen 2010, 2015a, 2015b). Big ideas are described as pedagogically powerful because they offer direction to the teaching (Mitchell et al. 2016). Furthermore, as Whiteley (2012) pointed out, big ideas can be considered significant patterns of knowledge, allowing for "connecting the dots of knowledge that would otherwise be fragmented" (42). In our proposal, we mixed Harlen's understanding of big ideas with our concept of fleta pedagogy as well as ideas coming from biology, to teach topics like sexual diversities, nonbinarism in nature, and other issues related to sex education and to dispute the use of the *o*—referred to at the beginning of this article—that serves to hierarchize the diversity of expressions in and out the science classroom. Ultimately, we aim to promote with this relationship the free expression of students' sexual orientations and gender diversities.

Our Practice: What Did We Do?

In 2020, in a course within a master's degree, C and P (teachers of the course, authors of this article) challenged F and T (students of the course, authors of this article) to build a big idea—in the sense of Harlen's framework—related to a topic chosen by the students and considering what Mitchell and colleagues (2016) referred to as pedagogically powerful ideas. After some discussion, the following big idea was developed:

> In nature, sexual behaviors are not presented in a binary, dichotomous, or absolute way. Yet, there is a gradient of possibilities that generates diversity and contributes to the survival of the species. Human sexuality is not exempt from such diversity, which is translated into intertwined sociocultural, affective, psychological, value, and political dimensions that, alongside shaping the sexuality of a subject, interact with each other. As a result, sexuality cannot be restricted to merely a reproductive function or a binary.[2]

This idea arises after analyzing the Chilean curricula, some recent hate speeches delivered in our context, and different cases where the binarism of sexual behaviors (male/female, homosexual/heterosexual, cisgender/transgender) is questioned. This proposal can be broken down into two parts. First, "in nature, sexual behaviors are not presented in a binary, dichotomous, or absolute way. However, there is a gradient of possibilities that generates diversity and contributes to the survival of the species," which refers to sexual and reproductive behaviors in nature. In contrast, the second part is, namely, "Human sexuality is not exempt from such diversity, which is translated into intertwined sociocultural, affective, psychological, value, and political dimensions that, alongside shaping the sexuality of a subject, interact with each other. As a result, sexuality cannot be restricted to merely a reproductive function or a binary," which refers to the multifactorial nature of human sexuality and the complex interaction between its dimensions.

To realize the big idea's pedagogical potential, a design of a sequence of lessons was necessary. The lesson plan was made considering the following questions: *What to teach?* (big idea and its sociopolitical dimension); *Whom to teach?* (knowledge of students' preconceptions and interests); *How to teach?* (knowledge of strategies in the discipline); *How to evaluate?* (knowledge about strategies of evaluation); and *How is it related to the curriculum?* (knowledge of the science curriculum).

Sociopolitical Aspects of the Big Idea: What Did We Consider?

We like to think this big idea is embracing everyone's diversity: men, women, cisgender, transgender, intersex, nonbinary, gay, lesbian, straight, pansexual, asexual, demisexual, and all other possible identities—because we are all human and we are all sexual beings. Even today, it is common to use the term "sexual minorities" to refer to any sexual orientation or gender identity that escapes the hetero-cis norm; however, this concept rests on the sexual hegemony that has been imposed in Western societies for a significant amount of time. As a result, this concept of "minority" is often used as a euphemism and has a discursive burden that marginalizes those pigeonholed to live under the eaves of the so-called majority, without its privileges.

We agreed with Long, Steller, and Suh (2021), who pointed out that teachers have a rich opportunity to include gender diversity in their lessons. In inquiry lessons for nature, we can teach what is evident in nature: for instance, that there are more than four hundred animal species that present homosexual behaviour (Bagemihl 2000; Coria-Ávila, Triana-Del Rio, and Manzo 2011; Roughgarden 2013); that there are neurobiological bases of homosexuality, which, although they do not fully explain male or female homosexuality, have shown essential correlations (Romi 2009; Coria-Ávila, Triana-Del Rio, and Manzo 2011); that epigenetics has shown how the silencing or overexpression of genes in embryonic development manages to modify the brain circuits expressing sexual orientation (Romi 2009);

amongst others. Thus, countless examples in nature escape from the hetero-cis norm by disputing not only heterosexuality but also how stable sex is (Bagemihl 2000; Romi 2009; Coria-Ávila, Triana-Del Rio, and Manzo 2011; Roughgarden 2013). The created idea supposes a strong emphasis on the critical emancipatory focus of Critical Scientific Literacy (Benzce and Carter 2011; Sjöström and Eilks 2018), since it seeks to make visible what many people experience; it allows for development of empathy, appreciation for individual freedoms, and respect for the freedoms of others—an ideal prelude generated by education while we wait for policymakers to take off the blindfold and begin to legislate for everyone and not just for the so-called majority.

Fleta Pedagogy in Action

Initially, the lesson plan considered six lessons of ninety minutes delivered in a classroom in Chile by T and F. In these lessons, preconceptions would be raised, and then the binarism in sex, gender, and sexual orientation would be discussed considering a repertoire of examples from nature, human sexuality, and the vision of the native people of Chile. However, applying this plan in 2021 was somewhat complex due to the pandemic. In the new scenario, the lesson plan changed to sixty minutes and was held in a hybrid format, meaning that some students were in the classroom while others were at home. For its application, T contacted a closely allied teacher (F), an LGBTQIA+ member too, who worked in a private school in Chile. Together, they changed the plan to only three lessons. They taught together in a tenth-grade course, and then F repeated the unit alone with another similar course.

The first lesson was based on raising the students' perceptions of human sexuality under four dimensions: biological, psychological, social, and affective (Mock 2005). During the second lesson, the idea of *nonbinary* in nature was reviewed. We questioned the idea of *dichotomous* in taxonomy, parental reproductive strategies, and sexual behavior such as types of asexual reproduction; vegetative reproduction in plants; sexual reproduction by external and internal fertilization; parthenogenesis in insects, birds, and chondrichthyans; different strategies of sex determination and differentiation; cases of homosexuality and bisexuality in primate and nonprimate mammals of all parenthood and family structures; cases of sex change in fish; and different types of intersexuality in humans. In the third lesson, we reviewed the principles of fleta theory in the context of biology and human behaviors, highlighting the visibility of nonbinary gender identities, nonconforming gender expression, and sexual orientations outside of the familiar opposite pairs like homosexual/heterosexual, such as intersex identities and bodies.

We ended up reconstructing the preceding big idea about sexuality and resignifying the four dimensions (biological, affective, psychological, and social) to a much more complex model, like a multicolored paint stain flowing constantly, considering sex, gender, identity, and expression as well as sexual, affective, and romantic orientation in conjunction with the social class, system values, and historical and sociopolitical contexts of the students. To assess the lessons, we asked open-ended questions that students had to answer critically. In the first question, three natural cases were posed (an androgynous wasp, a shark born in a pond with only females, and some specimens of transsexual palm trees), and the students were asked to choose between one of two questions: (1) How do these cases work as an argument to support the idea of nonbinary nature? and (2) How do you think these reproductive mechanisms propitiate the perpetuation of the population? One student, age fifteen, replied to the first question as follows:

> As we can see, the imposed binary system does not govern all living beings. If a wasp is androgynous, organizations of wasps do not come to say it has to identify with masculine or feminine traits only, or in the case of shark pups, other sharks do not come to take the pups from the females because "they are not capable of breeding and they are going to give the pup the wrong thoughts." We are shown that the binary system is the only "correct" system in our society, or the idea that one type of family is more correct than another. That is only a product of our intolerance as human beings and is not something happening in the rest of nature.

Another question was related to news about a politician from the Chilean Congress who recently argued against the Comprehensive Sex Education (CSE) Law in 2020. The question read: "On public television, a politician declares: 'Approving the Comprehensive Sex Education Law would be a mistake, since it violates the freedom of teaching and its traditional teaching modalities. Also, it tries to impose a gender ideology that goes against all natural laws. Write a brief paragraph about the sentence of the politician in question." A fifteen-year-old student replied as follows:

I think that by saying implementing CSE violates the freedom of education and imposes a gender ideology that goes against all natural laws, the politician is being hypocritical, because if CSE is not taught, it is a violation of the freedom to teach essential and fundamental topics to us, it does not show what is happening in nature, and they would be imposing a binary gender ideology. They would not open spaces to think or get to know each other, and they would be narrowing down to a single idea in the name of this supposedly biological argument, because CSE does not go against natural laws since nonbinary is something natural; it exists in animals and plants. By not approving the CSE Law, apart from allowing ignorance as an argument, we are deprived of important information we need as human beings. CSE is not only about sex but also about the affection, respect, and knowledge to avoid falling into discrimination due to ignorance.

In the first answer, you can see how the student satirizes the natural situation by comparing behaviors that do exist in society. The common factor of both answers is how they strongly criticize the idea of what is "imposed" and what is "correct," very much in accordance with what the theory proposes in its fundamental principles of breaking binaries, interrupting heteronormativity and its social deconstruction of reality (Snyder and Broadway 2004).

Recounting the Experience: What Happened Next?

We used a reflective written tool called a lesson story to analyze the lesson plan. Lesson stories were developed by a group of science teachers in Chile called PRETeC.[3] They define lesson stories as a tool to analyze and reflect on their pedagogical practice in the classroom, which is discussed collectively with other science teachers in bimonthly meetings (Acuña et al. 2016). For example, the lesson story resulting from the abovementioned practice of T and F was presented to PRETeC in a session in June 2022 as follows:[4]

> **T:** When I started developing the idea of nonbinary nature, I was full of doubts. I thought, "Am I being biased with the information that I am compiling?"; "Could it be it has no biological basis?" Yet I realized I was wrong. What I was doing was important. In the beginning, I was afraid, because in every scenario I imagined, someone questioned the proposal, and I found myself with no arguments to refute them. However, I kept going and found others who shared this idea. Together we built this big

idea of sexuality, which invites us to look at the world outside the lens of binarism to realize that out there, diversity prevails, while without diversity, there would have been no evolution, and, indeed, we would not be here.

F: I greatly admired the idea T was developing, because although I considered it fundamental in science education, I always felt I lacked the theoretical or curricular tools to address it in my classroom. In that light, I told T: "Do you mind doing your lesson plan of nonbinary nature in a course at my school?" T told me: "It's a Catholic school. Won't there be a problem?" I replied (with a small quantity of fear and uncertainty): "It should not be." After all, it is supported by the national curricular learning goal; anyway, I requested the appropriate authorizations, and my school did not have any problem with T and myself doing the lessons.

T: I designed a loop of—beautiful, in my head—six lessons, but we did not know if it would work until we tried it. Besides, we were in the middle of the pandemic, delivering lessons in a hybrid manner and with shorter hours, so it was a hostile environment to abruptly intervene in the traditional ways of doing lessons. Thus, we modified this original proposal into a shorter one.

F: I saw it as an exciting proposal when we specified the number of lessons and their objectives. However, I was afraid as we got closer to the day we would do the lessons. My fears were related to how my students would receive this, fear of the parents' reaction when they saw these lessons (all recorded), fear of the words we would use, and much more. However, something told me that T (no matter how sure T appears) would be much more afraid than me, and therefore, I must support them, and the least I can do is encourage T, telling them everything will be fine.

T: For me it was apparent even in 2021 that talking about sexuality is a complex and delicate matter, especially when one does not have complete knowledge of the course one is teaching. How would they react? What would they say? How can I motivate them if I do not know them? [. . .] During the development of the lessons, the hybrid regime was demanding. I was at my house, projected on the board with F as my interlocutor. Despite this, the students were quite motivated, they participated a lot, and they knew a lot! It was not like when I was at the school, when there were the so-called normal ones (straight) and the so-called sick ones (all the other, nonstraight people). These students wanted to discuss, talk, and criticize. So, the lesson became short, with some parts cut to make room for discussion. I remember feeling a sense of sufficiency, like, "Hey, I love what happened in these three lessons; we can do this." Let us see what happens in the assessment.

F: When T started the lessons, my students were very respectful and attentive, but my mind could only say, "If anything, this is part of the curriculum," like a mantra. I repeated that phrase during the first ten minutes. This insecurity disappeared when the students answered the survey questions in a way I did not expect. T's favorite time of the lesson was this closing time as we posed thought-provoking and conclusive questions, which were answered by the students.

T: When I read the answers, I thought: "they got it all; it made perfect sense; I was wrong in thinking this would not be important," and above all, it made me reinterpret the students' opinions. We tend to deny or ignore them, assuming they too young to know what they are doing. However, they are clearsighted and need good stimuli to generate deep reasoning. Ultimately, seeing how free they felt to express themselves was amazing. We also realized that comprehensive sex education is not only for LGBTQIA+ people attempting to feel more included but also helps foster empathy among hetero-cis people. It generates healthier, more accessible, and safer environments. At the end of the day, the aim was to discuss the ideas of normality, naturalness, and nonbinarism, and I think that was achieved. However, I think there is a long way to go, and it is necessary to continue theorizing, researching, and doing. The lesson plan was held in June, which is the time of year when we recognize how a community has been excluded, discriminated against, separated, and experienced violence on countless occasions, many of them in the name of religion and many others in the name of biology. Nevertheless, we stand up, we fight, we educate, and above all, we hope to do this kind of thing.

F: To be honest, my previous experience with sex education was awkward, because there was not much participation, but this time was not one of those occasions. I think the big idea was quite ambitious; it has much information, and it becomes very challenging for students to understand it 100 percent. However, the complexity of this idea is powerful; it leaves nothing out and is urgent. This topic is so diverse that we cannot simplify it; therefore, as teachers and social actors, we are called to bring this idea to the science classroom and not feel afraid to do so—mainly because our Chilean curriculum excludes many sexuality issues, so if we leave them in the hands of social media or TV series, it can get out of hand and we are going to live in a constant social decontextualization.

Nonbinary Nature in Initial Teacher Training: Closing Thoughts and Projections

During one author's master's thesis in 2021, research was conducted to analyze pre-service biology teachers and teacher educators regarding sex education and gender diversities, recognizing the relationship between those subjects and their possible tensions in a Catholic university in Chile. The results showed that the initial training in sexuality and gender issues in biology teachers is deficient, especially in constructing the teacher's personal and professional identity. As a result, sex education as content is delivered to the students as if disconnected from their life and experience, thus rendered insignificant for them. Therefore, they will not incorporate it into their future practices or repeat the teaching patterns received (Ardiles 2021). This work proposes that the initial teacher training of sexuality must be focused on fleta pedagogy, which means recognizing the self as a subject that teaches to other subjects or *yoes* that learn in dialogue and constant conversation. In the case of sex education, that also means understanding that sex education is content and experience while also reviewing the narrowed biological and scientific understanding (Ardiles 2021).

Recently, three of the authors of this article had the experience of teaching an optional course on sex education and biology teaching to pre-service teachers. One of the central axes was to discuss the binary construction of sexuality, but this time from a deeper perspective than in the school lesson plan mentioned above. In the course, there were also three lessons that ended with an essay. In the first lesson, we discussed nonbinarism in sex and the construction of the current model of sex education we teach in schools. We reviewed different types of intersexuality and analyzed the intersex population in Chile compared to a smaller context such as the school. We also discussed the provoking question of "which bathroom would an intersex person occupy?" to question the social logic we take for granted. The second lesson was similar to the story described above, which analyzed different species that challenge the (imposed) binary construction of reproduction and sexual behavior, but this time with a more critical focus on ecological and evolutionary aspects. The third lesson was focused on pleasure and bodies, discussing concepts such as "female orgasm" or "male orgasm" instead of talking about penile or clitoral orgasms. Likewise, we discuss the concept of a menstruating person and a pregnant person, disputing the binary idea of these concepts, which, although they seem purely biological, carry a social burden due to impregnation entirely by society. To finish this cycle, students were asked to bring cases of animal species that escaped the binary regime, write essays about them, and carry out short lesson experiences in groups, using their cases as a resource.

We want to share with you two excerpts from essays written by students of the course who recognized themselves as nonbinary people:

> Socially, it seems a lesbian person is expected to look like a "tomboy," or a gay person like an "effeminate," let alone the rest of the queer spectrum. I wonder if a nonbinary or intersex person should look like an undefined body. What, supposedly, should a bisexual person look like? Behind this pigeonholing question hides the deep-rooted heritage of binarism from the perspective of determining the gender of how a person should think or act, according to their biological sex. [...] Thus, it is not surprising that the binary perspective has penetrated so deeply into other spheres of the complex human experience, such as the experience of the body, sexuality, and gender. [...] Therefore, whenever we approach these dimensions, we do so from this fixed position reduced to two possibilities. [...] Fortunately for us, the "sexual and corporeal protists," nature has been shown more than once to be a fluid spectrum of possibilities promoted by natural selection, where binarism does not exist.

We find it especially interesting that this student calls themself a "corporeal and sexual protist," meaning they consider themself as someone that cannot be pigeonholed. This self-classification resonates with their initial question on appearance based on gender identity as opposed to sexual orientation. However, they find solace in biology, mentioning that nature has shown itself to be a fluid spectrum that, far from narrowing down, opens and generates possibilities. Another account was as follows:

> Throughout my childhood, I was pushed to choose between two options. However, one of these was already preestablished thanks to the organ I have between my legs. A male was born, a little boy, a baby who dressed in light blue and yellow but never pink or purple. [...] How nice it would have been to grow up knowing "either/or" could be "either/or" and also "neither this nor that." [...] The deer is my favorite animal; I always saw them as elegant beings, with strength, attitude, and fragility. [...] In nature we can find a universe of possibilities in terms of sexuality, and unfortunately it was we, as human beings, who imposed the norm, what is legitimate and what is not; I invite us to we question those who have separated us.

Here, something similar to the previous case happens. They repudiate what they have learned to be since childhood and find an example from biology—intersex deer—as a consolation allowing them to bring their own identity into existence.

Final Words

When I (T) started this tour, I was a gay man, I recognized myself as him, and I liked other "hims," or so I thought. In retrospect, I think I felt more like what the student mentioned as "a corporeal and sexual protist," "a neither this nor that, but at the same time this and that." However, I did not know how to express it or if it was "right" to feel it. At some point, I felt it was not my fight, because, beyond homosexuality, I wondered: who am I to question binarism, if I am within that regime? It turns out it was always my fight, and I became interested in the science behind everything—the argument and sustenance of my existence, as if it were not enough to exist. Then I found these other people with whom I can share these very worries. We took what we identified as fleta pedagogy, displaying it as a tool in different contexts, making sense in all of them. We realized with our experience that breaking binaries is crucial, questioning heteronormativity is necessary, and deconstructing social conceptions of reality is imperative. We apply fleta theory and pedagogy to teaching biology, without disputing existing biological knowledge. Instead, we contest how it came to be produced, what is being legitimated, and what is marginalized as power-sensitive questions applied to knowledge. Finally, we understand what *nonbinary* means in the context of biology teaching. It means being here and there, nowhere, and everywhere simultaneously. It means that there are not only light blue and pink shades but many other colors, that corporeal and sexual protists exist with many possibilities, and that the "o" is opposed to the "and"—though both options denote a binary system separated by a slash (x/y). Therefore, it is necessary to look for other options when dialoguing, because in nature there is less structure than we think, and the pedagogy must engage with it; if it was not taken care of in the past, let it be taken care of in the future.

Tebi Ardiles (they/them) is a chemistry and biology teacher with a master's in science education.They are currently directorx of education at Lab4U, and lecturer of biology teaching practice at Universidad Metropolitana de Ciencias de la Educación (UMCE). They can be reached at Tebi@lab4u.co.

Paulina Bravo (she/her) is a biologist with a master's in science education and PhD in science education. She is an assistant professor at the Universidad Católica del Maule (UCM) and a member of PRETeC (Teachers Reflecting for a Transformative Science Education). She is interested in the sociopolitical turn of science education, professional development of science teachers and teacher educators, and reflexivity and ethical-political positioning. She can be reached at pbravog@ucm.cl.

Fabián Fernández (he/his) is a biology and natural sciences teacher with a master's in science education. He is currently an academic in the Department of Biology at the Universidad Metropolitana de Ciencias de la Educación (UMCE), in charge of coordinating internships, and is a member of PRETeC. He can be reached at fabian.fernandez@umce.cl.

Corina González-Weil (she/her) is a professor of biology with a PhD in didactics of biology. She has been an academic at the Pontificia Universidad Católica de Valparaíso since 2005 and is a member of PRETeC. She is interested in the professional development of teachers and the processes of collaboration and reflection for science teachers. She can be reached at corina.gonzalez@pucv.cl.

Notes

1. In Spanish, *yo* is "I." In this case, we made up the word *yoes* to express the word "I" in plural.
2. In Spanish: "En la naturaleza, los comportamientos sexuales no se presentan de manera binaria, dictómica ni absoluta, sino que existe un gradiente de posibilidades que genera diversidad y aportan a la sobrevivencia de las especies. La sexualidad humana, en particular, no está exenta de dicha diversidad, lo que se traduce en dimensiones dinámicas como la sociocultural, afectiva, psicológica, valórica y política, las que, junto con configurar la sexualidad de un individuo, interactúan y se influencian entre ellas, por lo tanto, esta no puede ser restringida a lo meramente reproductivo ni binario."
3. PRETeC stands for Profesores Reflexionando por una Educación Transformadora en Ciencias.
4. This lesson story was written in two voices, and it was noninterruptedly read before the discussion with the whole group, which is the usual way in which PRETeC members share their practice.

Works Cited

Acuña, Teresina, Damián Avilés, Paulina Bravo, Delia Cisternas, Corina González-Weil, Camilo Henríquez, Lizzette Maldonado, Leopoldo Palacios, Exequiel Salinas, and Jonathan Santana. 2016. "Profesores Reflexionando por una Educación Transformadora en Ciencias (PRETeC)." *Revista Docencia*, no. 60: 42–53.

Ardiles, Tebi. 2021. "A Necessary Tension to Resolve in Biology Teachers: Fleta Exploration of Initial Teacher Training." MA thesis, Valparaíso University.

Bagemihl, Bruce. 2000. *Biological Exuberance: Animal Homosexuality and Natural Diversity*. New York: St. Martin's Press.

Bencze, Larry, and Lynn Carter. 2011. "Globalizing Students Acting for the Common Good." *JRST: Journal of Research in Science Teaching* 48 (6): 648–69.

Butler, Judith. 2006. *Deshacer el género* [*Undoing Gender*]. Barcelona: Paidós.

———. 2007. *El género en disputa: El feminismo y la subversión de la identidad* [*Gender Trouble: Feminism and the Subversion of Identity*]. Madrid: Paidós.

———. 2019. *Cuerpos que importan: Sobre los límites materiales* [*Bodies That Matter*]. Buenos Aires: Paidós.

Coria-Ávila, Genaro A., Rodrigo Triana-Del Rio, and Jorge Manzo. 2011. "Homosexual Behavior and Its Neural Bases." *eNeurobiología*, no. 1: 1–13.

Fifield, Steve, and Will Letts. 2014. "[Re]considering Queer Theories and Science Education." *Cultural Studies of Science Education* 9 (2): 393–407.

Gunckel, Kristin L. 2009. "Queering Science for All: Probing Queer Theory in Science Education." *Journal of Curriculum Theorizing* 25 (2): 48–61.

Harlen, Wynne, ed. 2010. *Principles and Big Ideas for Science Education*. Chilean Academy of Sciences.

———. 2015a. "Towards Big Ideas of Science Education." *School Science Review* 97 (359): 97–107.

———, ed. 2015b. *Working with Big Ideas of Science Education*. Trieste: Science Education Programme of IAP.

Jarpe-Ratner, Elizabeth. 2020. "How Can We Make LGBTQ+-Inclusive Sex Education Programmes Truly Inclusive? A Case Study of Chicago Public Schools' Policy and Curriculum." *Sex Education* 20 (3): 283–99.

Long, Sam, Lewis Steller, and River Suh. 2021. "Gender-Inclusive Biology: A Framework in Action." *The Science Teacher* 89 (1): 27–33.

Mitchell, Ian, Stephen Keast, Debra Panizzon, and Judie Mitchell. 2016. "Using 'Big Ideas' to Enhance Teaching and Student Learning." *Teachers and Teaching* 23 (5): 596–610.

Mock, Gloria. 2005. "Una Mirada a la Sexualidad: Del Nacimiento a la Pubertad." *Revista De Ciencias Sociales* 14: 22–39.

Movimiento de Integración y Liberación Homosexual (MOVILH). 2013. *First National Survey: Sexual Diversity, Human Rights and Law against Discrimination* [In Spanish]. Santiago. https://n9.cl/tn5mh.

Organisation for Economic Cooperation and Development (OECD). 2019. *Society at a Glance 2019: OECD Social Indicators*. Paris: OECD Publishing. https://doi.org/10.1787/soc_glance-2019-en.

Real Academia Española (RAE). 2019. s.v. "o." https://dle.rae.es/o?m=form.

Romi, Juan Carlos. 2009. "Bases neurobiológicas de la conducta sexual." *Revista de Psiquiatría Forense, Sexología y Praxis* 12: 42–77.

Roughgarden, Joan. 2013. *Evolution's Rainbow: Diversity, Gender, and Sexuality in Nature and People*. Berkeley: University of California Press.

Sjöström, Jesper, and Ingo Eilks. 2018. "Reconsidering Different Visions of Scientific Literacy and Science Education Based on the Concept of *Bildung*." In *Cognition, Metacognition, and Culture in STEM Education*, ed. Yehudit Judy Dori, Zemira R. Mevarech, and Dale R. Baker, 65–88. Switzerland: Springer Nature. https://doi.org/10.1007/978-3-319-66659-4_4.

Snyder, Vicky L., and Francis S. Broadway. 2004. "Queering High School Biology Textbooks." *JRST: Journal of Research in Science Teaching* 41 (6): 617–36.

Sumara, Dennis, and Brent Davis. 1999. "Interrupting Heteronormativity: Toward a Queer Curriculum Theory." *Curriculum Inquiry* 29 (2): 191–208.

Varela, Nuria. 2020. *Feminismo 4.0: la cuarta ola* [Feminism 4.0: The fourth wave]. Barcelona: Editions B.

Whiteley, Maree. 2012. "Big Ideas: A Close Look at the Australian History Curriculum." *Agora*, no. 47: 41–45.

#Nonbinary Joy—Tristan

Salgu Wissmath

This is an image from my personal project celebrating #NonbinaryJoy. #NonbinaryJoy is a series of joyful, colorful, fun portraits of nonbinary individuals!

Tristan
Gender: Trans Masc/Nonbinary
Pronouns: He/They

"To me it means I am not limited with how I express myself and am able to live my truth. Oftentimes I don't like to even identify my gender at all, but prefer to use the umbrella term 'trans,' since to me it's most inclusive."
—Tristan

Salgu Wissmath is a nonbinary Korean American photographer from Sacramento. They are currently a Hearst Photo Fellow at the *San Antonio Express News* and based in Texas. They are dedicated to decolonizing visual storytelling by engaging in ethical storytelling by and for people of color and the queer community. Their personal work explores the intersections of mental health, queer identity, and faith from a conceptual documentary approach. They studied at UC Berkeley and Ohio University's School of Visual Communication. Previously they interned at the *Kodiak Daily Mirror*, the *Fairbanks Daily News-Miner*, and the *Courier Journal*. They are a 2022 Gwen Ifill Fellow, 2021 California Arts Council Emerging Artist Fellow, and 2017 Women Photograph Mentee, as well as an alumnus of the Chips Quinn Scholar Program, AAJA Voices, Eddie Adams Workshop XXXI, and NLGJA's Connect Student Journalism Project. Salgu was recently recognized as AAJA's 2022 Emerging Journalist of the Year. Salgu is the communications director for Diversify Photo, a core team member with Ethical Narrative, and a member of AAJA, Women Photograph, Queer the Lens, and Authority Collective. They can be reached at swissmath@gmail.com.

WSQ: Women's Studies Quarterly 51: 3 & 4 (Fall/Winter 2023) © 2023 by Salgu Wissmath. All rights reserved.

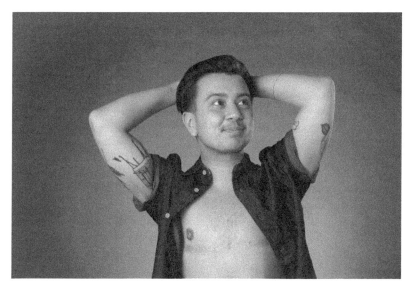

Salgu Wissmath. *#Nonbinary Joy—Tristan*, 2022. Digital photograph.

Nonbinary Epistemologies:
Refusing Colonial Amnesia and Erasure of
Jotería and Trans* Latinidades

Omi Salas-SantaCruz

Abstract: The author reflects on the experiences of teaching a Trans*
Latinx studies course, where students initially expressed discontent with
the syllabus for lacking legible trans subjects. By engaging with decolonial methodologies and theories, the author highlights the limitations of
"looking for" (Lugones 2020) trans in traditional archives and theories.
The author discusses the importance of embracing the nonsense within
the pluriverse of affective belonging and recognizing the possibilities that
emerge within the nonsensical and nonbinary theoretical subjectivities that
challenge conventional understandings of transgender phenomena. Engaging with U.S. women of color feminist theorizing—rooted in Black, Latinx,
Indigenous, and decolonial feminisms—the author discusses the importance of nonbinary thinking practices in confronting the epistemology of
ignorance in trans studies. Drawing upon the works of various decolonial
and trans* of color scholars, this paper explores the complex diasporic
relationality of *jotería* as a way of existing within coloniality, offering a critical lens to examine the diverse dimensions of queer and trans Latinx life.
Nonbinary thinking, in this context, is essential for learning from, alongside, and within oppressed trans of color knowledge, theories, strategies,
and ways of existing grounded in particular cosmologies, geographies, histories, and cultures. It also represents a vital political strategy for avoiding and
refusing discursive colonization. **Keywords:** decoloniality; trans studies;
jotería; trans of color critique; nonbinary

Nonsense: *Una Entrada*

In the winter of 2020, I taught my first course, Trans* Latinx Studies. During
the first two weeks of class, students voiced their discontent with the syllabus, claiming that the initial readings were mainly about gay and lesbian

WSQ: Women's Studies Quarterly 51: 3 & 4 (Fall/Winter 2023) © 2023 by Omi Salas-SantaCruz.
All rights reserved.

Latinos/as. One of the students, who identified as a mestizo mixed-raced trans and nonbinary student, shared the following: "I took a general intro trans studies class that at least had one week for us. It does not make sense to have the course titled Trans* Latinx Studies if we only read queer Latino history." In asserting "a week for us," the student referred to the usual single article or week focusing on trans-Latinx people within listed trans courses—a "week for us" that usually offers trans-Latinidad as simply a distinct voice or as a group of gender-variant people among various Latinx subcultures. I also understood the "us" as the students' desire to have me, a trans* Latinx instructor, help them find and look for trans-Latinx peoples' archives from Afro-Latinx and Central American perspectives. In other words, this student asked me for trans-legible archives arranged by neocolonial state and racial formations and categories of existence. I, however, was interested in foregrounding transnational and decolonial challenges to colonial binaries, identity categories, and forms of organizing the social, where students could encounter a more generous view of transing and transitions (Silva Santana 2017). My approach would enable students to interact with Afro-Indigenous and transgender *jotería* methodologies and practices throughout Abya Yala.

I asked my students, mostly trans Latinx, to keep reading, write down their thoughts, and return to this comment later in the semester. I knew my students were engaging with the ideological common sense of trans legibility that they had learned from trans curricula in the organization of their university and the field of trans studies as it begins to expand across university courses.[1] My reading choices were truly *nonsense*, as these readings, and the people and practices they carry within, exist unintelligibly, as nonsense, with respect to the concept of trans in most of early trans studies (Stryker 2004). By the fourth week, students had read decolonial methodologies and theory from prominent scholars such as M. Jacqui Alexander, Gloria Anzaldúa, and María Lugones. By then, the same student who had shared before left the following message on Canvas: "I was looking for trans Latinx [people], not recognizing that such imposition is another method meant to erase us. It is nonsense to think we are not there!" This "there" is the gender-queer, *travesti*, or trans* "we" in the *jotería* archive I had crafted for the class. The nonsense of *jotería* that presents a more complex understanding of *joto* as not just a "gay Latino" or even a "gay Mexican-American," as assumed under colonial epistemic frames of intelligibility, but *jotería* as a decolonial praxis (Alvarez 2014; Bañales 2014; Hames-Garcia 2014), as modes of thinking, being, and sensing among a group of Indigenous or mestizo,

Afro-Latinx, Central American, Caribbean, and ever-growing communities of gender "sexiles" (Cortez and Hebert 2004) interplanting themselves as guests in the settler U.S. state. I had given my students an archive of *jotería* as a "Brown commons" (Muñoz 2020), with unique modes of affective belonging (Muñoz 2000; Calvo-Quirós 2018; Ferrada 2018; Alvarez 2019a, 2019b, 2022; Alarcón 2020) despite the coloniality of gender and the ongoing colonization of transgender (DiPietro 2019; Salas-SantaCruz 2023). A "nonsense to think we are not there" that complicates the ontological and existential singularity found in the most prominent Anglo-Western trans archives and theories (Valentine 2007; DiPietro 2020; Salas-SantaCruz 2023). My students began to understand the discursive and methodological violence of "looking for" (Lugones 2020) transgender as well as the limits of common sense on what gets to count as transgender phenomena through either/or binaries in the archive.[2] I am interested in thinking beyond the binary of common and non-sense, but within the pluriverse of affective belonging within the nonsense. And the nonsense to think non-sense is an absence and not a possibility; in Anzaldúa's words (1987), the non-sense is *una entrada*.

Nonbinary Epistemic Refusals

Nonbinary epistemic refusals involve embracing decolonial methods, contesting Western dualities, and delving into the complex histories and archives of trans* people of color. This approach, inspired by Black, Latinx, Indigenous, and decolonial feminisms, opposes epistemic imperialism and seeks to understand the intricate borderlands of existence. Nonbinary epistemes offer alternative ways of reading, thinking, and sensing through decolonial methods, trans decolonial theories, and exploring different ways of being within gender coloniality. This enables a more profound understanding of complex existences that might be ignored when solely focusing on binary theoretical subjects described as the "evil twin of queer theory" (Stryker 2004).

This nonbinary pedagogical approach involves shifting and trespassing epistemic boundaries, enabling a more comprehensive understanding of complex histories, desires, knowledges, and identities. Throughout the course, we examined queer gender manifestations and resistant materiality in BIPOC Latinx communities in the U.S. and Latin America, learning to think beyond fragmented ontological categories. Nonbinary thinking explores power relations in shaping the common sense, good sense, and nonsense of gender coloniality. Nonbinary epistemologies demand innovative methodologies, going beyond the visual and visibility, where sensing trans involves engaging multiple senses to grasp social relations existing and arising within the dynamic of oppression, experiencing oppression, and resistance to gender coloniality (Lugones 2003, 2007). Nonbinary epistemes engage with pedagogies of crossings, shifting, and trespassing, refusing dualisms and categorical universality that obstruct grappling with intricate histories, desires, knowledges, identities, and beings/becomings. Moreover, I was teaching my students the importance of remembering "quare" (Johnson 2001), *jotería* (Hames-García and Martínez 2011), working-class "butch-femme worlds" (Alarcón 2020), and other worlds of sense that are not queer or trans but decolonial genres that refuse singular categorical logics. In other words, students began to engage with the practice of remembering as a trans* of color methodology (Salas-SantaCruz 2021). This approach involves uplifting queer and trans BIPOC histories, which is especially relevant when faced with intentional or unintentional ideological and discursive violence in the field of trans studies. In addition, the act of remembering serves as a nonbinary epistemic strategy to counter the various academic practices regarding trans phenomena that persistently position Black, Brown, and Indigenous trans feminisms and social practices as a mere afterthought and as belated arrivals within the white trans archive, as noted by Ellison, Richardson, and Snorton (2017, 162).

U.S. women of color feminism consists of epistemic shifting from studying the binaries of categorical logics to building bridges and coalitions, both as a political commitment to decolonial resistance and as a pedagogical practice for reimagining archives. By engaging with decolonial methodologies and BIPOC trans scholarship, we can understand the complex histories of Black feminism, borderland thinking, decolonial feminism, and Indigenous Two-Spirit theory and knowledge as precursors to understanding permeable bodies, histories, and subjective practices within modernity and coloniality. Transforming power relations is a critical aspect of decolonial work. It is worth noting that nonbinary thinking is not new. Binary thinking's discursive violence places us in an ideological war between hegemony and counterhegemony to arrive at a new common sense (Gramsci 1971). Nonbinary thinking necessitates our continuous remembrance of nonsense, as this is the knowledge that becomes looted and overlooked by the prevailing "common-sense" understanding of new terms and definitions. "New common sense" concepts have formed a crucial part of the theories and knowledge within racialized and marginalized communities of queer and trans BIPOC populations. In a roundtable discussion, Bacchetta, Jivraj, and Bakshi (2020) highlight how "white queer theory," and by extension, white trans theory, is what they describe as "colonial-and-race-amnesiac" (576). Bacchetta and colleagues explain that a principal component to white queer theory is the choice to "forget" and overlook "colonialism, racism, Islam-ophobia, capitalism, class relations and other relations of power," thereby reproducing these isms inside the theory itself (576). Settler-colonial common sense necessitates a decolonial approach to the trans imaginary, emphasizing remembering and contextualizing Black, Latina, and Indig-enous theories on bodies, practices, and responses to discursive violence within Western European universal frameworks. It is important to note that Bacchetta and coauthors (2020) describe white queer theory not as an essentialist, morphological term of racial positionality but as a white-ness based on what it epistemologically produces: approaches, definitions, presuppositions, categories, logics, and conclusions within a theory. The nonbinary thinking I ground in my work is the modes of thought estab-lished by theories in the flesh and Latina philosophy (Moraga and Anzaldúa 1983; Lorde 1984; Ortega 2016; Pitts, Ortega, and Medina 2020) and modes of refusal within settler coloniality that actively confront epistemic violence and erasures within colonial-and-race-amnesiac academic prac-tices on matters related to subaltern trans of color sociality, relationality, histories, and existence. The emergence of "la facultad" (Anzaldúa 1987), or my students' new consciousness, begins with a reaction against white-ness's amnesia—the whiteness that erases queer, trans, and nonbinary BIPOC knowledges and relegates them to marginalized zones of nonbe-ing and nonexistence while subjecting them to looting and silencing of their languages, histories, and ways of living (Alarcón 1990; Bey 2021; DiPi-etro 2020; Green 2016; Hayward 2017; Valentine 2007). An important element of this consciousness is the "half and half" gendered way of living, as described by Anzaldúa (1987), which allows students to constantly shift across and within histories of racialized gender embodiments to decolonize how we approach trans phenomena in academic practices.

To clarify, the epistemic shifts discussed here go beyond simply reori-enting towards intersectional approaches that gather data or learn about trans people of color experiences. Instead, these shifts involve fundamen-tally uprooting our understanding of trans phenomena within theory itself.

This entails committing to a trans* of color critique that recognizes the colonial and racial violence ingrained in settler colonialism (Morgensen 2016) and adopting "thinking within complexities" (Lugones 2003, 3), which embraces nonbinary meaning-making within coloniality. This pedagogy of nonbinary thinking is not merely a new horizon or orientation (Ahmed 2006), as these often remain rooted in binary logic and overlook overlapping horizons. Shifts are tectonic, involving multiple, disparate movements and collisions that defy common sense, good sense, and nonsense. Shifts occur in the spatial ground, what María Lugones (2003) describes as the oppressing/being oppressed ↔ resisting relation among those experiencing simultaneous fragmentation and multiplicity (12). Shifts propel us from the settled ground, such as the straightforward binary logic of oppression and resistance. The nonbinary and complex thinking that avoids "looking for" trans phenomena creates space for perceiving and sensing coloniality, as well as understanding genealogies, histories, vocabularies, and conceptualizations of intricate identities and embodiments. Accounting for coloniality in trans theory and pedagogical practices enables us to grasp other complex social relations emerging from within coloniality. By thinking from within the nonsense, we can start exploring other cosmologies of existence and relationality, such as those of the Muxes, Ipas, Waria, Phet Thi Sam, Bayot, or Nádleehi, among numerous collective beings/becomings that socially relate and resist coloniality rather than succumbing to a trans identity that has to be explained as a "gender within gender" in the face of social and political necessity or desire for legibility (Baderoon 2011). Unlearning the habit of looking for trans identities also demands confronting our complicity in perpetuating harm by attempting to fit trans experiences into narrow categories within diasporic and postcolonial peoples' archives. These categories often involve comparisons to trans experiences, overlooking the complexity of embodied practices and social relations that challenge individuality, the self, and gender as a universal. A nonbinary pedagogical framework urges us to engage in epistemic disobedience, reevaluating Black, Latinx, decolonial, and Indigenous concepts of being that account for intersecting oppressions, resistance, and ontological and existential plurality. This can lead to a more nuanced understanding of trans* as a multifaceted and "polyvalent consciousness" (DiPietro 2016).

To understand this complex polyvalent consciousness, the class read Omise'eke Natasha Tinsley (2018), who reminds us that our senses begin to listen to various voices when we shift our thinking. Tinsley (2018) cautions that searching for queer and trans Caribbean people using the vocabulary of trans and queer theory may not yield results, as its universalism may obscure the unique prisms in which Caribbean authors express creative genders and sexualities. Similarly, María Lugones warns that the colonizing practice of "looking for" further obstructs our perception of coloniality and the intricate and ongoing resistance within. When students initially looked for transgender, they assumed gender was a universally existing metacategory, leading to attempts at finding trans/gender comparisons across various societies and time periods. This assumption could imply that similarities in understandings and experiences of gender exist across diverse cultures and communities. However, prioritizing trans worldviews over trans worlds of sense may cause us to miss the politics of embodiment, being, and sociality, as well as cultural perspectives and experiences. These practices and embodied resistances transcend individuality, the self, and gender as a universal ontological category. Additionally, the act of looking for transgender perpetuates colonial-and-race-amnesia concerning the concept of trans-Latinidad, further enabling self-colonization. As a result, nonbinary thinking emerges as a critical epistemic shift for marginalized individuals to counter the ongoing structures that colonize our thought processes. These shifts are vital for learning from, alongside, and within oppressed trans* of color knowledge, theories, strategies, and ways of existing grounded in particular cosmologies, geographies, histories, and cultures. They also are essential political strategies for avoiding discursive colonization.

Start Here: Return until You Shift ↔ Within
Shifting is a process that challenges ideological violence and epistemic imperialism, transitioning from the fragmentation of knowledge to the reintegration of all knowledge and all bodies. It involves rejecting the "common sense" dictated by coloniality and embracing the varied perspectives within.

Remembering is intertwined with the past, present, and future, defying binary constraints such as cis/trans, gender/sex, and human/nonhuman, and acknowledging the perpetual existence of Black, Brown, and Indigenous resistance to gender coloniality.

Shifting moves from documenting trans phenomena as potential avenues for new horizons within (settler) territories, to concentrating on tangible practices that defy settler logic and elevate sovereignty.

Methodological shifts involve moving from searching for trans phenomena (as ontologically singular or separate) and employing intersectionality, to actively listening to remember and acknowledge ontological and existential diversity, multifaceted transformations, and interconnected selves that account for coloniality and resistance.

The purpose of shifting is to uncover coloniality and ground knowledge of being in complex forms of relationships, co-constructions, assemblages, cosmologies, and multiple systems that structure social organization.

This pedagogical shift transitions from binary thinking focused on agency, identity politics, and anthropocentrism to building coalitions, acknowledging nonhuman complexity, and accounting for "infra-human, near-human, permeable, and [other forms of] carnal inconformity" (DiPietro 2020).

In the Nonsense: Arrivals as Departure

We can now begin to study *jotería* scholarship. *Jotería* scholarship embraces M. Jacqui Alexander's (2002) call to remember the bridge as a method of suturing, healing, and reclaiming the "coalitional body dismembered by a history of ideological violence" (Hames-García and Martinez 2011, 4). This method, as Hames-García and Martinez (2011) argue, brings together, names and sutures, repopulating the knowledge and forms of *jotería* criticism that have been denied and appropriated by white queer theory (Hames-García 2013). *Jotería* scholarship not only mends the ideological dismemberment that constructs *joto* as just an ethnic gay identity, but it also elevates *jotería* as a complex way of existing within coloniality and as a social diasporic relationality.

Listening becomes seeing, feeling, smelling, touching, tasting, and hearing "the sounds of black queer world-making" in the Caribbean (Tinsley 2018, 2). My students are now listening to what *jotería* in the U.S. borderlands is saying (Anzaldúa 1987). We begin to sense the rhythms silenced and obscured by universalist assumptions of trans materiality and embodiment (DiPietro 2016, 2019). *Jotería* is not simply gay or trans-Latinx but rather a complex way of being, relationality, resistant consciousness, and healing pedagogies (Cruz 2019; Galarte 2014a, 2014b, 2021; Hames-Garcia 2014; Bañales 2014; Alvarez 2019a; Caraves 2020; Gonzalez, Orozco, and Gonzalez 2023). I had shared with my class that during my undergraduate years, the *jotería* group in my college called themselves Young Queers

United for Empowerment, or "YQUE!", and we had a chant: *"Joto, Y que?*
Jotería y que? Yque? Yque? Yque!!!!" The chant of "Yque?" is a queer Latinx
resignification (Ferrada 2018) that transforms Yque from a question to a
statement, a defiant play of words: yque! or a "so what?" that challenges
ideological common sense and invites us to listen. The chant refers to a dissident sonic and corporeality that trespasses the common sense of Latina/o
hegemony, urging us not to be silent or ashamed. The "Y que?" confronts
the cisheteropatriarchal common sense of Latinidad, which often perceives
jotería and *joto* as nonsense. By then, the students had learned to grapple
with the kind of senses needed to understand the complexity of social life
within gender coloniality, like the use of the concept of *travesti así* as a dissident expression of corporeality from the geopolitics of the infrahuman in
the Andean mountains (DiPietro 2019). This *jotería* and the "so what?"
forms of beings and becomings offer complex approaches to understanding
multiple worlds of sense, questioning how we know and perceive the power
dynamics that erase a long history of dissident and permeable Latinx corporeality (Rodríguez 2003; Ochoa 2008; La Fountain-Stokes 2011; DiPietro
2016). *Jotería* exists as a way of living in the borderlands, a genderqueer diasporic existence that moves, shifts, expands, and migrates through constant
shifts in consciousness from living within gender coloniality, U.S. imperialism, and endless displacement(s) and exiles. Yes, some *jotxs* are simply
vestidas, some queer, some trans, and some nonbinary, but all are part of
a discursive community of "queer/trans Latinidades" who exist and resist
despite antiblackness, the colonial/modern gender system, and heterosexualism (Lugones 2007).

In my course, nonbinary epistemic refusals opened the space to return to
U.S. women of color feminist theorizing and engage with what my student's
common sense had labeled as the "nonsense of reading gay/lesbian Latinx
history" and the non-senses needed to understand the importance of such
archives, to grasp coloniality and the power of the coloniality of knowledge
and of being. The constant epistemic shifting allowed my class to understand
jotería as a social and complex relationality that provides glimpses into how
we understand ourselves, our bodies, our relations, our movements, our
desires, and how we love, dance, smell, connect, and create through other
senses: the nonsense within coloniality that resists and imagines an otherwise from within modernity/coloniality. A way of life that exists within the
contradiction and multiplicity within the borderlands that came before a
white trans scholarship and discourse that attempted to fragment its meaning

and foreclose its rich trans analytic. *Jotería* is a type of trans-theorizing, specifically a borderland theorizing of *"los atravesados"* (Anzaldúa 1987). It exists within the context of "No/Otras (Us/Other)" (Anzaldúa 2015), a nonbinary other, which encompasses those who cross over the boundaries of gender coloniality and the coloniality of being. *Jotería* emerges to decolonize dichotomies of what it means to be human/nonhuman, near-human, and infrahuman (DiPietro 2020) and honor the complexity of queer and trans diasporic people and organisms so as to directly confront categorical separations of gender, sex, sexuality, race, and land. More recently, *jotería* scholarship has confronted the hegemonic trans and Latinx imaginaries that structure how we discuss trans-Latinx philosophy, relations, and strategies in their relationship to trans theory and cisnormative Latinx studies, specifically when *jotería* epistemologies are constantly erased in both Chicana or Latina philosophy and feminist perspectives on trans issues (Pérez 2003; Galarte 2014a, 2020; Cruz 2012; Cuevas 2018).

Finally, nonbinary thinking practices confront the epistemology of ignorance in trans studies, as the process of shifting is a never-ending pedagogical practice. Shifting is a social and political commitment to trespassing into forms of knowledge that have been foreclosed and silenced despite the loud and long history of Indigenous, decolonial, and U.S. women of color scholars that have given us numerous accounts of historical and political configurations of the social and how these operate politically, collectively, and subjectively in the ongoing structures of colonial power and settler colonialism (Combahee River Collective 1977; Moraga and Anzaldúa 1983; Anzaldúa 1987, 1990; Spillers 1987; Minh-ha 1989; Smith 1999; Moallem 2002; Mohanty 2003).

I now depart with my arrival into my first encounter with *Trans Studies Quarterly* "keywords" (Stryker and Currah 2014) during my first year of graduate studies. I, too, was "looking for" *jotería* and did not find it. While I found the term "Latinas/os," *jotería* as a genderqueer/trans Latinidad remained elusive. It took the course of my graduate career to arrive to decoloniality and learn how to shift and think with and along nonbinary ways of conceptualizing living within and despite the coloniality of gender. After my class, I revisited *TSQ* and found *jotería* hidden in the seemingly nonsensical word of "tatume" in the eponymously titled article by Vic Muñoz (2014). "Tatume, tatuma or calabacita," they write, "is a keyword for transing land, decolonization, diaspora, the meaning of seasons, and growing food" (214). *Jotería*, like *calabazitas*, unsettles and confuses Western categories of existence, of culture, and of growing. *Jotería* is related to tatume through decolonial resistance, as it disrupts and challenges Western ideas of being, identity, gender, and sexuality. *Jotería*, like squash, has been inter-planted and is growing in *el norte* looking for a home, patiently waiting to be remembered.

Acknowledgments

I would like to express my sincere gratitude to the early readers of this article and those who have contributed to its successful completion: Dr. Gabeba Baderoon, Dr. Hil Malatino, Dr. Melissa Wright, and Dr. Mariana Ortega. I extend my appreciation to the editorial board and the anonymous reviewers, whose constructive feedback and thoughtful suggestions have been instrumental in refining and enhancing the quality of this paper.

Dr. Omi Salas-SantaCruz is the inaugural President's Postdoctoral Fellow in Trans Studies at Penn State University in the Department of Women's, Gender, and Sexuality Studies. They earned their PhD in education with a designated emphasis in critical theory and gender, women, and sexuality from the University of California, Berkeley, and a master's degree in sociology from Columbia University. Their research examines questions at the intersections of coloniality, race, Latinidad, the epistemology of trans inclusion, and practices of being. They can be reached at oss5057@psu.edu.

Notes

1. For a sample reading list of trans studies and course listings offerings across U.S. and Canadian universities, see Jeremy Gottlieb's list of courses and readings in transgender studies: https://humanitiesfutures.org/wp-content/uploads/2019/10/Trans-Courses-GSF-FHI-Gottlieb-Wilson.pdf.
2. Either/or "binary thinking" produces trans knowledge or trans analytics in binary terms. Such analytical categories tend to show up in terms of normal/abnormal, livable/unlivable, sex/gender, normative/nonnormative, and human/nonhuman. On the contrary, Black and Indigenous trans analytics tend to provide modes of "trans* imaginations" (Pelaez Lopez 2023) that are more complex and multiple and move away from epistemic limitations imposed by coloniality (see also Baderoon 2011).

Works Cited

Ahmed, Sara. 2006. *Queer Phenomenology: Orientations, Objects, Others*. Durham, NC: Duke University Press.

Alarcón, Norma. 1990. "The Theoretical Subject(s) of *This Bridge Called My Back* and Anglo American Feminism." In *Making Face, Making Soul / Haciendo Caras: Creative and Critical Perspectives by Feminists of Color,* ed. Gloria Anzaldúa, 356–69. San Francisco, CA: Aunt Lute Books.

Alarcón, Wanda. 2020. "Reading and Remembering Butch-Femme Worlds." *Association of Mexican American Educators Journal* 14 (2): 145–71.

Alexander, M. Jacqui. 2002. "Remembering *This Bridge*, Remembering Ourselves: Yearning, Memory, and Desire." In *This Bridge We Call Home: Radical Visions for Transformation,* ed. Gloria Anzaldúa and AnaLouise Keating, 81–103. New York: Routledge.

Alvarez, Eddy Francisco, Jr. 2014. "Jotería Pedagogy, SWAPA, and Sandovalian Approaches to Liberation." *Aztlán: A Journal of Chicano Studies* 39 (1): 215–28.

———. 2019a. "Finding Sequins in the Rubble: Stitching Together an Archive of Trans Latina Los Angeles." *Transgender Studies Quarterly,* no. 3/4: 618–27.

———. 2019b. "I Pray: Un Rezo of Healing pa' lxs Mariconxs." In *Voices from the Ancestors: Xicanx and Latinx Spiritual Expressions and Healing Practices,* ed. Lara Medina and Martha Gonzales, 330–32. Tucson: University of Arizona Press.

———. 2022. "Embodied Collective Choreographies: Listening to Arena Nightclub's Jotería Sonic Memories." *Performance Matters* 8 (1): 109–24.

Anzaldúa, Gloria. 1987. *Borderlands / La Frontera.* Aunt Lute Books.

———. 2015. "Geographies of Selves—Reimagining Identity: Nos/Otras (Us/ Other), las Nepantleras, and the New Tribalism." In *Light in the Dark / Luz en lo Oscuro: Rewriting Identity, Spirituality, Reality,* ed. AnaLouise Keating, 65–94. Durham, NC: Duke University Press.

Bacchetta, Paola, Suhraiya Jivraj, and Sandeep Bakshi. 2020. "Decolonial Sexualities: Paola Bacchetta in Conversation with Suhraiya Jivraj and Sandeep Bakshi." *Interventions* 22 (4): 574–85. https://doi.org/10.1080/13 69801X.2020.1749710.

Baderoon, Gabeba. 2011. "Gender within Gender": Zanele Muholi's Images of Trans Being and Becoming." *Feminist Studies* 37 (2): 390–416.

Bañales, Xamuel. 2014. "Jotería: A Decolonizing Political Project." *Aztlán: A Journal of Chicano Studies* 39 (1): 155–66.

Bey, Marquis. 2017. "The Trans*-ness of Blackness, the Blackness of Trans*-ness." *Transgender Studies Quarterly* 4 (2): 275–95. https://doi. org/10.1215/23289252-3815069.

———. 2021. *Black Trans Feminism.* Durham, NC: Duke University Press.

Calvo-Quirós, William A. 2018. "The Aesthetics of Healing and Love: An

Epistemic Genealogy of Jota/o Aesthetic Traditions." In *Routledge Handbook of Chicana/o Studies*, ed. Francisco A. Lomelí, Denise A. Segura, Elyette Benjamin-Labarthe, 345–54. London: Routledge.

Caraves, J. 2020. "Centering the 'T': Envisioning a Trans Jotería Pedagogy." *Association of Mexican American Educators Journal* 14 (2): 104–23.

Combahee River Collective. 1977. "The Combahee River Collective Statement." Library of Congress. https://www.loc.gov/item/lcwaN0028151/.

Cortez, Jaime. 2004. *Sexile*. New York: Institute for Gay Men's Health.

Cruz, Cindy. 2012. "I Grew Up Un-doing Colonized Gender." In *Speaking from the Heart: Herstories of Chicana, Latina, and Amerindian Women*, ed. Rose Borunda and Melissa Moreno. Dubuque, IA: Kendall Hunt Press.

———. 2019. "Reading *This Bridge Called My Back* for Pedagogies of Coalition, Remediation, and a Razor's Edge." *International Journal of Qualitative Studies in Education* 32 (2): 136–50.

Cuevas, Jackie T. 2018. *Post-Borderlandia: Chicana Literature and Gender Variant Critique*. New Brunswick, NJ: Rutgers University Press.

DiPietro, P. J. 2016. "Of Huachafería, Así, and M'E Mati: Decolonizing Transing Methodologies." *Transgender Studies Quarterly* 3 (1/2): 65–73. https://doi.org/10.1215/23289252-3334211.

———. 2019. "Beyond Benevolent Violence: Trans* of Color, Ornamental Multiculturalism, and the Decolonization of Affect." In *Speaking Face to Face: The Visionary Philosophy of María Lugones*, ed. Pedro Javier DiPietro, Jennifer McWeeny, and Shireen Roshanravan, 197–216. Albany, NY: State University of New York Press.

———. 2020. "Neither Humans, nor Animals, nor Monsters: Decolonizing Transgender Embodiments." *Eidos: A Journal for Philosophy of Culture*, no. 34: 254–91.

Ellison, Treva, Kai M. Green, Matt Richardson, and C. Riley Snorton. 2017. "We Got Issues: Toward a Black Trans* Studies." *Transgender Studies Quarterly* 4 (2): 162–69. https://doi.org/10.1215/23289252-3814949.

Ferrada, Juan Sebastian. 2018. "Resignifications: Linguistic Resistance and Queer Expressions of Latinidad." In *The Oxford Handbook of Language and Sexuality*, ed. Kira Hall and Rusty Barrett. New York: Oxford University Press. 10.1093/oxfordhb/9780190212926.013.73. Online publication June 9, 2021. https://academic.oup.com/edited-volume/42645/chapter-abstract/358161188.

Galarte, Francisco J. 2014a. "On Trans* Chican@s: Amor, Justicia, y Dignidad." *Aztlán: A Journal of Chicano Studies* 39 (1): 229–36.

———. 2014b. "Pedagogy." *Transgender Studies Quarterly* 1 (1/2): 145–48. https://doi.org/10.1215/23289252-2399857.

———. 2020. "Transgender Studies and Latina/o/x Studies." *Oxford Research Encyclopedia of Literature.* https://oxfordre.com/literature/view/10.1093/acrefore/9780190201098.001.0001/acrefore-9780190201098-e-349.

———. 2021. *Brown Trans Figurations: Rethinking Race, Gender, and Sexuality in Chicanx/Latinx Studies.* Austin: University of Texas Press.

Gonzalez, Ángel de Jesus, Robert C. Orozco, and Sergio A. Gonzalez. 2023. "*Joteando y Mariconadas*: Theorizing Queer *Pláticas* for Queer and/or Trans Latinx/a/o Research." *International Journal of Qualitative Studies in Education.* https://doi.org/10.1080/09518398.2023.2181433.

Gramsci, Antonio. 1971. *Selections from the Prison Notebooks of Antonio Gramsci.* New York: International Publishers.

Green, Kai. 2016. "Troubling the Waters." In *No Tea, No Shade: New Writings in Black Queer Studies,* ed. E. Patrick Johnson. 65–82. Durham, NC: Duke University Press.

Hames-García, Michael. 2013. "What's after Queer Theory? Queer Ethnic and Indigenous Studies." *Feminist Studies* 39 (2): 384–404.

———. 2014. "Jotería Studies, or the Political Is Personal." *Aztlán: A Journal of Chicano Studies* 39 (1): 135–41.

Hames-García, Michael, and Ernesto Javier Martínez. 2011. "Introduction: Re-membering Gay Latino Studies." In *Gay Latino Studies: A Critical Reader,* ed. Michael Hames-García and Ernesto Javier Martínez, 1–18. Durham, NC: Duke University Press.

Hayward, Eva S. 2017. "Don't Exist." *Transgender Studies Quarterly* 4 (2): 191–94. https://doi.org/10.1215/23289252-3814985.

Johnson, E. Patrick. 2001. "'Quare' Studies, or (Almost) Everything I Know about Queer Studies I Learned from My Grandmother." *Text and Performance Quarterly* 21 (1): 1–25. https://doi.org/10.1080/10462930128119.

La Fountain-Stokes, Lawrence. 2011. "Translocas: Migration, Homosexuality, and Transvestism in Recent Puerto Rican Performance." *Emisférica* 8 (1). https://hemisphericinstitute.org/en/emisferica-81/8-1-essays/translocas.html.

Lorde, Audre. 1984. *Sister Outsider: Essays and Speeches.* Trumansburg, NY: Crossing Press.

Lugones, María. 2003. *Pilgrimages/Peregrinajes: Theorizing Coalition against Multiple Oppressions.* Lanham, MD: Rowman & Littlefield.

———. 2007. "Heterosexualism and the Colonial/Modern Gender System." *Hypatia* 22 (1): 186–209. http://www.jstor.org/stable/4640051.

———. 2020. "Gender and Universality in Colonial Methodology." *Critical Philosophy of Race* 8 (1/2): 25–47. https://doi.org/10.5325/critphilrace.8.1-2.0025.

Minh-ha, Trinh T. 1989. *Woman, Native, Other: Writing Postcoloniality and Feminism*. Bloomington: Indiana University Press.

Moallem, Minoo. 2002. "Women of Color in the U.S.: Pedagogical Reflections on the Politics of 'the Name.'" In *Women's Studies on Its Own: A Next Wave Reader in Institutional Change*, ed. Robyn Weigman, 368–82. Durham, NC: Duke University Press. https://doi.org/10.1215/9780822384311-021.

Mohanty, Chandra Talpade. 2003. "'Under Western Eyes' Revisited: Feminist Solidarity through Anticapitalist Struggles." *Signs* 28 (2): 499–535. https://doi.org/10.1086/342914.

Moraga, Cherríe, and Gloria Anzaldúa. 1983. *This Bridge Called My Back: Writings by Radical Women of Color*. Watertown, MA: Persephone Press.

Morgensen, Scott L. 2016. "Conditions of Critique: Responding to Indigenous Resurgence within Gender Studies." *Transgender Studies Quarterly* 3 (1/2): 192–201. https://doi.org/10.1215/23289252-3334379.

Muñoz, José Esteban. 2000. "Feeling Brown: Ethnicity and Affect in Ricardo Bracho's The Sweetest Hangover (and Other STDs)." *Theatre Journal* 52 (1): 67–79.

———. 2020. *The Sense of Brown*. Durham, NC: Duke University Press.

Muñoz, Vic. 2014. "Tatume." *Transgender Studies Quarterly* 1 (1/2): 213–16.

Ochoa, M. 2008. "Perverse Citizenship: Divas, Marginality, and Participation in 'Loca-lization.'" *WSQ: Women's Studies Quarterly* 36 (3–4): 146–69. https://doi.org/10.1353/wsq.0.0102.

Pelaez Lopez, Alan. 2023. "Trans* Imagination." *WSQ: Women's Studies Quarterly* 51 (12): 233–40.

Pérez, Emma. 2003. "Queering the Borderlands: The Challenges of Excavating the Invisible and Unheard." *Frontiers: A Journal of Women Studies* 24 (2/3): 122–31. http://www.jstor.org/stable/3347351.

Pitts, Andrea J., Mariana Ortega, and José Medina. 2020. *Theories of the Flesh: Latinx and Latin American Feminisms, Transformation, and Resistance*. New York: Oxford University Press.

Rodriguez, Juana Maria. 2003. *Queer Latinidad: Identity Practices, Discursive Spaces*. New York: New York University Press.

Salas-SantaCruz, Omi. 2021. "Queer and Trans* of Color Critique, Decolonization, and Education." In *Oxford Encyclopedia of Gender and Sexuality in Education*, ed. Cris Mayo. New York: Oxford University Press. https://doi.org/10.1093/acrefore/9780190264093.013.133.

———. 2023. "Decoloniality and Trans* of Color Educational Criticism." In "Queer and Trans* Futurities in Educational Research and Practice," ed. Karen Zaino and Jordan Bell, special issue, *Theory, Research, and Action in Urban Education* 8 (1). https://traue.commons.gc.cuny.edu/decoloniality-trans-of-color-educational-criticism/.

Silva Santana, Dora. 2017. "Transitionings and Returnings: Experiments with the Poetics of Transatlantic Water." *Transgender Studies Quarterly* 4 (2): 181–90. https://doi.org/10.1215/23289252-3814973.

Smith, Linda Tuhiwai. 1999. *Decolonizing Methodologies: Research and Indigenous Peoples.* London: Zed Books.

Spillers, Hortense J. 1987. "Mama's Baby, Papa's Maybe: An American Grammar Book." *Diacritics* 17 (2): 65–81. https://doi.org/10.2307/464747.

Stryker, Susan. 2004. "Transgender Studies: Queer Theory's Evil Twin." *GLQ: A Journal of Lesbian and Gay Studies* 10 (2): 212–15. https://www.muse.jhu.edu/article/54599.

Stryker, Susan, and Paisley Currah. 2014. "Introduction." *Transgender Studies Quarterly* 1 (1/2): 1–18. https://doi.org/10.1215/23289252-2398540.

Tinsley, Omise'eke Natasha. 2018. *Ezili's Mirrors: Imagining Black Queer Genders.* Durham, NC: Duke University Press.

Valentine, David. 2007. *Imagining Transgender: An Ethnography of a Category.* Durham, NC: Duke University Press. https://doi.org/10.1215/9780822390213.

Tracing "Gender Critical" Ideology in Turkey: A Study of the Feminist Movement on Sex/Gender in Relation to Trans and Queer Inclusivity

Denis E. Boyacı and Aslıhan Öğün Boyacıoğlu

Abstract: Drawing from queer theory and transfeminism, this article discusses whether queer- and trans-inclusive feminism is a possibility within the contemporary feminist movement in Turkey by analyzing its approach to the concept of sex/gender. In this context, in-depth interviews were conducted with activists who took part in the feminist movement and the LGBTQIA+ movement in Izmir, Turkey. These interviews reveal that the feminist movement bases its understanding on the sex and gender distinction and heteropatriarchy's gender binarism, questions the identities of trans subjects, and establishes power domains in terms of being white and cishet. The present study has concluded that the feminist movement does not build sufficiently on transfeminism and queer theory, and reinforces a cisnormative sex/gender approach. **Keywords:** feminism in Turkey; queer theory; transfeminism; TERF; cisnormativity

Disclaimer: This article may trigger some readers as it analyzes transphobic views and contains participant quotations expressing such attitudes.

Introduction

The notion of sex/gender has been conceptualized in various ways through the history of feminism in the Global North.[1] With the influence of Simone de Beauvoir's famous remark "one is not born, but rather becomes, a woman" (2011, 330), the second-wave feminists have approached sex and gender separately, where sex is biological and gender is the cultural construction built on it. A radical interpretation on this distinction has been made with the emergence of queer theory in the '90s. Judith Butler, in their epochal work *Gender Trouble* (2006), criticizes the binary distinction of sex and

WSQ: Women's Studies Quarterly 51: 3 & 4 (Fall/Winter 2023) © 2023 by Denis E. Boyacı and Aslıhan Öğün Boyacıoğlu. All rights reserved.

gender. According to Butler, sex is also a social construction, and defining gender over an already socially constructed (and gendered) category loses its meaning (2006, 10). When it comes to feminism in Turkey, it is possible to say that it has been influenced by these globally resounding perspectives. The feminist movement in Turkey adapted the Western second-wave approaches in the '80s and was challenged by "different conceptualizations of the 'woman' question and the politics of identity/difference" in the '90s (Diner and Toktaş 2010, 41–42). With the rise of conservative right-wing populism in the Global North after the 2008 crisis, anti-gender campaigns have proliferated in a transnational manner (see Kováts and Pōim 2015), and this has echoed in the rise of biological reductionism and trans-exclusionary rhetoric in feminism (see Burns 2019; Hines 2020; Pearce, Erikainen, and Vincent 2020). Gender critical arguments also have had their impact on the feminist movement in Turkey—a nation-state in the grip of political Islam and nationalist right-wing populism that heavily relies on the gender binary system to maintain its power and imposes it through its various institutions, especially since 2018 when the TERF ideology drawn upon from the U.K. context started to circulate (Özlen 2020). These arguments intervened in feminist politics in a way that made trans, nonbinary, and gender nonconforming subjects' lived experiences a target. Amid these current tensions, questioning the sex/gender approach of the contemporary feminist movement has become essential in order to trace the correspondence of these discourses, if they had any. Therefore, this article asks two main questions within the context of the contemporary feminist movement: (1) How does the feminist movement in Turkey engage with the production of knowledge on being sexed/gendered? and (2) Does the feminist movement in Turkey have cisnormative tendencies, as observed in some gender critical discourses?

To answer these questions, first the theoretical framework is addressed with reference to transfeminists who influenced the trans struggles in Turkey and to Butler's views around sex/gender and their critique of feminism.[2] Then the methods and background of this study are explained. Next, the findings are presented, and in the conclusion the above questions are answered with a discussion of the queer- and trans-inclusive possibilities of the feminist movement in Turkey.

Theoretical Framework

Through the '60s and '70s, with respect to the sex and gender distinction, Western feminists used the term *gender*, as Joan W. Scott says, "as a way of referring to the social organization of the relationship between the sexes" (1986, 1053). Most of the theory and politics were produced over this distinction, whether with nuances or not (see Daly 1990; Dworkin 1991; Rich 1995; Firestone 2003; Rubin 2011; Millett 2016). Contextualization in Turkey also was influenced by these second-wave productions of knowledge, especially after the 1980 coup d'état, when feminism started to grow as a political movement (Diner and Toktaş 2010). Producing theory and politics over this distinction was about showing that male dominance in society was socially and historically established and that therefore we should not seek the reasons for this in the "biological differences" between women and men. Making feminist politics solely over this binary distinction was not enough, with the result that trans activists started to make their voices heard in feminist spaces. In 1987, trans activists attended the first feminist mass demonstration in the history of Turkey, the March for Solidarity against Battering, and a trans woman made a speech at the protest (Şakir 2020). This visibility is historically noteworthy, because it shows that the coexistence of feminism and trans people goes back a long way; moreover, trans folks have always been feminist subjects when they stood side by side with cis women in their joint struggle against patriarchy, and "trans entities have always been present inside feminist spaces" (Noble 2012, 51). However, this involvement has led to tensions between trans, queer, and cis feminists from time to time. When we look at the Western context, we see that transfeminists have criticized feminism for being cis-centric and trans-exclusionary (see Stone 1991; Bornstein 1994; Feinberg 1996; Halberstam 1998; Koyama 2001). TERFs have accused trans men of betraying the women's movement, citing a position of masculine privilege (Halberstam 2018, 114), and marked trans women as men trying to invade the spaces of "real" women (Stone 1991; Serano 2007, 2013; Stryker 2017). Similar to these contexts, the history of feminism in Turkey has its conflicts with trans existence (see Zengin 2016). The Ülker Street Incidents in the '90s and the Esat-Eryaman Incidents in the 2000s (for a brief overview, see Kaya 2022), where trans women were subjected to systematic violence, were not paid much attention by the cis feminists. At the International Women's Day parade of 2011, a trans person was asked to leave the demonstration by cis feminists since it was a woman-only space (Zengin 2016, 266). In

2018, some cis feminists in academia started to circulate anti-trans texts from Western contexts, and eventually Turkey's own TERF debates blew up in 2019,[3] mostly on social media platforms. In these debates, TERFs have taken a standpoint in which they equate sex with being inherent and fixed,[4] and have subjected trans people to transphobia over "male social-ization," "invading women's spaces," and so on (for a detailed analysis, see Özlen 2020). In 2021, a nonbinary activist was misgendered and subjected to cissexist attacks on social media by gender critical feminists, because they were giving a workshop at a women's conference and questioned another participant's transphobic tweets. In 2022, for the first time in the history of feminism in Turkey, an anti-trans feminist group tried to sabotage the March 8 parade with transphobic placards and by threatening trans subjects. These debates and incidents continue today and impact the agency of trans, nonbi-nary, and gender nonconforming people in the feminist movement. With the rise of queer theory in the Global North and Butler's interventions in the '90s, feminism received criticism for its binary normativity of sex and gender and for presupposing a monolithic feminist subject. Butler's views found a place in Turkey, too, especially within the relationship of feminism and LGBTQIA+ politics.[5] Although the discussions and their impacts are relatively new and not yet theorized for the context in Turkey, they are still effective in the expansion of nonbinary, gender nonconforming, or other antinormative gender identities in these social movements. For Butler, sex, as a cultural norm like gender, does not refer to prediscursive or preconstruc-tive categories of woman and man (1993, 1–2). These categories do not have to refer to certain bodies (Butler 2006, 9). The fact that the social regula-tion of these forms is limited to two categories also is problematized (Butler 2006, 31). These binary frameworks are regulatory constructs that natural-ize and thus consolidate the cisheteropatriarchal regime (Butler 2006, 45). This practice of regulation is also found in discussions about the subject of feminism. Butler states that "it may be that only through releasing the cate-gory of women from a fixed referent that something like 'agency' becomes possible" (1992, 16). The category of women as the subject of feminism is not stable and consistent, though the feminist tendencies that Butler crit-icizes restrain and immobilize it in a presupposed fixed natural position. Butler clarifies in *Gender Trouble* that "there is the political problem that feminism encounters in the assumption that the term *women* denotes a common identity" (2006, 4). This political stance is not inclusive of femi-nist subjects such as some trans, nonbinary, and gender nonconforming people who do not share these predetermined commonalities transcribed on the category of "woman," or who do not define themselves as women at all, but are still affected by patriarchal oppression. Butler takes a stance on the potential for the denaturalization, multiplication, and destabilization of identities in order to unveil the constructed nature of cisheterosexuality. For Butler, "construction is not opposed to agency; it is the necessary scene of agency, the very terms in which agency is articulated and becomes culturally intelligible" (2006, 201), and furthermore, the deconstruction of the subject does not mean to discard the subject (1992, 15). It is worth remembering this premise, especially regarding the "concerns" which assert that feminist spaces and the feminist subject are being hijacked.

Methods

This qualitative research was conducted through participatory observation, a phenomenological approach, and autoethnography. The idea of this research formed around the TERF debates of 2019. During these debates, one of the authors of this article, being a queer and feminist activist, started to question whether the contemporary feminist movement in Turkey was actually trans-exclusionary like it seemed on social media, because prominent feminist academicians have exposed their transphobia in these debates and it had a shocking effect on the queer community in Turkey. Trans-exclusionary attempts have been made before by cis feminists, such as forcing trans people to leave the March 8 protests because they "look like men," as mentioned in the theoretical framework, but it was never this systematic and persistent. Thus, a need arose to ask this broad question: What is today's feminism's take on sex/gender? While, on the one hand, keeping up with the gender critical arguments of feminists who say that sex is biological and does not change whatever trans people call themselves or identify themselves with and, on the other hand, having more antinormative conversations with queer activists, it was observed that the above question was essential to ask in this political climate. Was it a handful of anti-trans feminists exchanging these essentialist discourses, or was cisnormativity predominating over the movement?[6] Was an inclusive feminist movement on the horizon for trans, nonbinary, or gender nonconforming subjects? With these questions in mind, the author determined the problem sentences, formed the framework, and started seeking participants. The aim was to interview activists from feminist and women's organizations.

Participant	Activism area	Gender	Age range	Education level
B.	LGBTQIA+	Agender	30–39	Secondary school grad
D.	LGBTQIA+	Cis woman	20–29	MA degree
N.	LGBTQIA+	Trans woman	20–29	Undergraduate student
Y.	LGBTQIA+	N/A	20–29	MA student
Z.	LGBTQIA+	Gender-fluid	20–29	Bachelor's degree
F.	Feminist	N/A	20–29	Bachelor's degree
G.	Feminist	Cis woman	20–29	Bachelor's degree
K.	Feminist	Cis woman	40–49	Bachelor's degree
İ.	Feminist	Cis woman	30–39	MA degree
R.	Feminist	Cis woman	40–49	Bachelor's degree
S.	Feminist/ LGBTQIA+	Cis woman	20–29	Bachelor's degree

Table 1. Information of participants

Then, the activists from LGBTQIA+ organizations were included, too, as it would be more comprehensive for the research to question them about the feminist movement's approach on trans, nonbinary, and gender noncon-forming subjects. First, the author contacted four of their fellow activists in a committee that organized Pride marches together to do the interviews and recruit participants. They suggested activists from feminist and women's organizations in Izmir, and these participants suggested others, so snowball sampling was used. No prior knowledge of the gender identity of the partici-pants was known, or they were not selected accordingly. In-depth interviews were held with eleven activists in the twenty-to-fifty age range, of which one was engaged in both the feminist and LGBTQIA+ movements (see table 1). Interviews lasted an average of one hour, and they were mostly conducted face to face, in cafés or offices, in December 2019. With the semistructured interview form, questions were adapted to the varying social and academic backgrounds of the participants. Interviews were audio-recorded and tran-scribed verbatim. Data were organized under specific categories, and then the findings were reached. Findings were classified into five main themes, and these are displayed in the next section.

Results

Five interrelated themes emerged during the field study regarding feminism's sex/gender approach and the possibility of a queer- and trans-inclusive feminism: (1) feminist movement's distinction of sex and gender,

(2) transphobia and the feminist subject, (3) feminism in the grip of the gender binary, (4) power domains of the feminist movement, and (5) abstaining from the LGBTQIA+ movement. The study was conducted under the permission of the institute's ethics committee. The names of the participants were not explicitly included, since the queer and feminist community in Izmir (although it is the third largest and most populous city in Turkey) is relatively small, so abbreviations were used when quoting them. Quotes were translated from Turkish to English, and an effort was made to convey the spirit of the language.

The Feminist Movement's Distinction of Sex and Gender

Participants were first asked about their views on the concept of sex/gender. For most of the participants from the feminist movement, there was a distinction between sex and gender in terms of being biological and cultural, as seen in R.'s view:

> What is sex? Things that are innate. We have biological sex: women have breasts, vaginas; men have penises. But what we name as gender is the roles that society imposes on women because of the different bodily structures of women and men.

K. duplicated this view by adding an example to clarify the distinction: "The gays act feminine, but they were born male after all, right? It is a social issue." Feminist activists deem sex as an innate biological concept and gender as a socially constructed one. Accentuating this distinction, İ. explained, "Biological sex and gender, of course, are not the same thing; one has become an indicator of the other." These views point to the binary of sex and gender; a dichotomy of biology versus culture. For Butler, gender should not merely be understood as "the cultural inscription of meaning on a pregiven sex" (2006, 10), as gender is a cultural instrument that produces a prediscursive natural perception of sex. Butler adds in the same paragraph that "gender must also designate the very apparatus of production whereby the sexes themselves are established," so sex is not an empty surface on which gender is built (10). When asked about their views on sex/gender, almost all the participants from the LGBTQIA+ movement answered in a Butlerian manner. They also offered a common critique of the feminist movement's sex/gender approach, as seen in D.'s statement: "They are woman-centered and this woman is heterosexual woman." Seeing sex/gender as indefinable,

Z. also expressed the following about the feminist movement's sex/gender understanding: "Totally formalistic. Mustache, penis-like appearance, hairiness, rough movements, muscles, et cetera, for men; big breasts, bare skin, makeup, wearing heels for women." Being active in both the LGBTQIA+ movement and the feminist movement, S. supported this claim: "Unfortunately it is (straightly) a man with a penis and a woman with a vagina."

Transphobia and the Feminist Subject

To research the possibility of a more inclusive feminism, it is important to ask who the subject of feminism is and to consider how trans, nonbinary, and gender nonconforming subjects are addressed by the feminist movement. For Butler, the subject is "the linguistic occasion for the individual to achieve and reproduce intelligibility, the linguistic condition of its existence and agency" (1997, 11). Individuals must go through a process of subjectivation to become subjects (11). This process occurs by challenging domination and oppression. Through the history of feminist movements, it is seen that the instrument of domination has been the patriarchy and that the subjects have mostly been cis women. Participants from the feminist organizations see the subject of feminism as women and occasionally as people who have experienced womanhood (by which they mean those who are oppressed because of their gender, while mostly mentioning trans women), and a problematic relationship with trans men is emphasized. R. stated her views on trans men as follows:

> How sincere will they be? They gave up on their womanhood. He is a man. Secondly, this male image in trans men . . . It looks repulsive to me. When we're in the same place together, I really think I'm with a guy. Of course, he was a woman. But no, it feels repulsive to me.

K. also pointed out the "masculine styles" of trans men and added: "If one came to a meeting and sat in a corner, I would be nervous frankly." Both participants also complained about the presence of trans men in feminist marches and found it troublesome since they think it allows cis men to intervene. Additionally, F. admitted that they wave aside trans men in the calls of the workshops they organize. Different opinions also are revealed about trans women's position in the feminist movement. As a feminist activist, R. sees trans women as closer to the movement than trans men. However, she still expressed a doubt regarding "masculinity," as follows:

How much of the masculinity codes that they had in the past have trans women left behind? Sometimes I see them act rough. . . . This sounds bad to me. It is not like a female culture. That's masculine. Them being too aggressive, too quarrelsome, and producing a different language, etc.

These views echo in the attitudes of trans-exclusionary feminists like Janice Raymond, who typify trans people in a monolithic and stereotypical way (Bettcher 2007). As seen in R.'s views and in our observations over the years, trans women are being artificially homogenized and portrayed as aggressively masculine in feminist circles. TERF arguments also resonate in K.'s views:

So, they get their boobs done, grow their hair, and say they're a woman. Is that so? Yup, they are what they feel, but I think they are not exactly like us. We can't speak of a complete womanhood. Okay, if they say they're a woman, then they are a woman, but not a womanhood like mine.

There is an implication of the supposed naturalness of cis women in this view. Julia Serano states that the feminist movements tend to "create hierarchies, where certain gendered and sexual bodies, identities, and behaviors are deemed more legitimate than others" (2013, 5). Acknowledging cis women as natural and thus legitimate results in and from cisnormativity. Cisnormativity presents cis people as "real" while marking trans, nonbinary, and gender nonconforming folks as "fake" and sets sex/gender as a bodily position having an essence. K.'s view of a trans woman being "not a complete woman" supports this normative structure. Another participant, G., stated that trans women are reinforcing gender roles:

All the trans women I've met so far were very coquettish. As if femininity is to wear high-heeled shoes, to put on makeup all the time, and to show your breasts. Is this really what womanhood is? Or is it the femininity gender norms give you?

This is another common argument made by most of the trans-exclusionary feminists; for instance, Janice Raymond says in *Empire* that "most transsexuals conform more to the feminine role than even the most feminine of natural-born women" (1994, 79), and Robin Morgan sees this reemphasizing of gender roles as a parody of female oppression (2014, 180). Participants from the LGBTQIA+ movement verified that transphobia is intrinsic to the feminist movement and that it is directed especially towards trans men; as D. said, "They still see trans men as if they choose to be a man over being a woman, and think they cannot take part in feminist activism," and S. added: "Feminism advanced merely to a degree where they can accept the trans people only in a way they know." The interviews clearly show that the participants from the feminist movement question trans women's and mostly trans men's positions as subjects and that their views align with the trans-exclusionary arguments. It is also important to underline that, regarding the question of the feminist subject, none of the participants from the feminist movement explicitly mentioned nonbinary or gender nonconforming subjects.

Feminism in the Grip of the Gender Binary

When asked about their understanding of feminism, almost all the participants from the feminist movement said more or less the same thing: it is women's struggle for equality. They take "woman" as the primary subject and interpret power relations through binary oppositions where "man" is at the top. While their approach is over the binary categories of woman and man, LGBTQIA+ activists perceive feminism as a struggle against power. Z. sees it as an ideology that defends the rights of all individuals in terms of gender identity and sexual orientation. S. supported this with a nuance: "It is a movement that instrumentalizes bringing identities to a level of equality in order for all gender codes to be abolished and aspires to make a revolution in this entire cycle; it's never just an ideology." D. epitomized this view:

> What feminism tells me is to fight against the power, but I'd like to underline that by this power, I do not mean men; because there are women who carry that power and hold on to it.... For a really long time there was a mention of male violence, but this power could actually be held by a woman, too. We have recently seen the violence perpetrated by women against women.

The general idea in this passage has been supported by numerous feminists throughout feminist history, as seen in the theoretical framework. Concordantly, Y. agreed that feminism cannot be seen only as a matter of inequality of two things, and, they added, "limiting it to this context prevents us from seeing the whole." Throughout the interviews, it became apparent that the feminist movement approaches feminism as a struggle for equality sustained by instrumentalizing the gender binary system that, as we know, cisheteropatriarchy employs. The complex structures of power, including any policymaking outside of the gender binary, are mostly not taken into account.

Power Domains of the Feminist Movement

Regarding pervasive discourses, knowledges, and truth regimes, and being embedded in these, Butler writes that "power is not simply what we oppose but also, in a strong sense, what we depend on for our existence and what we harbor and preserve in the beings that we are" (1997, 2). Participant statements reveal significant information about the power domains of the feminist movement, where certain subjects are in the position of power-holders. S. described these subjects as "white, straight, and economically strong women" and continued: "They almost became the owners of the movement." As seen here, this monolithism, which has dominated throughout feminist history, is still maintained today. It is clear that while campaigning a resistance against a certain power, the feminist movement itself reproduces and maintains power relations. R. made the following criticism regarding the movement:

> I think they support the moral sentiment imposed on us by the State. . . .
> They do this both to Kurds and to gays. They equate Kurds with terrorists.
> They are criminalizing the LGBT movement. Like, trans people are doing
> prostitution. Sometimes accusing lesbians of perversion.

This criticism on the influence of state power is supported by the other participants as well, as Z. exemplified: "Feminism is also fed by the political power: I remember very well, in the 2000s, some feminists saying 'gay cancer' to refer to HIV and AIDS in Turkey." That the discourses of the feminist movement parallel those of the dominant political power is clearly not a coincidence.[7] These narratives can be approached with an exegetical reading of Butler: in order for the feminist subject to continue to exist, it consistently needs to reenact the requirements given by the operation of power, and this includes the repetition in a performative way of the norms upheld by that power, as well as a state of referentiality to norms. These norms reproduce themselves through this constant referentiality, and also, the performativity here "must be understood not as a singular or deliberate 'act,' but, rather, as the reiterative and citational practice by which discourse produces the effects that it names" (Butler 1993, 2). What underlies the feminist movement's rendering of these discourses is its referring to cisheteropatriarchy's norms and reiterating them for its own status. D. elaborated on this matter:

> I think what heterosexual women have been doing lately by saying "you experienced maleness, you don't know what we've been through" to trans women and "you're not subjected to male violence" to lesbian and bisexual women is actually protecting their own power domains.

Because of internalizing cisheteropatriarchy's norms, they form power relations that circulate the knowledge that the perpetrator is always a male and that the political ground should be established solely against this, by ignoring the identities which deviate from the female and male axis imposed by the norm. Such a power relation marginalizes LGBTQIA+ subjects in various ways while locating cis women to a more privileged and enclosed position. This situation can also be read in N.'s criticism, pointing to TERFs in Turkey:

> The reason there is such a crisis in the field is the people who have academic authority and power. They are the people who utter threats such as "we will not admit you to the academy, just watch!" It's an act of power to the core.

This also can be read as a discursive effect of cis women's exertions to maintain their power as they think their privileges and comfort zones are under threat in the face of trans, nonbinary, and gender nonconforming people. This discursivity establishes itself within the gender binary system and reinforces it.

Abstaining from the LGBTQIA+ Movement

Both feminist theory and queer theory address intersecting gender and sexuality issues. It is possible to see the LGBTQIA+ movement and feminist movement as linked, since they are closely related to each other.[8] An emerging pattern in the interviews is the close contact of these movements. The commonality between the two movements is addressed mostly by LGBTQIA+ activists. As Y. put it:

> Both movements are in elbow-contact. They are also aligned in terms of opposing the cisheteropatriarchy. . . . I think they are feeding each other in a way.

D. also emphasized that the LGBTQIA+ movement has always been feminist and that although there are some divergence points (she mostly referred
to TERFs), they are always in solidarity, by giving an example: "We're also
fighting against those guys like alimony victims; marriage is not legal for us,
no one will have children, it's forbidden, et cetera. But we're already dealing with it as if it's our own problem." Despite these views, there are some
blockages—mostly addressed by the feminist activists—in the interactions
of these movements. R. admitted that LGBTQIA+ people "are not so much
on the agenda" of the feminist movement and explained that she sees the
LGBTQIA+ movement as closer to the Kurdish movement. İ. described
the priorities of the feminist movement as a segregation point: "Why are
we talking about lesbianism when women are being killed?" This resonated
in R.'s words, too:

> In the founding process of organizations, different genders—that is,
> non-women—are not included. I mean, the subject of this was (always)
> women. It wasn't lesbians or anything.

Another recurring observation was made regarding the feminist movement's unfamiliarity with the ever-changing concepts of gender and sexuality.
For F., the feminist movement has not fully grasped the self-identification
issue: "They can assign gender to a person based on their appearance.
Segregation occurs because of these gender assignments." Throughout the
interviews, some confusion about "gender" and "sexual orientation" was also
observed when the feminist activists used these concepts interchangeably.

Conclusion and Discussion

This article explored how the feminist movement in Turkey engages with the
notion of sex/gender and whether this engagement offers a possibility for
a queer- and trans-inclusive feminism, through the views and experiences
of eleven participants from both the feminist movement and LGBTQIA+
movement in the city of Izmir. The data collected through in-depth interviews and participatory observation provided information to reach themes
that align with the literature. Participants revealed that the contemporary
feminist movement's sex/gender understanding is in line with the conceptualization of the second wave—the dichotomy of biology and culture,
with sex established as innate. As stated in the theoretical framework, queer
theory has criticized feminism's instrumentalization of this binary; assuming

the category of sex as natural and immutable produces power and oppression (Butler 2006). According to the participants, the feminist movement in Turkey deems its subject as cis women and sometimes includes trans women. Although some feminist circles in the Global North have reached a certain level of acceptance towards trans men over the years (Serano 2013, 23), findings show it is not the case in Turkey, where trans men are stereotyped based on their appearances and perceived as having switched to the oppressor's side (see Halberstam 2018). Transmisogyny also is evident in the participants' statements portraying trans women as aggressive and hyperfeminine (Serano 2013) and cis women as natural. These all show that the feminist movement in Turkey has a homogeneous perception of these binary sex/gender categories and that it creates a tendency to absolutize the movement around cisnormativity. Such cisnormative feminism becomes an instrument of patriarchy. For an antinormative feminism, the establishment of "women" and "men" as binary, mutually exclusive, and oppositional natural categories needs to be problematized. A struggle conducted through the gender binary already designated by heteropatriarchy will be inadequate in demolishing this system, which is based on reproduction. It will continue to exist without losing its legitimacy to affect the existences and narratives of trans, nonbinary, and gender nonconforming people. This study shows that the feminist movement in Turkey has power domains defined by being white and cishet. Participants expressed the movement's problematic relationship with Kurdish people, which is that at best it ignores them. This white- and cis-centric movement fortifies its privileged space by excluding subjects who pose a threat to its power and self-isolates itself by overlooking the intricate oppression mechanisms that feed each other, such as racism and cissexism. It also is suggested that feminists in Turkey are avoiding the LGBTQIA+ movement, resulting in the feminist movement being deprived of the information produced by certain gender terms, politics, and theories that trans, nonbinary, and gender nonconforming people and activism utilize. The lack of communication between the movements delays discussions on normativities and allows gender critical ideology imported from the West to enter into circulation for the purpose of establishing its knowledge regime. Turkey is a highly binary-gendered and reactively polarized nation-state, and transphobia and cissexism have destructive consequences for its trans, nonbinary, and gender nonconforming citizens. These imported TERF discourses also fuel social and institutional discrimination. TERFs in Turkey are mostly reiterating the Western anti-trans and anti-gender discourses circulated consciously by trans-exclusionary academicians in privileged and influential positions, which leads to the institutionalization of these stances. The formation and functioning of anti-trans groups and ideology in the Western context has a transnational impact and therefore requires a transnational solidarity, especially with the trans movement in Turkey. Since this article concludes that the feminist movement in Turkey perpetuates the cisheteropatriarchy's production of knowledge on sex/ gender by reinforcing the gender binary system in various ways, transnational and intersectional implications for both the feminist movement and the LGBTQIA+ movement to outflank the globally influenced and pervasive conservative and far-right policies will be a reference point for searching and finding new ways to articulate an inclusive struggle against this rigid system. For a future in which the gender binary system is subverted and the movement becomes a locus for a radical change, embodying the policymaking of trans, nonbinary, and gender nonconforming subjects is vital.

Denis E. Boyacı is a queer feminist activist and researcher from Turkey. They received a bachelor's degree in English language and literature and a master's degree in women and gender studies from Hacettepe University. Their work focuses on transfeminism, queer theory and politics, LGBTQIA+ resistance, and intersectionality. They can be reached at deeboyaci@gmail.com.

Aslıhan Öğün Boyacıoğlu is an associate professor of sociology at Hacettepe University in Turkey. Her research focuses on the sociology of crime, and gender studies. She can be reached at ogun@hacettepe.edu.tr.

Notes

1. Apart from referring to certain feminist approaches, the terms *sex* and *gender* are used in this article with a slash between them. The reason for this is a concern for not creating a dichotomy between them, as this article argues that sex is a fiction, just as gender is, regardless of our bodily traits. It is asserted here not that these terms correspond to identical concepts in our socially structured worlds, but that the purpose of using them in this way is to at least emphasize the social constructedness of both concepts, in order to envision a discursive future in which the concept of sex already is understood to be social.

2. This article utilizes Butler's views because they had and still have an important influence on feminist thought in Turkey, especially when considering the ongoing tension between queer theory, feminist movement, and LGBTQIA+ movement. The elucidations are based on Butler's ideas in an ironic sense as well, since TERFs in Turkey refer to queer activists who

oppose their anti-trans rhetorics by saying, "Butler is their prophet; *Gender Trouble* is their holy scripture." Transfeminism, also, is an underresearched area in Turkey. It can be said that trans and queer struggles are stronger on the street, but academic works—which are few—largely rely on Western theories and views. The focus is mostly on the commonality and shared experiences of being trans* rather than the discrepancy and differentness of being Western. Instead of viewing the circulation of Western-oriented theories as one-sided, it is approached more like a potentiality for trans-forming politics that can inform both the global and the local on the basis of reciprocity, depending on the context in which they are employed.

3. These debates were especially active on Twitter. They started when some feminists brought anti-trans propaganda made mostly in the U.K. to Turkey. Some cis feminists in academia made transphobic claims and spread fake news about trans lives—especially about trans children and their right to access puberty blockers—and transfeminists responded to these claims, ex-posing the transphobia. During these debates, trans activists were portrayed by TERFs as aggressive usurpers who seek power over feminism and as misogynist beneficiaries of masculinity.

4. Although there is a general nomenclature worldwide of *gender critical*, this acronym has been kept, since a considerable amount of these people refer to themselves as TERFs, whether in Twitter spaces or in their account bios.

5. After the trans-exclusionary attitudes in 2011, monumental meetings were organized by Amargi (a feminist collective in Istanbul) in 2011 and 2012 where cis, trans, and queer feminists came together and formed a dialogue. In these meetings, transfeminism, queer theory, the gender binary, and the fluidity of gender have started to be discussed, mostly with reference to Butler. These discussions are important because they show that feminists can stand side by side and inform each other about these theories in an intersectional way in Turkey (see Özdemir and Bayraktar 2011, 2012).

6. Although it is uttered by some of the trans activists in Turkey that TERFs in Turkey are limited in their number and not to be taken seriously, this article does not share this stance since their networking is having a notable effect on lives and politics.

7. This is of course a reciprocal interaction: for instance, the gradual increase of gender critical arguments and the proposals of "bathroom bills" in some U.S. states. These arguments are useful for the conservative far-right politi-cal actors to spread their ideologies by using them as justification.

8. This connection between queer theory and the LGBTQIA+ movement is made because it is observed that, compared to the feminist movement in Turkey, the LGBTQIA+ movement is more informed by queer theory.

Due to the connection between the emergence of queer theory and the lesbian and gay movements, over time, the gender binary system has been questioned and normative identity categories have started to be destabilized by the LGBTQIA+ movement. In Turkey, for instance, nonbinary activism is becoming more effective and is challenging normativities as a result of LGBTQIA+ activism.

Works Cited

Beauvoir, Simone de. 2011. *The Second Sex*. New York: Vintage Books.

Bettcher, Talia Mae. 2007. "Evil Deceivers and Make-Believers: On Transphobic Violence and the Politics of Illusion." *Hypatia* 22 (3): 43–65.

Bornstein, Kate. 1994. *Gender Outlaw: On Men, Women and the Rest of Us*. New York: Routledge.

Burns, Katelyn. 2019. "The Rise of Anti-trans 'Radical' Feminists, Explained." *Vox*, April 2, 2019. https://www.vox.com/identities/2019/9/5/20840101/terfs-radical-feminists-gender-critical.

Butler, Judith. 1992. "Contingent Foundations: Feminism and the Question of Postmodernism." In *Feminists Theorize the Political*, ed. Judith Butler and Joan W. Scott, 3–21. New York: Routledge.

———. 1993. *Bodies That Matter: On the Discursive Limits of "Sex."* New York: Routledge.

———. 1997. *Psychic Life of Power: Theories in Subjection*. Palo Alto, CA: Stanford University Press.

———. 2006. *Gender Trouble: Feminism and the Subversion of Identity*. New York: Routledge.

Daly, Mary. 1990. *Gyn/ecology: The Metaethics of Radical Feminism*. Boston, MA: Beacon Press.

Diner, Cagla, and Şule Toktaş. 2010. "Waves of Feminism in Turkey: Kemalist, Islamist and Kurdish Women's Movements in an Era of Globalization." *Journal of Balkan and Near Eastern Studies* 12 (1): 41–57.

Dworkin, Andrea. 1991. *Woman Hating*. New York: Plume.

Feinberg, Leslie. 1996. *Transgender Warriors: Making History from Joan of Arc to Dennis Rodman*. Boston, MA: Beacon Press.

Firestone, Shulamith. 2003. *The Dialectic of Sex: The Case for Feminist Revolution*. New York: Farrar, Straus and Giroux.

Halberstam, Jack. 1998. *Female Masculinity*. Durham, NC: Duke University Press.

———. 2018. *Trans*: A Quick and Quirky Account of Gender Variability*. Berkeley: University of California Press.

Hines, Sally. 2020. "Sex Wars and (Trans) Gender Panics: Identity and Body Politics in Contemporary UK Feminism." *Sociological Review Monographs* 68 (4): 699–717.

Kaya, Efruz. 2022. "Brief Past and Present of Transgender People in Turkey: Ülker Sokak (Street), Esat and Eryaman, Bayram Sokak (Street)." *Çatlak Zemin*, April 8, 2022. https://en.catlakzemin.com/brief-past-and-present-of-transgender-people-in-turkey-ulker-sokak-street-esat-and-eryaman-bayram-sokak-street.

Kováts, Eszter, and Maari Põim. 2015. *Gender as Symbolic Glue.* Budapest: FEPS.

Koyama, Emi. 2001. *Transfeminism: A Collection.* Portland, OR: Feminist Conspiracy Press.

Millett, Kate. 2016. *Sexual Politics.* New York: Columbia University Press.

Morgan, Robin. 2014. *Going Too Far: The Personal Chronicle of a Feminist.* New York: Open Road Integrated Media.

Noble, Bobby. 2012. "Trans. Panic. Some Thoughts toward a Theory of Feminist Fundamentalism." In *Transfeminist Perspectives in and beyond Transgender and Gender Studies,* ed. Anne Enke, 45–59. Philadelphia, PA: Temple University Press.

Özdemir, Esen, and Sevi Bayraktar. 2011. İstanbul *Amargi Feminizm Tartışmaları.* İstanbul: Amargi.

———. 2012. İstanbul *Amargi Feminizm Tartışmaları.* İstanbul: Kumbara Sanat.

Özlen, Lara. 2020. "'No TERFs on Our TURF': Building Alliances through Fractions on Social Media in İstanbul." *Kohl* 6 (3): 369–87.

Pearce, Ruth, Sonja Erikainen, and Ben Vincent. 2020. "Terf Wars: An Introduction." *Sociological Review Monographs* 68 (4): 677–98.

Raymond, Janice G. 1994. *The Transsexual Empire: The Making of the She-male.* New York: Teachers College Press.

Rich, Adrienne. 1995. *Of Woman Born: Motherhood as Experience and Institution.* New York: W. W. Norton.

Rubin, Gayle S. 2011. *Deviations: A Gayle Rubin Reader.* Durham, NC: Duke University Press.

Şakir, Şükran. 2020. "17 May 1987: March for Solidarity against Battering." *Çatlak Zemin.* April 8, 2020. https://en.catlakzemin.com/17-may-1987-march-for-solidarity-against-battering.

Scott, Joan W. 1986. "Gender: A Useful Category of Historical Analysis." *American Historical Review* 91 (5): 1053–75.

Serano, Julia. 2007. *Whipping Girl: A Transsexual Woman on Sexism and the Scapegoating of Femininity.* Emeryville, CA: Seal Press.

———. 2013. *Excluded: Making Feminist and Queer Movements More Inclusive.* Emeryville, CA: Seal Press.

Stone, Sandy. 1991. "The Empire Strikes Back: A Posttranssexual Manifesto." In *Body Guards: The Cultural Politics of Gender Ambiguity*, ed. Julia Epstein and Kristina Straub, 280–304. New York: Routledge.

Stryker, Susan. 2017. *Transgender History: The Roots of Today's Revolution.* New York: Seal Press.

Zengin, Aslı. 2016. "Mortal Life of Trans/feminism: Notes on 'Gender Killings' in Turkey." *TSQ: Transgender Studies Quarterly* 3 (1/2): 266–71.

Gender Transgressions:
Nonbinary Spaces in Greco-Roman Antiquity and Ancient China

Lou Rich

Abstract: Nonbinary presentations, behaviors, and spaces have been observed transculturally throughout history. Whilst historical manifestations differ from our modern notions of nonbinary, this article examines instances of nonbinary transgressions that may have been previously consigned to homoerotic histories. This article deploys such a nonbinary lens to discuss instances that relate to the body, gender presentations, social roles, and language, for the purpose of problematizing both notions of transgender history and binary assumptions of gender as untransmutable and immutable. **Keywords:** nonbinary; gender transgressions; transgender history; gender; Ancient Greece; Ancient Rome; Ancient China

Situating Gender Diversity

Whilst nonbinary as an identity has existed throughout history, the ancient world had no basis for understandings of gender as it has come to be understood in the past decades. The heterosexual matrix, as defined by Judith Butler in their germinal 1990 book *Gender Trouble*, not only influences our perception of desire, attraction, and sexual acts but additionally distorts and ratifies gender as a binary construct. *Nonbinary* is an umbrella term for gender identities that fall outside of the modern binary of male or female, and this term entered the transnational public lexicon within the last decade. With transgender studies emerging as a field spearheaded by authors such as Halberstam, Stryker, and Serano, identities such as transgender women and men have taken the forefront, with nonbinary identities slower to gain traction. Transgender is often defined as "an umbrella term that refers to all identities or practices that cross over, cut across, move between, or otherwise queer socially constructed sex/gender boundaries" (Stryker 1994,

WSQ: Women's Studies Quarterly 51: 3 & 4 (Fall/Winter 2023) © 2023 by Lou Rich. All rights reserved.

251). Transgender may encompass the nonbinary identity, but some nonbinary individuals do not identify with the term.

Whilst we may deploy a transgender lens to this article, I contend that a nonbinary lens further widens the scope within historical contexts. In removing the modern, Eurocentric assumptions of categories and binaries, whilst the experiences remain situated in their cultural contexts, a nonbinary lens allows scholars and readers to consider the absence of gender alongside constructions of genders, particularly in cultures where language and its deployments were intrinsically ambiguous. These Eurocentric assumptions of gender, sexuality, and binarism have been endorsed through the Western colonial spread of philosophy, science, and religion, resulting in the matrix becoming codified in many modern societies. Scholars such as Patil (2018) have examined such a colonial effect concerning the heterosexual matrix and yet have critically scrutinized its universality, or rather lack thereof, and its dis/connection to the larger network of imperial relations. Oyèrónkẹ́ Oyěwùmí (1997) notes that this ethnocentric presumption of the universality of gender, and therefore transgressions, does not apply to all cultures and societies, reinforcing the need for a nonbinary lens that accounts for cultural and historical contexts.

Indigenous gender systems outside of Western sexological colonial ideas existed in antiquity and continue to the present day. Examples of these nonbinary cultural spaces include the Bugis peoples of Indonesia and their conceptualization of five genders encompassing cisgender, transgender, and nonbinary genders (Davies 2007); the Hijra people in India, who have a degree of national legal recognition of their nonbinary gender identities (Reddy 2005); and the Muxe people of Zapotec cultures in Oaxaca, who are diverse in their gender identities and presentations in people who were assigned male at birth (Stephen 2002). Critically, the introduction of Western, colonial, and religious gender identities and the heterosexual matrix has caused these previously long-held diverse cultures to become subject to attack or erasure. Scholars have undertaken extensive work to document colonial changes to preexisting cultural notions of gender and sexuality. Guardeño (2020), examining the British Raj and the import of colonial-era ideas in China, definitively mapped the repercussions both socially and legally for gender/sexual diversity in both experiences and individuals. He found that the ushering in of legislation such as Article 377 in the British Raj upheld the heterosexual matrix and condemned previously accepted diverse behaviors and identities not only in colonized India but also in China, which was never formally colonized. It is, therefore, incorrect to say that only those who were directly colonized were influenced by the Western ideals that upheld the nuclear, heterosexual, binary-gendered family unit; notably, we see the lines of gender and sexuality blur within these nonbinary spaces and cultures, as with the Muxe peoples. For instance, in Nigeria, the yan daudu appear to straddle a line between "men who act like women" and gay men (Gaudio 2009, 218). Gender is a societal and temporal construct intrinsically intertwined with race, locale, and culture. Therefore, it can be considered under a nonbinary lens to uncover performances of gender both individually and culturally. In finding or revisiting scholarly works that uncover and reclaim queer histories (read: typically, homosexual histories with scant attention to other identities), we may expose nonbinary spaces. Doing so may lead us to acknowledge nonbinary experiences, acts, rules, and indeed, to an extent, requirements that had previously been relegated under the realm of homosexual or homoerotic. Through unearthing nonbinary readings, and revisiting thought surrounding the constitution and performance of gender, we may create room for nonbinary spaces in the present and the future.

In uncovering these experiences previously relegated to the homoerotic, it is observable that nonbinary spaces, language, and experiences have existed throughout history. In the last decade, there has been an upshift in scholarship concerning transgender people in history or antiquity (Campanile, Carlà-Uhink, and Facella 2017; Blood 2019; Ruffell 2020; Surtees and Dyer 2020), although such scholarship has largely focused on the binary notion of what it means to be transgender, rather than allowing nonbinary spaces to be just such—outside of any binary. Whilst sparsely investigated then, most transgressions of our modern gender norms have been relegated to being what we now term transgender, or subsumed under the homoerotic, with very few investigated from a nonbinary lens. Marianna van den Wijngaard's 1997 study on how biomedical science used transgender people to construct categories of masculinity and femininity illuminated, along with queer theory's early beginnings, how the body, organs, and brain were thought of as crucial to dissecting the queer experience. Gender essentialism, as Lennon and Alsop illuminate, often anchors itself through sexed identification in biology, language, and the self (2020, 2). A nonbinary lens, therefore, does not ignore biological differences or symbolic structures but rather takes these into account in the production of discursive spaces and experiences.

Connotations of both gender and being transgender therefore have always been culturally and historically specific to the moment of their production. To theorize a nonbinary space, we must acknowledge that the systems and social cultures which enable such a space to exist are often at the expense of the feminine. These spaces are often masculine-dominated not just in terms of social status but also in the realm of recorded history itself. Historical scholars since Hayden White have emphasized history as postmodern storytelling, with historians as the selectors of events that should, in theory, offer "a return to an emphasis on the uncertainty of our knowledge about the past, and on the ways in which our conceptions of the past are embedded in our present" (Curthoys and McGrath 2011, 15). It is within this uncertainty that nonbinary spaces reemerge from the previous relegations to binary heterosexual and homosexual histories. While recent scholars such as Leah DeVun (2021) have uncovered nonbinary identities in historical spaces such as the late Middle Ages and early Renaissance, antiquity remains largely untouched. In this continued research into historical contexts of intersections between Greece, Rome, and China, we unearth discursive possibilities through the discussion of nonbinary spaces. A nonbinary lens does not subscribe to applying modern identity terminology towards historical situations that fell outside of the recognized binary of permitted social actions, roles, and determinations. Before the efforts of transgender and queer scholarship, most societies were thought to have recognized only two distinct, broad classes of gender roles, and gender had been thought of as a fixed social role rather than an internal identity linked to biological sex. That does not, however, mean such transgressions were uncommon or nonexistent, but rather that they had been relegated to "cross-dressing" or even subsumed under the umbrella of homoeroticism. Chris Cagle (1996, 236) employs the term "monosexual gay historiography" to describe situations where bisexuality is rendered epistemological or a byproduct of historical culture. I contend that the same happens with instances of nonbinary spaces: they are either subsumed under the homoerotic, argued over semantically within transgender histories, or simply erased. In unearthing two potentials for nonbinary spaces—the physical body and the social role—we thereby discover discursive spaces for nonbinary understandings that can inform past, present, and future discussions of intersections of culture and identity.

Gender and the components of its performance allow us to look at gender transgressions throughout history and theorize nonbinary spaces.

We may find evidence of these resultant nonbinary spaces when we examine language, clothing, social roles, sexual organs, and sexual acts. The parameters of these nonbinary transgressions may also differ depending on the culture—what some may consider a transgression in their culture could be a common occurrence in another. Therefore, not only historical context but cultural context must be considered when illuminating nonbinary spaces. If we consider the ancient world, we find much evidence for the potential of a nonbinary view of gender. Sexual practices differ from the "established" protocols of masculinity and femininity and thus can be seen as gender transgressors (Pinto and Pinto 2013). The concepts of the body, sex, and gender, as well as transgressions of all three, allow for greater dialogue between historical scholars and those in transgender and nonbinary studies as they investigate the (dis)continuities. To pinpoint three ancient cultures, for the sake of brevity, this paper focuses on gender-transgressive behaviors within Ancient Greece, Rome, and China to illuminate nonbinary spaces of gender questioning. I illuminate the transgressive periods of Greco-Roman culture due to the syncretism between them, and their lasting impacts. Due to the Greek influence on Roman culture, and vice versa, it is, I believe, not possible to see one as fully distinct from the other regarding societal representations of gender. When we look at representations of the social, the cultural, and the physical (that is, societal expectations, cultural expectations, and both the physical body and the concept of the body), there are transgressions to be illuminated. These locales are selected in comparison for a breadth of reasons. The Greco-Roman world and Ancient Chinese cultures, with their literary languages in use for several millennia, have been analyzed by scholars such as Lloyd and Zhao (2017). This article focuses largely on the periods of the Greco-Roman world and the Han dynasty of Ancient China, as this was when most accounts were written into literary history, by Sima Qian—note: written, not observed. These rich and influential literary traditions make it possible to consider their social structures, queer and gender-transgressive histories, and classical traditions. Heuristically, such a comparison assists in illuminating spaces that would otherwise remain unclear. It also destabilizes the idea of linear progression and naturalizations within societies and cultures and is an approach that liberates us from conventional spaces of time and place (Scheidel 2018, 43). In other words, this comparative approach offers the potential to liberate us from a binary approach to events and experiences. It is within these ideas of social identity, language, and tradition within Greco-Roman culture and Dynastic

China, then, that we may unearth commonalities and differences using a nonbinary lens.

Bodily Androgyny

Observing the connections between the body, social roles, and discursive nonbinary spaces, eunuchs in Ancient China chose castration as a means to transition from one social role to another. In one of the most detailed investigations into (trans)gender China, Howard Chiang (2018) troubles the perception of eunuchs as transhistorical "third sex" subjects, as China did not have a word for the concept of "sex" until the 1910s. Chiang also posits that the notion of the third sex consolidates the binary of male and female and universalizes a supposed transgender experience. Such argument supposes that eunuchs were outside of the binary of male and female, which were the sexes noted at the historical moment. Their role was predicated on the condition of not being classed as "fully" male by the standards of society. Significantly, there were two subsets of eunuchs, further solidifying their nonbinary space within the permitted sex classifications of China. Some self-castrated and in doing so chose to make themselves eligible for the eunuch role, and others, termed "natural eunuchs," were born intersex or with ambiguous genitalia. However, it also was noted in metamorphosis stories that some individuals were born as one sex and during puberty physically transitioned to another (Milburn 2014, 5). Despite their adherence to either male or female social roles, this showcases that there was a spectrum when it came to human reproductive anomalies and thus nonbinary transitions and spaces. Regardless, castration in Ancient China was seen as an accepted transgression of gender roles and supposed sexual norms—castration provided a path to alternative roles in society, rather than expulsion or exclusion.

The motivation for self-castration varies from culture to, indeed, individual—eunuch as a nonbinary category was both personal and public. The personal category was the signification that the loss of biological fertility for a man signified the birth of his all-encompassing eunuch life, affecting both the work, the place of living, and the quality of the eunuch's life after castration. On a public level, the loss of fertility and masculinity meant that the subject gained a social role that was contingent on their new lack of genitals, creating a space for a nonbinary social role of masculinity. Although some scholars such as Wassersug, McKenna, and Lieberman (2012) have proposed that "eunuch" become its own identity, eunuchs ordinarily continued to occupy a male social role, as their masculinity was not undermined by their lack of genitals. It remains, however, that the premise of their identity as eunuchs was based on genital preconditions, creating an ambiguous and nonbinary space. In addition, male favoritism was linked to the social role of the eunuch. Male favoritism was a sexual relationship with the emperor, often between a eunuch and the ruler. This role of the male favorite would lead to further social mobility, as they occupied their own space within the Imperial court. The eunuch role, therefore, transferred and enabled both gender and social mobility, whether natural (by birth) or through transformation (through castration). Thereby, this role can be seen as creating a truly nonbinary space that facilitates further discussions of relationships between masculinity, nonbinary transgressions, and the body.

Likewise, within the Greco-Roman period, eunuchs occupied their own social role, although often tied to priesthood. During the Greco-Roman period, we can find the cult of Cybele and Attis, whose worshipers were known to castrate themselves and subsequently dress in women's clothing and present as feminine from that day forward—known as the Galli. Such worshipers were, additionally, buried with female funeral items when they died, prompting archaeologists such as Hilary M. Cool to posit that "if they wore these ornaments in life, as well as in death, then their fellow citizens would undoubtedly have considered . . . the man in grave 951 to be a transvestite" (Cool 2002, 29–30). Whilst we may not know the true motivation for castration, what is apparent is that the implication of such gender transgression was ostracization from larger society. Rather than relegate these gender transgressions to the act of exotic religious rituals, however, it is important to see the Galli in context—they had previously adhered to societal expectations of gender yet chose a life of transgression. Some scholars, indeed, have stated that they believe this self-castration to have been related to our modern concept of dysphoria: "under the influence of alcohol or drugs to dull the pain, [they] had voluntarily castrated themselves because they wanted to be women in shape as well as spirit" (Conway 2006, 367).

However, this is not a universal opinion amongst scholars, and some believe that castration merely served a religious, gatekeeping purpose. If we are to discard the possibility that the individual was indeed satisfying some gender-transgressive desire for the fact that such castration was merely a precondition of religious fervor, we must pause. For nonbinary and transgender individuals now, such methods of alteration, whether social or bodily, in order to reinforce a desired identity are reminiscent of such gender-transgressive behavior, and they should not be dismissed in antiquity. Another such example of gender transgressions relating to the body is the Anarieis, who are noted in Hippocratic texts to be impotent, wear women's garments, "speak like women," and work with other women, doing women's work (Penrose 2020, 37). Hart (2017) suggests that the Anarieis raised intersex individuals rather than practicing infanticide, unlike the Ancient Greeks, and that within Scythian culture, many possible practices indicated permissible nonbinary, transgressive acts such as the ones mentioned above. Therefore, it is prudent to assert that although Ancient Rome did make room for gender-diverse cultures and expressions, gender nonconforming people were not free from judgment on both a social and legal level. Much like today, philosophy's significant role in society and social norms was divided on the treatment and conception of such gender transgressions, and therefore the treatment and representation of such individuals meant that gender-diverse representations have often been subsumed or relegated as unimportant.

Regarding bodily transformation and gender troubles, it is also prudent to note that as with Ancient Greece, the surviving accounts of living persons who transgress defined gender roles are few, if any. Milburn (2014), however, examines Early and Imperial Chinese accounts of intersex peoples and bodily transformations, which are key to discussing a potential history of nonbinary spaces. Several bodily transformations from one gender to another have been observed, such as that of Zhuang Qisheng and Li Liangyu, and as Milburn accounts, such metamorphoses and gender transgressions were reacted to by scholars at the time in two main trends: some saw it as an omen of dynastic change, and some were simply curious. In Taoism, gender and the concept of yin and yang were also linked to masculine and feminine social roles (Wu 2010). For example, see the below passage:

> According to the *Shiji* (Records of the grand historian), in the thirteenth year of the reign of King Xiang of Wei (322 BCE), there was a woman in Wei who was transformed into a man. The *Jing Fang yizhuan* (*Traditions of the [Book of] changes*, by Jing Fang) says: "When a woman is transformed into a man, this means that *yin* is in the ascendant and a person of humble origins will become king. When a man turns into a woman this means that *yin* has conquered [*yang*] and that [portends] disaster." (Milburn 2014, 9)

Such transitions, in this manner, were to be reflected as an omen and therefore negative. Beginning in the Han dynasty, a negative correlation began showcasing that the appearance of nonbinary gendered individuals or intersex peoples during times of turmoil supposedly predicted the collapse of a dynasty. However, as Milburn proposes, it raises the possibility that during times of peace, such gender-transgressive individuals were not recorded, as they were seen as unimportant when not interpreted as an omen. We can also turn to the genre of *zhiguai xiaoshuo* (志怪小說) or "tales of the strange," which first appeared in the Han dynasty. Within this genre, strange, miraculous, or ghostly counter accounts to official dynastic records were chronicled. We see the record of Zhou Shining, among others, in the following passage:

> In the Yuankang reign era (291), there was a girl called Zhou Shining in Anfeng who [starting] at the age of eight sui gradually turned into a boy. When he reached the age of seventeen or eighteen, he finished puberty. His female bodily transformations were not complete and his male characteristics had emerged but were not dominant. [Zhou Shining] took a wife but they never had a child.
> 元康中, 安豐有女子曰周世寧, 年八歲漸化為男. 至十七八而氣性 成. 女體化而不盡, 男體成而不徹. 畜妻而無子. (Liu Jiangguo, *Xinji Soushen ji* 227 in Milburn 2014, 17)

This account in the *zhiguai* differs from its account in official dynastic history, in which all accounts of ambiguous gender were removed. Zhou Shining's nonbinary sex and, perhaps, gender provide us with a recorded account of transgression that differed from other gender transformations, as in virtually all other accounts they are stated to have married and had children in their later life, validating their gender recategorization (Milburn 2014, 18). Thus, Zhou Shining's gender transformation can be read as nonbinary, not belonging to full recategorization, and crucially, the omission of this gender ambiguousness from dynastic history allows room for the thought that such nonbinary identity lay outside of permissible transformations. If one had nonbinary genitalia at birth, they might come to be a eunuch. However, it appears that if this nonbinary transformation occurred later in life, as is possible in some intersex people during puberty, it was considered a bad omen. The social role of nonbinary gendered people, regardless of whether that be in terms of genitalia or bodily transformation, appears to have been precarious. Though recorded, it appears that their acceptance was predicated on many variables, such as religion or an established social or historical precedent. Nevertheless, reflecting on these spaces provides us with invaluable accounts of binary gendered lines becoming blurred and allows us to transculturally trouble expectations of gender. A nonbinary lens troubles the dominance of hetero/homo and cis/trans binaries as frames of interpretation regarding the body in these cultures and offers a space for transgressions to exist and trouble preconceptions surrounding gender in antiquity.

Social Trouble

Moving away from transformations of genitalia, we can examine how language, and thereby the larger concept of gender, within these cultures permitted the nonbinary historically. Many scholars and audiences think of language as a clear vehicle to accurately communicate social ideas, norms, and stories. In calling this certainty into question regarding ungendered language, we unveil nonbinary spaces in which the audience is left with the scope to interpret the significance of the text according to their own inter-pretation—signs are only ever what they mean to someone individually or collectively (Short 2007). In Ancient Greece, the concept of a neuter or androgynous gender, whilst holding negative connotations, allows room to explore the concept of nonbinary thought. This concept of the neuter gender, outside of the binary of feminine and masculine, was also accompa-nied by its own set of language and grammar rules. Aristotle (fourth century BCE), for example, categorized spoken gendered language with three such labels: masculine, feminine, and "in-between" (μεταξύ). Conversely, we see that Dionysius Thrax (second century BCE) termed this third gender as "neither" (οὐδέτερον) (1874). Rich (2023) illuminates a possible read-ing of how neuter pronouns in Sappho's work are a deliberately nonbinary deployment of language to forsake the gender of the subject. Exploring Sappho's work from a gender-neutral subject view, for example, illuminates many lyrics composed by her that could be considered nonbinary in both object of desire and gender of voice, such as Fragment 31 and Fragment 102. As Sappho had used explicitly gendered terms in other lyrics, such as that of Fragment 94, it is not out of the ordinary to assume that her un/ gendered deployment and its transgression of gender were deliberate. It is within such language deployments that we can unearth a nonbinary narra-tive. The neutrality deployed by authors was for bi-eroticizing their works,

thereby leaving the genders of those involved fluid and open to interpretation, allowing for the listener or reader to imagine themselves and the
character as any gender. This deployment of ungendered language created
nonbinary spaces that opened the piece to a wider audience. This ambiguity has been contested and seen as a problem by historians and linguists, yet
I contend that even when perceived as a problem this language has value.

Another poet who played on the concept of gender in Ancient Greece
was Ovid in his *Metamorphoses*. In this story, Iphis, who held a gender-neutral
name and was assigned female at birth, was raised as male by their mother to
prevent their death. Over the coming years, they fell in love with a girl named
Ianthe, yet before their wedding, Iphis underwent a sex change divinely
ordained from Isis. Quentin Stickley proposes that Ovid, despite the misog-
yny within *Metamorphoses*, imagines a "lack of understanding of gender as
an immutable fact set at birth" (2020, 65). Sex and gender identity are also
explored throughout the piece, with gender transgressions and transformations used to resolve problems about social gender dynamics such as
violence against women and disputes between genders. Such transgressive
bodily acts denote the fluidity permitted by Greek authors when it came
to the concepts of gender and the body, allowing the audience or reader
to imagine nonbinary spaces outside of the gender roles of Greek society.

Regarding gender diversity within Ancient Greece, language was often
used transgressively to label individuals outside of their assumed gender,
based on social characteristics—for example, in *On Regimen*, courage was
viewed as a masculine trait, and bold women were often called "masculine" by the authors' contemporaries. Female masculinity was seen as either
a compliment and an insult to one's femininity, depending on the situation. Critically, opinions on the distribution of masculinity and femininity
between genders were not universal—whilst Plato's Socrates asserted that
"men and women *can* have the same virtues, including courage," Aristotle,
Xenophon, and others disagreed (Penrose 2020, 30–33). Further examples
of female masculinity lying outside of gender norms of the time would be
Athenian playwright Aeschylus's *Oresteia,* in which the character Clytem-
nestra killed her husband to avenge her daughter's death, with her actions
(revenge-taking) described as improper for a woman, leading to her subse-
quent death (31). This concept of gender dependent on language, status,
and acts means that for Greeks, gender transgressions, whilst limited, were
a part of the Greek canon and were a factor in the historizing of the nonbinary. Additionally, Ctesias, a Greek physician, tells us that the Babylonian

satrap Nanarus was called an *androgynos* by his rival (Penrose 2020, 40). Nanarus lived luxuriously, wearing feminine clothing, shaving, and using cosmetics, but was offended by his rival calling him such a term (Hart 2018, 62–66). This alerts us to the cultural implications of being an *androgynos*, showing that, indeed, such a term was reserved for those who indulged in transgressive behaviors. Upon further reading, it becomes clear that the *androgynos* concept was embedded into the culture already, alongside the *andreiai* (masculine) female. *Androgynos* is generally understood to refer to feminine men rather than intersex individuals, and Greek thought understood such nonbinary presentations to be set prior to birth, as we can see in the below passage:

> If male seed is emitted from the woman, and female from the man, and the male seed wins the battle, the foetus grows in the same manner as the former, while [the latter] is lessened. These become *androgynoi* and are rightly called so. (Joly 1.28.4 qtd. in Penrose 2020, 33)

Therefore, within these Greek works of literature and other documents, we see early manifestations towards a medicalization of gender, transgender, and intersex individuals alongside an acknowledgment that nonbinary spaces within such a binary existed and that there were many examples. It appears that authors, in particular the author of *On Regimen*, understood gender diversity to be related to traits rather than physical attributes, such as courage or boldness rather than strength versus weakness, and intelligence, allowing for the deployment of a nonbinary lens. Such a lens has the potential to trouble social characteristics and traits, which could be said to have applied regardless of the gender of the subject at which the observation was leveled, allowing for more discursive potentials to be unveiled.

   In Ancient China and towards the present day, representations of nonbinary individuals and practices must be recovered from the realm of the homoerotic, as performance and presentation are often intrinsically assumed to be tied to sexuality. Whilst this can be the case, gender also may stand alone and allow the opening of further discussion related to gender during such times. From a Chinese perspective, the concept of gender as a social role is fundamental in the Taoist notion of yin and yang; for example, we find an emphasis on masculine and feminine energy, although this is not a strict relation, as mentioned prior. This concept of energy regarding the masculine and feminine is not unlike the concepts proposed by Greek philosophers. For example, an empress could be yang, whilst her male ministers could be yin, although this held negative connotations and was permissible only in certain social contexts. As Doran (2016) clarifies, a female ruler such as Wu Zetian (武则天) was seen as unusual, with her masculine construction of power at odds with the norms surrounding gender and sex and scorned by those who wrote about her. Buddhist and Taoist thought, then, allowed for nonbinary spaces of observation through notions of transformation and energy, although typically this was only thought to have occurred after the human life span of the individual—in particular, it is noted that Buddhists stressed that religious practice could lead to rebirth in the desired gender (Schuster 1985). In terms of presentation rather than energy-based nonbinary space, androgyny as a deployment has been observed within China since the fall of the Han dynasty. Cross-dressing as a cultural practice within Chinese literature enables gender ambiguity yet simultaneously may serve to enforce gender binaries. In reading these deployments with a nonbinary lens, we may see them as attempts to deconstruct the strict gender norms of the dynastic times, which were held in relation to the naturalized concepts of yin and yang, as explored earlier. For example, in *The Butterfly Lover*, protagonist Zhu Yingcai dresses as a man, without detection, to become a scholar and only reveals such disguise after her graduation. It is made believable, as the scholarly figure is more on the wen side of the wen-wu masculinity binary, lending themselves more to the arts rather than being a warrior (Kam 2002). Such a transformation in the context of the wen masculinity, however, troubles the lines between masculinity and the supposed feminine subject. It suggests that the male and female subject can look the same, in spite of their sex, and that wu can indeed belong to the female figure. Cross-dressing as a nonbinary expression in China, as recorded within the realm of the arts, is similar to the practices common in Ancient Greece. Deploying a nonbinary lens towards transcultural concepts of language and presentation may unearth nonbinary spaces in which previously static categories of history (i.e., homoerotic, cross-dressing, or fully subsumed under "queer") become fluid once more to allow for further examination of just what constituted and was performed as gender in ancient cultures.

Conclusion

Crafting nonbinary spaces within antiquity provides us with an opportunity to revisit previous scholarship to unearth new discursive readings of gender and social structures. The nonbinary social space of the eunuch is thereby troubled—in the Greco-Roman world, such chosen castration often led to feminine presentation in both the social and bodily sphere, whereas in Ancient China the eunuch was a royal social role that remained masculine. In addition, seemingly spontaneous bodily transformation is shown to be tied to myth. In Ancient China the transformation from male to female or vice versa was seen as an omen, and in Ancient Greece and Rome, the literary or stage transformation was a vehicle for allegory. The language surrounding a nonbinary concept of gender was present throughout all three cultures, and such language was often tied to traits rather than the body, like it is in sexological thought, as with the concepts of androgynoi, andreiai, yin, yang, and wen-wu. Further analysis of such language terms may offer nonbinary spaces that make it possible to examine the concepts of masculinity and femininity as well as spaces in between and outside of these terms. In examining body alteration, language, and gender presentation, we may further trouble notions of gender that are deemed culturally and historically intransmutable and untouchable. Rather than immediately ascribing a possible gender identity to the individuals who partake in such acts or performances, we may find that a nonbinary reading unlocks a space in which to consider what gender, or the lack of it, constitutes, provides, and ratifies. Such considerations allow for a transnational, transcultural discourse that accounts for cultural aspects and troubles categories of gender binaries.

Lou Rich is a PhD candidate in the Department of Comparative Literature at the University of Hong Kong. Their current research focuses on bisexuality—and other nonbinary sexualities and genders—in historical, literary, cinematic, and new media contexts. They can be reached at slrich@connect.hku.hk.

Works Cited

Blood, H. Christian. 2019. "*Sed Illae Puellae*: Transgender Studies and Apuleius's The Golden Ass." *Helios* 46 (2): 163–88. https://doi.org/10.1353/hel.2019.0009.

Cagle, Chris. 1996. "Rough Trade: Sexual Taxonomy in Postwar America." In *RePresenting Bisexualities*, ed. Maria Pramaggiore and Donald E. Hall, 234–52. New York: New York University Press. https://doi.org/10.18574/nyu/9780814768839.003.0016.

Campanile, Domitilla, Filippo Carlà-Uhink, and Margherita Facella, eds. 2019. *TransAntiquity: Cross-Dressing and Transgender Dynamics in the Ancient World*. London: Routledge.

Chiang, Howard. 2020. *After Eunuchs: Science, Medicine, and the Transformation of Sex in Modern China.* New York: Columbia University Press.

Conway, Lynn. 2006. "Historical and Cross-cultural Evidence of Transsexualism." *Basic TG/TS/IS Information,* part 2. http://ai.eecs.umich.edu/people/conway/TS/TS-II.html#anchor172830. Accessed April 17, 2023.

Cool, H. E. M. 2002. "An Overview of the Small Finds from Catterick." In *Cataractonium: Roman Catterick and Its Hinterland,* ed. P. R. Wilson, vol. 2, 24–43. York: Council for British Archaeology.

Curthoys, Ann, and Ann McGrath. 2011. *How to Write History That People Want to Read.* Basingstoke: Palgrave Macmillan.

Davies, Sharyn Graham. 2007. *Challenging Gender Norms: Five Genders among Bugis in Indonesia.* Belmont, CA: Thomson Wadsworth.

DeVun, Leah. 2021. *The Shape of Sex: Nonbinary Gender from Genesis to the Renaissance.* New York: Columbia University Press.

Dionysius, Thrax. 1874. *The Grammar of Dionysios Thrax.* Vol. 1. St. Louis, MO: Studley.

Doran, Rebecca. 2016. *Transgressive Typologies: Constructions of Gender and Power in Early Tang China.* Cambridge, MA: Harvard University Asia Center.

Gaudio, Rudolf Pell. 2009. *Allah Made Us: Sexual Outlaws in an Islamic African City.* Chichester: Wiley-Blackwell.

Guardeño, Jaime Manuel Navarro. 2020. "How Did Colonization Affect the Perception of the LGBTIQ+ Community in Asia?" Madrid: Comillas Pontifical University.

Hart, Rachel. 2017. "(N)either Men (n)or Women? The Failure of Western Binary Systems" (abstract). Paper presented at 148th annual meeting of the Society for Classical Studies, January 5–8, 2017, Toronto, Ontario. https://classicalstudies.org/annual-meeting/148/abstracts.

———. 2018. "More than Meets the Eye: Autopsy and Physicality in Herodotus and Ctesias." PhD dissertation, University of Wisconsin, Madison.

Lennon, Kathleen, and Rachel Alsop. 2020. *Gender Theory in Troubled Times.* Cambridge: Polity.

Lloyd, G. E. R., and Jingyi Jenny Zhao, eds. 2018. *Ancient Greece and China Compared.* Cambridge: Cambridge University Press.

Louie, Kam. *Theorising Chinese Masculinity: Society and Gender in China.* Cambridge: Cambridge University Press, 2002.

Milburn, Olivia. 2014. "Bodily Transformations: Responses to Intersex Individuals in Early and Imperial China." *Nan Nü* 16 (1): 1–28. https://doi.org/10.1163/15685268-00161p01.

Oyěwùmí, Oyèrónkẹ́. 1997. *The Invention of Women: Making an African Sense of Western Gender Discourses*. Minneapolis: University of Minnesota Press.

Patil, Vrushali. 2018. "The Heterosexual Matrix as Imperial Effect." *Sociological Theory* 36 (1): 1–26. https://doi.org/10.1177/0735275118759382.

Penrose, Walter, Jr. 2020. "Gender Diversity in Classical Greek Thought." In *Exploring Gender Diversity in the Ancient World*, ed. Allison Surtees and Jennifer Dyer, 29–42. Edinburgh: Edinburgh University Press.

Pinto, Renato, and Luciano C. G. Pinto. 2013. "Transgendered Archaeology: The Galli and the Catterick Transvestite." *Theoretical Roman Archaeology Journal*: 169. https://doi.org/10.16995/TRAC2012_169_181.

Reddy, Gayatri. 2005. *With Respect to Sex: Negotiating Hijra Identity in South India*. Chicago, IL: University of Chicago Press.

Rich, Lou. 2023. "Fluid Movements: Representing Bisexuality in World Literature, Film, and New Media." PhD dissertation, University of Hong Kong, Hong Kong.

Ruffell, Isabel. 2020. "Poetics, Perversions, and Passing: Approaching the Transgender Narratives of *Thesmophoriazousai*." *Illinois Classical Studies* 45 (2): 333–67. https://doi.org/10.5406/illiclasstud.45.2.0333.

Scheidel, Walter. 2018. "Comparing Comparisons." In *Ancient Greece and China Compared*, by Qiaosheng Dong, ed. G. E. R. Lloyd and Jingyi Jenny Zhao, 40–58. Cambridge: Cambridge University Press. https://doi.org/10.1017/9781316091609.003.

Schuster, Nancy. 1985. "Striking a Balance: Women and Images of Women in Early Chinese Buddhism." In *Women, Religion, and Social Change*, ed. Yvonne Y. Haddad and Ellison B. Findly. Albany, NY: State University of New York Press.

Short, T. L. 2007. *Peirce's Theory of Signs*. Cambridge: Cambridge University Press. https://doi.org/10.1017/CBO9780511498350.

Stephen, Lynn. 2002. "Sexualities and Genders in Zapotec Oaxaca." *Latin American Perspectives* 29 (2): 41–59. https://doi.org/10.1177/0094582X0202900203.

Stickley, Quentin A. 2020. "Gender Transformation and Ontology in Ovid's *Metamorphoses*." Austin Peay State University.

Stryker, Susan. 1994. "My Words to Victor Frankenstein above the Village of Chamounix: Performing Transgender Rage." *GLQ: A Journal of Lesbian and Gay Studies* 1 (3): 237–54.

Surtees, Allison, and Jennifer Dyer. 2020. *Exploring Gender Diversity in the Ancient World*. Edinburgh: Edinburgh University Press. https://doi.org/10.1515/9781474447065.

Wassersug, Richard J., Emma McKenna, and Tucker Lieberman. 2012. "Eunuch as a Gender Identity after Castration." *Journal of Gender Studies* 21 (3): 253–70. https://doi.org/10.1080/09589236.2012.681178.

Wijngaard, Marianne van den. 1997. *Reinventing the Sexes: The Biomedical Construction of Femininity and Masculinity*. Bloomington: Indiana University Press.

Wu, Chia-Chi. 2010. "Queering Chinese-Language Cinemas: Stanley Kwan's *Yang ± Yin*: Gender in Chinese Cinema." *Screen* 51 (1): 38–53. https://doi.org/10.1093/screen/hjp054.

You entice me with but one of your eyes

Maya von Ziegesar

You entice me with but one of your eyes is named for a verse from *Song of Songs* and modeled after the Ain Sakhri figurine, also known as the Ain Sakhri Lovers. The Ain Sakhri figurine is the first artistic portrayal of sex, between two embracing, genderless figures. The sculpture also depicts ambiguous sex organs depending on the angle from which it is viewed. It was carved eleven thousand years ago in what is now Palestine. It was discovered by a Bedouin, whose name was not recorded, and identified to be of immense historical importance by a French archeologist. In 1958 Sotheby's sold the Lovers to the British Museum, where they remain to this day.

The cave in which the Lovers were discovered sits in an Area C zone of the occupied West Bank, halfway between Ramallah and Tel Aviv. The Israeli state has a massive interest in excavating and exploring sites of biblical significance in order to emphasize Jewish history and their claim to the land. Archeological sites from before and after the biblical period serve no nation-building purpose and are therefore often overlooked. In 2012 Israel built a road above Ain Sakhri Cave and now pays a small fee to the occupied Palestinians for the right to dump trash into the valley below.

You entice me with but one of your eyes is made of plaster gauze and string. Both are medical materials, evoking conflict, rupture, and repair. I made the piece after an extended educational trip to the West Bank and most particularly as a response to Avi Mograbi's documentary *Avenge But One of My Two Eyes*. Mograbi uses this biblical verse (Judges 16:28) as a guiding lens to understand mutually destructive impulses in the Arab-Israeli conflict. I try to reimagine the liminal space of occupied Palestine through a verse from *Song of Songs* (Song of Songs 4:9) and through an acknowledgment

WSQ: Women's Studies Quarterly 51: 3 & 4 (Fall/Winter 2023) © 2023 by Maya von Ziegesar. All rights reserved.

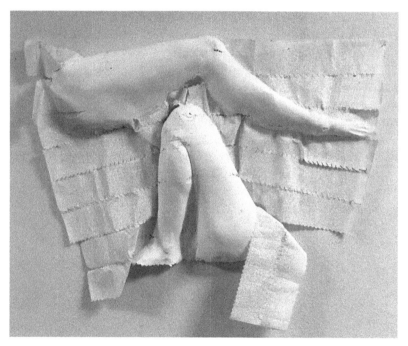

Maya von Ziegesar. *You entice me with but one of your eyes*, 2019.
Plaster gauze, string.

of the land's continuous history, which predates monotheistic religion and dualistic conflict. The Ain Sakhri figurine is a piece of this new historical narrative.

Maya von Ziegesar is a sculptor and philosophy PhD student from New York City. Her philosophical work explores coloniality, ideology, and practices of epistemic resistance, especially in Asian diasporic communities. Her artwork explores surface, volume, and skin. Before starting her PhD studies at the CUNY Graduate Center, she worked at Humboldt-Universität in Berlin, taught English in South Korea, and got a degree in philosophy and visual art from Princeton University. She can be reached at mvonziegesar@gradcenter.cuny.edu.

Works Cited

Boyd, Brian and Jill Cook. 1993. "A Reconsideration of the 'Ain Sakhri' Figurine." In *Proceedings of the Prehistoric Society* 59: 399–405.

Boyd, Brian, Hamed Salem, and Sophia Stamatopoulou-Robbins. 2015. "Toxic Ecologies of Occupation." *EnviroSociety*. http://www.envirosociety.org/2015/04/toxic-ecologies-of-occupation/.

MacGregor, Neil. 2010. *A History of the World in 100 Objects*. London: Allen Lane.

Noegel, Scott B., and Gary A. Rendsburg. 2009. "The Song of Songs: Translation and Notes." In *Solomon's Vineyard: Literary and Linguistic Studies in the Song of Songs*. Atlanta: SBL Press. http://faculty.washington.edu/snoegel/PDFs/articles/Song%20of%20Songs%20Translation.pdf.

Pardes, Ilana. 2013. *Agnon's Moonstruck Lovers: The Song of Songs in Israeli Culture*. Seattle: University of Washington Press.

Transition and Trans*lation beyond Binary History in Mid-century Upper Egypt; or, Portraits of Transfemininity in Asyut

Beshouy Botros

Abstract: In 1958, the popular Egyptian magazine *Ākhir Sā`ah* ran a story about four people designated "men donning dresses and living as women" in the Upper Egyptian town of Asyut. *Ākhir Sā`ah* presented brief profiles explaining these people's gender expression alongside staged photographs and opinions from an Egyptian psychiatrist, the local minister of education, a lawyer, and a social scientist. This article departs from that one. By annotating my trans*lation of the Arabic text, I interrupt its binary logics. Trans*lation is an idiomatic meaning-making process that is in intimate dialogue with the process of transition itself. In the source text, Egyptians living in tension with the gender binary were made legible through the relay of pseudoscientific evidence and details about their early childhood experiences, or in one instance, through a story about a deal between the subject and a spirit, a jinn. My analysis denaturalizes the publication's ethnographic documentation and teleological narration of these people's lives. Working through the Arabic text and departing from the Orientalist fixation with philology, I consider the possibilities of rendering gender alterity across languages and employ trans*lation as a method to engage narratological and historiographical processes. In my treatment of these biographies, I clarify how "nonbinary" challenges the emplotment of gender transition and the work of translation as linear processes, and I motion towards its potential to evacuate the overlapping transitions to modernity and the emergence of the postcolonial nation-state, which the aforementioned transfeminine individuals also lived, from similarly teleological narrations and binary logics. Ultimately, I situate these four subjects beyond the interlocking binaries of man/woman, human/spirit, cis/trans, modern/traditional, and East/West. In so doing, I collapse these structures and offer alternative portraits of transfemininity in Asyut. **Keywords:** trans*lation; nonbinary; translation; teleology; historiography; gender transition; emplotment; performance; photography; Arabic; Modern Egypt

WSQ: Women's Studies Quarterly 51: 3 & 4 (Fall/Winter 2023)

FIGURE 1: The full two-page spread in *Ākhir Sāʿah*

Phallogocentric language, not its particular speaker, is the scalpel that defines our flesh.

— Susan Stryker, "My Words to Victor Frankenstein"

The task of the translator is to facilitate this love between the original and its shadow, a love that permits fraying, holds the agency of the translator and the demands of her imagined or actual audience at bay. The politics of translation from a non-European woman's text too often suppresses this possibility because the translator cannot engage with, or cares insufficiently for, the rhetoricity of the original.

— Gayatri Spivak, "The Politics of Translation"

Introduction: Are They Doing It for *Luqmat ʿAysh*, a Morsel of Bread?

This is a history of language. The subtitle of the magazine article, pictured above, poses the question "What does psychology have to say about what these people are doing because of their professional commitments . . . and those doing it for a morsel of bread?" The author underscores that these people's transfeminine embodiment is rooted in material realities and needs. The popular expression *luqmat ʿaysh*, "a living wage," and the dual meaning of *ʿaysh* as "bread" and "life" in Egyptian colloquial Arabic makes the opening question especially pointed. Are they doing it for bread? Or life? Both? This opening question is one that I upend because of the farcical *why* it entails.[1] The more fruitful, but perhaps equally blunt, question is how they managed to do it, to live their lives. This question can also be misplaced. The graphic blurb beneath the subtitle addresses the reader even more directly: "Believe it or not these four 'men' [problem quotes in the original] live in the heart of Upper Egypt . . . in Asyut!" Here, the magazine's Cairene headquarters and the educated-Egyptian vernacular Arabic in which it is written are emphasized— can you *believe* what they're doing down there: "They don women's clothing and they live as women . . . carrying themselves as women do!" I have no trouble believing that these individuals lived full, complex lives in Asyut. It is often regarded as the capital of Upper Egypt, and in the mid-twentieth century its population was over one hundred thousand.[2]

In 1958, the Egyptian reading public, roughly 18 percent of a population of over twenty million, might have reacted with some incredulity. That is the tone taken up in much of the article as it reifies distinctions between the strange traditions of Upper Egyptians in the mostly rural, southern and central parts of the country, also known as al-Saʿīd, and its readers. By the second half of the 1940s, the daily circulation of Arabic press in Egypt had ballooned to over five hundred thousand, and *Ākhir Sāʿah* was, and remains, a referential magazine.[3] The exhibition of gender alterity in its pages, as an example of the queer customs of the saʿīd, speaks to the hypervisibility of transfemininity. An easy target for the ethnographic gaze, its representation demands spectatorship and not just readership. While this article might be said to uniquely command the spectatorship of mid-twentieth-century readers, it also fits within an already well-established genre of Egyptian ethnographic writing on Egypt.[4] Any details about these individuals' lives must be understood in the context of the voyeuristic framing of the magazine, which also leads me to reject the ethnographic impulse and trans-historical reflex of connecting these mid-twentieth-century transfeminine subjects with others from pre-Islamic Egypt or with Sufi dancers, whose whirling skirts captivated Orientalists. This is to say that the *Ākhir Sā`ah* article, and this one, should not be read with the primary goal of understanding indigenous perspectives on gender nonconformity in Egypt.[5] However, both present distinct local perspectives and textured accounts of four lives lived with intention and in tension with the gender binary.

In what follows, I read closely against and along the bias grain of the *Ākhir Sā`ah* article so that I might find the edges where the meanings of these peoples' lives were made and might be remade. I engage "nonbinary" less as a designation for who these people were or how they lived and more as a reading technique to interrupt the teleological narrations of gender transition as it intersects with Egyptian modernity. I present the four accounts of these individuals' "becoming-trans" in Asyut.[6] Their lives trouble the interlocking binaries of man and woman, human and spirit, modern and traditional, East and West, and cis and trans—critically historicizing them involves unlearning these binary logics. Only then can one appreciate the beauty of the lives these four individuals crafted in the middle of the century and in the heart of Egypt. After sketching out their contours, I examine the staged photographs to disrupt how these people were posed as questions, questions that a social scientist, lawyer, psychiatrist, and education minister were quick to address as they diagnosed the aforementioned ontological problem: why do these people live this way? To wield language deftly, as a surgeon might a scalpel, is to repurpose its tools by rewriting the expert opinions and breaking down the linear narrative structure in which trans and nonbinary people were emplotted. Throughout this piece, I punctuate and rhythmically interrupt the translation of the Arabic original as I weave my analysis into the text. I write around the masculine pronouns of the original and avoid using any pronouns to refer to the individuals in my own sentences; this includes dispensing with the use of the singular *they*. I trans*late, moving through an experimental writing exercise whose purpose is not to eliminate pronouns or rectify the magazine's representations but rather to hold complex narratives through meaningful interjection and syncopated prose and to write beyond binary gender by writing through and around it. Trans*lation is an idiomatic meaning-making process in intimate dialogue with the process of transition itself; it does not seek to define shifts from one language or gender to another, as if there were only one or the other, but instead insists on being polyglottal and multidirectional, lexical and sensual. Trans*lation *feels for language*, its plurality, its possibility, and its imperfection, and in order to deal with the inevitable imperfection of any and every language, trans*lation feels *across* languages. Unlike translation, which traditionally works to transfer meaning from a source text to a "destination language," trans*lation reaches beyond the binary logic that inheres the parallelism and parity that most translators seek to convey. In so doing, a trans*lation begins to account for the valences of gender and sexuality across linguistic and cultural differences. This definite article is therefore a trans*lation, one that functions through interruption, problematizes the teleological narration of gender and other transitions, and acknowledges that translation is itself based on the false teleological promise of moving meaning across semantic, social, and discursive frames.[7] Its argument is not predicated upon the location of any authentic meanings of nonbinary gender in Egypt, but is deeply concerned with the predicates themselves and with their expression.

Biographies on the Verge of Meaning, Teleology, Transition, Trans*lation

In what follows, any and all gendered pronouns are not my own, but come from citations of the source text. I engage in this practice of critical translation, or trans*lation, as I work through a source that can be hard to read. It is hard to read because its descriptions reproduce the language of sexism and transmisogyny. My rewriting breaks the flow of the primary source as I offer a series of linguistic and historical annotations. This is not just about contextualizing the original article's contents. It is a practice rooted in the understanding that translations are live processes, that translators are never idle, and that linguistics is to translation what biology is to gender; it belies unidirectional root systems and fixed patterns of meaning and change. At the level of word choice, my reflexive fixation with language plays off of the philological and etymological drives of Orientalist literary scholarship that scrutinizes the definitions of different sexual acts within (pre)modern vocabularies and taxonomies of deviance and desire.[8] A different reading would make words play in order to affirmatively critique the futile attempts to locate the origins or fix the meanings of terms for gendered and raced categories and sexual acts in Arabic. At the level of sentence construction, my prose bends to move alongside the Arabic original while my trans*lation accounts for but does not provide an account of the development of gendered grammar in Arabic, so as not to further reify the linguistic-cum-biological yoking of sex and gender in language.[9] Such an account would pander to two farcical questions: why these transfeminine people were living the way they were and why they were referred to in a certain way in a sentence in Arabic. It might be fair to claim that these people were misgendered in every line of the *Ākhir Sāʿah* article. Before making such a claim, it is important to see how they were gendered in every sentence, and how that gendering happened at the level of word choice, sentence structure, and (extra)narrative superstructure. By referring to them differently and putting trans*lation to work in narration and as method, I invite the reader to learn and unlearn the morphology of gender in the Arabic language. I invite the reader to feel across languages.

The first person is introduced in the third-person under the heading "They Compelled Him to Dance so He Became a Professional." The verbs in this sentence and throughout the article are conjugated around a singular masculine predicate, *agbarūh*, rather than the feminine *agbarūhā*, and an unspecified collective "they." Verbs in Arabic are conjugated according to the gender and number (singular/plural) of their subject, and if the verb's direct object is reducible to a pronoun, it can be attached as a suffix. For example, in the verb *agbar*, meaning to coerce or compel, "he" is the suffix and the direct object of a recurring proverbial "they," the Upper Egyptian townsfolk; in the second clause, *aṣbaḥṣa*, "he became," instead of *aṣbaḥit* (conjugated in the feminine), *aṣbaḥū* (conjugated in the plural, "they") or *aṣbḥatoma* (conjugated in the *muthanna*, gender-neutral dual). These gendering verb-subject-object forms were standard across the four profiles; singular masculine pronouns and conjugations of verbs were ascribed to transfeminine people. This creates a discordance between the subjects and their verbs that I proceed to break down, but cannot redress. I flag this discordance because it demands that the reader engage language by looking at the text and photos, discussed later on, and listening for their harmony, or lack thereof. Noting the sharp edges where pronouns, subjects, and verbs do not seem to agree with one another is a way of deconstructing the hegemonic gendered grammar that makes trans* inclusive language sound "awkward."[10] We might become attuned to the singular plural or neutral *muthana* in Arabic, and other forms as we read, look, and listen, anew.

The *Ākhir Sāʿah* article opens with the "first problem," that of Husayn Mahmoud, who worked as a dancer at weddings. It states, "Behind his dedication to this profession is a strange story related to his upbringing. During his childhood, people would bully him for his bad looks [*damātihi*]... and he had a sister who was distinguished from him through artificial beauty [*gamal masnūʿ*], her powders and rouge and brightly colored clothing. When he would go out with her, he would hear the Upper Egyptian townsfolk [*Saʿayda*] say, 'Oh wow, what a pretty thing,' and he started to envy her. Why doesn't he attract their attention like her, why is he unable to choose admirers in the same way?! And this thought continued to perturb him," literally "to return to him" (*tarawiduh*). The article stages a seemingly classic psychoanalytic case of childhood cross-gender identification. It also flags Husayn Mahmoud's dysphoric feelings, feelings that persisted "until one night, some of his friends came to him and requested that he dance at one of their weddings [*yiʿūm bi-iḥyāʾ faraḥ bi-al-raqṣ*]," literally "to take up the task of enlivening a wedding by dancing." Husayn Mahmoud "immediately accepted and went to the wedding after putting on a full feminine outfit and makeup." There, "he danced for the first time and received admiration that he was not expecting, and from that night on he became a professional dancer." As someone assigned "male" at birth, Husayn Mahmoud was later required to submit for mandatory military service. The article explains that upon being conscripted, "he tried to leave his profession but was unable to, so he secretly brought along his feminine clothing to the army base and would dress covertly until one night an officer found him and punished him, and this punishment was repeated until his military service ended." The term of Mahmoud's conscription was between two and three years, and this unspecified punishment recurred throughout. It takes no stretch of the imagination to glean that it likely involved sexual violence, but narrating and translating Mahmoud's sentence *stretches language*. Even in the hostile environment of the military base, Mahmoud could not leave behind the vestments of the dance floor. A flowing skirt, bangles, and a well-cut blouse were all tucked away. Mahmoud went stealth. Far from any fans, Mahmoud remained a dancer; this was more than a job.

The next individual was introduced under the heading "He Beats the Drums and Treats Seizures." Each of these people poses a problem, or a set of linked linguistic and interpretive dilemmas, for the mid-century reader and the contemporary translator. They were each introduced as having a problem: "The second problem belongs to Bayoumi Hashim; he is married and has six children, and he is a professional *zar* musician." Noting Hashim's apparent heterosexuality throws this subject's work life into further relief. The article further describes that "his reason for being in this profession is that his mother was a *zar* master and the head of a band [*gawqat zar*], and she would take him to all of the sessions she arranged until *zar* began to run through his veins [*yagri fī ʿurūquh*]." In her recent ethnographic study, Egyptian anthropologist Hager el-Hadidi defines *zar* as "both a possessing spirit and a set of reconciliation rites between the spirits and their human hosts. . . . Originally spread from Ethiopia to the Red Sea and the Arabian Gulf through the nineteenth-century slave trade, in Egypt zar has incorporated elements from popular Islamic Sufi practices" (2016). The leaders of *zar* ensembles are almost always women, who create sacred performance spaces and intercede between spirits and humans. While it is not uncommon for young boys to be present, it is rare for men to act as their conductors. The *Ākhir Sāʿah* article explains that Hashim "was prohibited from attending these sessions when he grew older, because they are exclusively for women and children, and because of this he had to accompany his mother covertly in women's clothing to participate alongside her in the beating of the drums and treatment of the patients. And when his mother passed away, he became the head of the ensemble [*raʾīs al-gawqah*], and since then he has not taken off feminine clothing." Hashim remained a practitioner of *zar*, a conductor—*raʾīs*, masculine, rather than *raʾīsat*—of the ensemble (*al- gawqah*). Hashim did not become a woman, but remained a devotee of *zar*. In keeping with this professional work and these spiritual practices, Hashim transitioned into a unique transfeminine position in the interstitial spaces between spirits and humans, and men and women. In this role, Hashim found patrons seeking ritual healing and was able to raise a family.

The third story brings the reader into even closer contact with the supernatural. It is narrated under the heading "She Married Him and Ordered Him to Wear Makeup." Each of these people was presented with a problem and a masculine name, even if they had taken on a new name. The article proceeds: "And the third problem belongs to Ismail Raza, and he has a strange story. They call him Abū al-Sibāʿ, 'The Father of the Lion,' and they say that he married a woman from the underworld [*sayyidah min taht al-ard*]. This woman brings him food and clothing and all he requests without receiving anything in return." In exchange, this feminine spirit commanded that Abū al-Sibāʿ "wear women's clothing and apply makeup, so that earthly women would not look upon him with desire." This transhuman and feminine injunction was a way of delimiting desire in exchange for care labor. Abū al-Sibāʿ was obliged to fulfill her orders, to maintain their connection and avoid her punishment. This became the stuff of local legend, as "all the people of Asyut say that he is forced into performing transfemininity," literally *al-tashabbuh bi-al-nisa*, "so that he is not harmed by the jinn." The townsfolk would, "tell weird stories about him and testify that they saw her [the jinn] with their own eyes. One of them says that Abū al-Sibāʿ gave him a handful of sand and told him to blow in it and open his hand—the man did as he was told and found in his hand a ten-*qirsh* silver coin."

The article's narrator and the people of Asyut tried to explain things that stretched the imagination: this person's gender expression and magical powers. The journalist interviewed another man, who recounted how Abū al-Sibāʿ used "incredible physical strength" to single-handedly end the celebrations of the Moulid of Sidi al-Galal. After hearing this, the journalist asked Abū al-Sibāʿ to perform a miracle, at which point "he turned away and said, 'I don't have time; what's your deal, and what business do you have with me.'" The reporter then asked for a photograph, and Abū al-Sibāʿ refused. He goes on to explain how he tried to snap a picture while Abū al-Sibāʿ was not paying attention, but "he was faster than I was, and he covered his face with a pillow." Here, too, a transfemme in Asyut troubled the boundaries between gendered categories, spirits and humans, and between cisness and transness. Abū al-Sibāʿ was capable of great displays of strength, ending a major saint's festival with the crack of a whip and doing so with a full face of makeup. It is one we are not allowed to see.

The last entry is the shortest of the four: "Zar . . . Another Time!" Perhaps the journalist had gotten used to the reappearance of transfeminine *zar* performers. It starts as follows: "And the fourth problem belongs to Sultan Ibrahim. His father passed away, so he had to help his mother in cleaning houses and laundering the neighbor's clothing, and he felt that this work was not fit for him." The article then notes the traditional garb worn by *zar* devotees, while narrating this person's transition across different forms of feminized labor: Sultan Ibrahim "began working with a *zar* group after changing his clothing completely to women's dress, and he began to wear a *tarḥa* [headdress] and atop it a *mandil abū ūyah* [a scarf with spangles]." These sartorial details, and others about the family's economic straits after the death of Ibrahim's father, laid the groundwork for the experts' interventions on the next

FIGURE 2: *Top left,* image of Husayn Mahmoud and caricature; *Top right,* Abū al-Sibā' with child; *Bottom left and right, zar* performers Bayoumi Hashim and Sultan Ibrahim

page, in which they sought to explain these as natural cases of gender deviance caused by nontraditional family structures and the backwards customs of upper Egyptians. Ibrahim's story was concluded with this general statement and segue in bolded letters: "And there are many other cases everywhere, similar to these and with their own difficult and specific circumstances, most dealing with seeking income. And all need explanation and treatment. So, what are the opinions of the psychiatrist and social scientists?"

Posing Questions, Composing Photographs

There is a unique grammar to how the visual and verbal content of the *Ākhir Sāʿah* article was arranged. "Grammar" here refers to the mid-century graphic design and editing that coordinate the article's affective structure.

In each of the four stories, the journalist provided details meant to provoke shock and sympathy and preempt answers to the aforementioned "why" questions. In so doing, the article scaffolds four narrative arcs that were meant to, first, trouble the sensibilities of readers by exhibiting these people and, subsequently, placate those sensibilities by providing rational explanations. If these individuals were living as they did out of desperation or due to the particular conditions of their upbringing, then they could be made to make sense, trans panic averted. Panning out, the divide between the first page, which profiles the four transfemmes, and the second, which details the opinions of the four experts, also clarifies. Before getting to this asymmetry, it is worth considering that more than half of the space of this two-page spread in *Ākhir Sāʿah* is devoted to photographs, whose layout directs readers' eyes. While this is nonunique in comparison with the rest of the magazine, both the position of transfeminine people within the visual economy and their responses to the camera demand special attention.

Obviously, these photos underscored the transmisogynistic and sexist language of the article. The juxtaposition of Husayn Mahmoud, the dancer, and this caricature is perhaps the most egregious example. Mahmoud's uncomfortable pose and the proximity between the photograph and the graphic speak loudly. The editors drew these figures and made connections between what they rendered as caricatures of femininity. Still, it may be counterproductive to discard the photos as transphobic media matter. The image the journalist attempted to take of Abū al-Sibāʿ is placed with the caption "Abū al-Sibāʿ refused to be photographed, and he placed a pillow over his face because these are the orders of the jinn." In place of the pillow, the editors placed the name "Abū al-Sibāʿ." Abū al-Sibāʿ rejected the conditions of visibility proffered by the magazine; this photograph is a testament to Abū al-Sibāʿ's quick reflexes (or the camera's slow shutter-speed) and the spirit's ability to impose her will on the mortal world.

The others did not refuse to be photographed. On the next page, a much larger picture of Husayn Mahmoud appears, and it is framed by the remainder of the article, which comprises the experts' opinions (see figure 1). In it, Mahmoud gives a coy, knowing glance. Looking dignified and pretty, Mahmoud was posed and composed, holding a small bottle of perfume and the viewer's gaze. This picture is flanked on the bottom with images of the *zar* performers. Bayoumi Hashim, pictured beating a drum, might be proclaiming the text of the caption: "So what, brother [*ummal ayh ya khūya*]? Zar runs in my veins." The other caption describes the headdress worn by Sultan Ibrahim. Both look entranced by the *zar* and not the camera. These people were posed not just as subjects in a photograph but as questions that needed answers. Statements like Bayoumi Hashim's give a taste of their responses. It is as if together they were able to say, in their own words, actions, and images, "These are our lives. So what?"

Expert Rules, Narration, and the Telos of Transition

By detailing aspects of these subjects' experiences in childhood and adolescence, the *Ākhir Sā'ah* piece furnished comfortable, convenient explanations for these aberrations in a sexual order dominated by the gender binary. Four experts, a psychiatrist, a social scientist, the local minister of education, and a lawyer, further buttressed these explanations. They were pictured in passport-sized photographs at the top of the page. First was "the psychological point of view [*ray' 'ilm al-nafs*]": "The psychiatrist Doctor Sabri Girguis took up these cases. . . . he continues to search for an answer as to why they are spreading in Asyut and not Qena or Girga or Sohag. Perhaps this is because we only looked in Asyut." The "we" writing in *Ākhir Sā'ah* was aware of one obvious source of confirmation bias, that these cases appeared wherever they were sought out, but there is another more fundamental source of confirmation bias: seeking out the supposed reasons for or causes of an individual's nonbinary or trans becoming always yields results, especially when the individual examined is already visibly flouting the norms of binary gender. And this is part of what makes the aforementioned "why" questions so farcical!

The plot points of this confirmation bias thicken as the experts elaborate. The *Ākhir Sā'ah* article breaks the block text of Girguis's explanation with the bolded quote "Nero the Roman Emperor was afflicted by it!"—the reflex to historicize trans embodiment is an old one indeed. He continues, "An individual's tendency for cross-dressing [*irtda' malabis al-gins al-akhar*, literally wearing the other sex's clothing] is a form of sexual deviance, the result of a mental illness [*halah nafsiyah mardiyah*] . . . and we are unable to provide an opinion applicable to all cases, because each should be studied separately in order to discern the individual's reasons for deviating from the comportments [*al-sulūk*], pertaining to his sex. . . . In real cases of illness, the afflicted [*al-marīd*, masculine] must always imagine himself in these clothes as though he were of the other sex." Girguis distinguished between those seeking pleasure or economic gain through "cross-dressing" and those, afflicted, who imagined themselves as always being in the clothes of the other sex. The conditions of the aforementioned individuals' labor made for uneasy slippages between what they did for a living, who they were, and what they became. They never left their work clothes; their jobs as dancers and spiritualists engendered them.[11]

The next expert, the social scientist Hassan al-Saʿti, had more specific things to say about the causes of these cases, diagnosing them under the heading "The Mother Might Be a Reason." The first aspect he identifies is "the concern of most mothers for their male children and their raising them as girls; they dress them up in girls' clothing, and this weakens their sense of self . . . and the young boy finds this sweet [*yastatīb hadhihi al-hālah*] and so he grows accustomed to being spoiled through being treated and dressed like a girl." Dressing infants and young children assigned "male" at birth as girls and piercing their ears was and remains a significant practice in Upper Egypt. It is done in order to protect the child and mother from the wandering and prying eyes of distant relatives and neighbors who might look upon a healthy baby boy with envy. Feminine attire wards off *ḥasad*, the hex of the evil eye. Kohl, a cosmetic made of frankincense or charcoal, is also applied to the newborn's eyes so that they might grow big and wide. Are Upper Egyptians bringing up their kids trans? No.[12] What the social scientist Hassan al-Saʿti put his finger on was a preference for boys among (Upper) Egyptians, manifesting in how they were prized, protected, and spoiled. Girguis further claims that "an excess of primping leads to deviance." The second aspect al-Saʿti describes "relates to imitation, and it shows up in the case of the conscript who wanted to imitate his sister . . . here, too, the youth's concern for primping during puberty is a factor" because it "causes them to deviate by making them obsessed with self-beautification, even if it demands that they imitate women." These "expert" opinions build upon one another. The psychiatrist offered a general appraisal of the perceived affliction, while the social scientist [*ustadh al-ijtimaʿ*] pointed to problematic child-rearing practices. Together they described a slippery slope between provincial metrosexual behavior and trans embodiment. But if the gender creativity of childhood was a widespread phenomenon and the aforementioned customs for child-rearing in Upper Egypt were at least somewhat common, then none of the aspects they flagged can be clear indicators for trans becoming. Their diagnoses thereby extended this fundamental fallacy: seeking the causes for the conditions of the four transfeminine people profiled, and others, would always yield results. This is because the nonbinary gender trouble of children in Upper Egypt came into fuller view from the vantage point of their physical appearance and their personal and professional lives as adults.

Third to report was Ahmed Hamza, the director of education and *tarbiyah* in Asyut.[13] He identified more general factors under the heading "The People of Asyut," reporting that "these cases are the result of the social environment [*al-bi'ah*] that people lived in . . . and that education is not related to this matter." Hamza recommended that these individuals and others like them be placed under surveillance in order to "prevent them from infecting others." Here, the article presents the state's reading and prescribed redress. For this official, trans embodiment was as an infectious disease, one that was the product of the cultural/natural environment [*al- bi'ah*] and one whose spread had to be curtailed through quarantine. Hamza sidestepped education, the charge of his ministry, by making the people of Asyut the problem. He reiterated the point that these aberrations in gender were an indicator of Upper Egypt's underdevelopment relative to Cairo. Adherence or nonadherence to the gender binary was mapped onto the binary between traditional, retrograde Upper Egyptians and modern, progressive Cairenes.

The last expert excerpted is the lawyer Kamal Ayad. Ayad states "that these cases are caused by many factors; among them is that these individuals were raised in a feminine atmosphere [*wasat nisawiyah*, literally amidst femininity]," and submits that "in this feminine atmosphere they were exposed to what in psychology is called a 'lifestyle' [*uslub al-hayah'*], in which the mother had imprinted a feminine character on these men since early childhood. And through this the boy is raised intersex [*nash'ah mukhannathah*]." Even as modern psychological terms, such as "lifestyle" (*'uslub al-hayah*), were being translated into Egyptian understandings of the self and the social, Ayad still relied on the word *mukhannath*, an old word derived from the Arabic root for bending or flexibility and used in Islamic jurisprudence (*fiqh*) to describe intersex people. I offer this etymological detail not because it contains some kernel of truth about gender in Arabic but because the interplay between the psychiatric and *fiqh* terms helps to unfurl the binary modes for understanding the four people on the page. Both local and Egyptian adaptations of Western epistemologies were deployed to contain these transfeminine people, while practices such as *zar* and schools of thought like *fiqh* persisted and evolved. Although the article sought to apprehend them using the tools of modern science, ethnography, and photography, these disciplinary structures could not capture the complexity and creativity of the lives of Husayn Mahmoud, Hashim Bayoumi, Abū al-Sibāʿ, and Sultan Ibrahim.

Conclusion: With Intention, In Tension With

Reading about these apprehensions of transfemininity in mid-century Upper Egypt demonstrates the limitations of "what" and "why" questions as they relate to nonbinary gender expression. This is also to say that in defining the meanings of "nonbinary," asking what it is or why certain people come to express a gender in tension with binary masculinity or femininity are similarly limited endeavors. My rewriting has sought to create space to appreciate the "how" of these people's lives while clarifying how they were represented in the magazine and in my own process of resignification and trans*lation. "How did they live?" is also a pretty blunt and potentially harmful question, but addressing it while scrutinizing and resisting the source text opens up these individuals' histories, allowing them to impart lessons from beyond the binary. These lessons challenge the ethnographic impulse to locate transness in indigenous contexts, and they invite critical reflection on how biographies and other historical narratives are assembled.

As they were told, the stories of Husayn Mahmoud, Hashim Bayoumi, Abū al-Sibāʿ, and Sultan Ibrahim have much to teach about the narration of nonbinary gender expression and modernity in Egypt. First, reading about these transfemmes in Arabic, or in a thoughtful translation, is not enough to understand them on their own terms. Foremost is that the emergence of nonbinary and transgender expression congeals by way of retrospective examination, in which the causes of a given individual's gender alterity are identified through the application of medical (especially psychological) discourses. The histories presented in *Ākhir Sāʿah* show the fallibility of that logic. If all Upper Egyptian "boys" whose mothers doted on them turned out to be transfeminine, Asyut would be a very different place. The *Ākhir Sāʿah* article occluded this, because its narration of trans becoming was necessarily teleological; in each case, specific biographical details were emphasized in order to justify a fait accompli. This involved reductive retrospective readings that made individual trajectories towards trans embodiment legible within the language of dysphoria and reified transness as a singular and seemingly inevitable telos.

Similarly, histories that seek to narrate Egypt's transition from its status as a semiautonomous Ottoman province to a British protectorate and then an independent Arab republic by emphasizing how masculine anxieties or motherly representations were central to emergent nationalist movements risk reproducing narrative structures that are consonant with those binary logics encircling the four individuals profiled above.[14] These logics were applied by four experts, belying a pernicious parity between the psychiatrist, lawyer, social scientist, and minister, and the dancer, the two *zar* performers, and the spirit and her possessed. Narrating their meeting, I have strategically elided how the 1952 Free Officers Movement, which antedates the publication of the *Ākhir Sā`ah* article, led to the deposition of the Egyptian monarchy and inaugurated an era of Nasserist decolonization. I have also completely ignored that in 1958, Egypt was not Egypt, or not just Egypt. Only months prior to the article's publication, a treaty was ratified to form a new sovereign state, the United Arabic Republic, a short-lived political union of Egypt, Syria, and later, the Gaza Strip. It is not that these are unimportant facts but rather that casting these biographies of transition within the drama of the (super)nation-state would be petty, because my point has not been that these four transfeminine people in Asyut were significant to modern Egyptian history or that the panic that they provoked was somehow symptomatic of the literati's gendered anxieties six years after the ouster of their puppet-prince-king, two years after the standoff between Egypt, Israel, France, and England known as the Suez Crisis and two months after they technically became citizens of a new postcolonial polity. Nor has my point been that these transfeminine people were a significant part of the history of gender or sexuality but rather that they might show us how to move history beyond binary logics, revealing that it is in fact worthwhile to resist the teleological impulses driving the narrations of their embodied realities and the other (meta)physical, psychosocial, political, economic, and cultural transitions that they lived through. Histories, theirs as well as ours, must not always be made to seem so inevitable, nor their endings so predetermined.

A trans* theory of history would make way for interruptions. To spurn rulers and experts, to reject their working definitions of the gender-expansive lives discussed here, is to unsettle questions of modernity, medicine, race, sexuality, and coloniality in Egypt. The language of "nonbinary" offers a way out of the seemingly endless feedback loops structuring histories of trans becoming, especially as they relate to the emergence of postcolonial nation-states. I struggle to read these individuals as either cis or trans. Working with "nonbinary," a fraught and occasionally oxymoronic designation, while honoring these people's transfemininity, I have sought to attend to their ways of living with intention and in tension with binary gender norms. Although their biographies were published in *Ākhir Sā`ah* shortly after the first clinic offering gender-affirming care was established in Cairo, I am not sure they could have wanted to transition medically by seeking out hormonal treatment or surgical procedures. Here, medical transition should not demarcate a barrier between trans and nonbinary people but instead evince the complex ways in which trajectories of transition are shaped by the lifeworlds that people occupy. Such uneven topographies of transition provide an opening to carefully account for the diversity of gender alterity, to trans*late and to relate to the past and present on less binary terms.

Husayn Mahmoud, Hashim Bayoumi, Abū al-Sibā`, and Sultan Ibrahim did transition. And each of their transitions involved more continuity than change. Husayn Mahmoud took clothing to dance in as a conscript. Sultan Ibrahim and Hashim Bayoumi were raised on *zar* and remained practitioners of the art. Abū al-Sibā` complied with the orders of the jinn in order to maintain their relationship. Another lesson their stories might impart is about seeing transition not just through the prism of change but also as a way of staying in and inhabiting one's gender, body, and lifeworlds without having them predetermined or posteriorly made to make sense. This reconfiguration alters the terms by which we understand trans and nonbinary subjects by changing the kinds of questions we ask. Instead of asking questions *of them*, "what" or "why," these stories ask us to reflect on how we are accustomed to explaining change and continuity and giving shape to a biography. "Nonbinary," then, poses a challenge that is more narratological and historiographical than linguistic or ontological, one that is less about how a subject is gendered in a given sentence in Arabic or English and more about where that sentence leads.

Beshouy Botros is a PhD student working across the History and Women's, Gender, and Sexuality Studies Departments at Yale University who is researching coloniality, race, and trans* medicine in Northern Africa, is more broadly interested in cultural and intellectual history, and can be reached at Beshouy.botros@yale.edu. Beshouy does not always avoid pronouns.

Notes

1. It gives me joy to express deep thanks to Zayn Kassam, Sana Khan, Alan Mikhail, Niyati Shenoy, and Kyla Wazana Tompkins for their advice and readings of the first and last versions of this article; Maryam and Theresa

Abdelshaheed for helping me acquire an original copy of the magazine; Robin Dougherty for assistance with preservation and transliteration; and my great-aunt Samiha Hanna, for speaking with me about Asyut as she lived it. I am also grateful to have workshopped this piece at the Women's, Gender and Sexuality Studies Colloquium at Yale University, where Regina Kunzel, Dara Strolovitch, Daniel Swain, and Minh Vu were generous facilitators; and Fisayo Akinlude, Creighton Baxter, Bhasha Chakrabarty, Yung In Chae, and Colton Valentine generous interlocutors. Over the last two years, Carolyn Dean, Anne Eller, Greta LaFleur, Nana Osei-Quarshie, Chitra Ramalingam, Carolyn Roberts, and Evren Savcı's scholarship and teaching have propelled my writing and reading. Eva Pensis talked me through key points, sharing her careful, critical eye in a critical time. Gervais Marsh walked with me through some rough patches. Finally, I am thankful for the feedback and attention to detail of the anonymous reviewers and the gracious stewardship of the editors of *Women's Studies Quarterly*.

2. Peter Gran has recently written about Asyut's importance and underrepresentation in Egyptian historiography in "Asyut in Modern Times: The Problem of Invisibility" (2021).

3. Nancy Reynolds provides details on the Egyptian press in *A City Consumed: Urban Commerce, the Cairo Fire, and the Politics of Decolonization in Egypt* (2012, 122). Mahmud Faksh provides data on literacy and education in Egypt; see "The Consequences of the Introduction and Spread of Modern Education" (1980, 46–49). In 1960, illiteracy was registered at 83.8 percent among females and 56.6 percent among males, so the category "reader" skews male, or assigned male at birth. And although "readers" does not necessarily mean city-dwellers, in lieu of a mapping of literacy rates, I operate with the assumption that the category "reader" in the 1950s entailed some degree of interpellation into Egyptian modernity and metropolitanism regardless of where specific readers resided.

4. See Omnia el-Shakry's *The Great Social Laboratory: Subjects of Knowledge in Colonial and Postcolonial Egypt* (2007) for a rich history of human geography, demography, and other social sciences in Egypt.

5. Earlier scholarship describes manifestations of gender diversity across geography and time and problematizes the coloniality of the gender binary; see Nanda 2014 and Zeb Tortorici for a theorization of the archive through sexuality and on cross-dressers and hermaphrodites in *Sins against Nature: Sex and Archives in Colonial New Spain* (2018, 100–15). See also Jacqui Alexander's account of Vasco Núñez de Balboa's 1513 massacre of "cross-dressing" Indians during the Spanish conquest of Panama and her theorization of the ideological traffic between postcolonial state's regulation of sexuality, sexual violence and contemporary/colonial militarism (2005, 183–205). For

Alexander, the pedagogies of crossing are a methodological and theoretical response to the violence of ideological traffic. All of this is critical work, but it is not a solely colonial gender binary that I am problematizing with respect to Asyut in 1958, it is primarily an Egyptian one. To understand how the Egyptian and European colonial forms of binary gender were co-constitutive, one must look to the late eighteenth and nineteenth centuries. I am also informed by work critiquing the application of queer theory to "area studies" and attentive to how the homoerotics of Orientalism in North Africa subsume trans* gender/sexual difference within a discourse about sexuality (Arondekar and Patel 2016; Boone 2014).

6. Language is vexed and imperfect, and the use of certain terms is historically contingent and sometimes contested. In describing these Egyptians as transfeminine people and writing about their "becoming-trans," I deploy *trans, femme,* and *transfemme* as adjectives and not as nouns that refer to modern identitarian, sexological, or medical designations, which have themselves shifted. I thank Greta LaFleur for helping me work through this conundrum and that of the use of the singular *they* for historical figures; it is one I have engaged but also strategically sidelined in this piece.

7. In *trans*lation*, as in *to trans*late*, the asterisk interrupts the verb at the point of its syllabic fold. It also, in Eva Hayward and Jami Weinstein's formulation, "starfishes trans, literally making trans a radiated reach—a reach through yet another reach" (2015, 198). In my formulation, *to trans*late* also refers to the temporal arrangement of transition itself, as in to trans*, late. In trans*lating, I hold space for lags in meaning and I am inspired by Cole Rizki reminder that "translation's refusal as a critical mode of accompaniment and care can signal a commitment to copresence as affiliation that does not collapse, meld, or erase ways of organizing experience" (Rizki 2021, 534). Hil Malatino describes "trans care" in relation to archival praxis; see *Trans Care* (2020). I see this form of reading and narration as deeply informed by interventions made by Black feminist scholars, as Jennifer Nash outlines in "Writing Black Beauty." She writes that "to do justice to her shape and his hand," through moving prose and risky disclosure, is "an effort to do justice to loss" (Nash 2019, 103).

8. In the second chapter of *Orientalism* (1979), Edward Said critiqued the central role of philology in the work of Silvestre de Sacy and Ernest Renan. However, Said returned to philology in his last book, *Humanism and Democratic Criticism* (posthumously published), in which he advocated for "detailed, patient scrutiny of and a lifelong attentiveness to the words and rhetorics by which language is used by human beings who exist in history" (2004, 61). A fixation with the (mis)usages of specific words has remained central to work on the histories and literatures of the Middle East and

Northern Africa, especially when it comes to gender and sexuality. Everett Rowson offers a series of close readings of erotic poetry, sexual humor, and legal texts to understand the meanings and regulations of sexual behavior (1991). Paula Sanders discusses how jurists regulated the ungendered bodies of hermaphrodites when ruling on matters of inheritance, marriage, and even where someone was to stand in a mosque during prayer (1991). Joseph Massad has analyzed the mistranslation of terms like *homosexuality* into Arabic and the discursive transits of the Gay International (2007). Kadji Amin makes a resonant point in problematizing the paradoxical proliferation of taxonomies to describe queer, trans, and asexual identities and advocates, centering "Indigenous, non-Western, and historical ontologies of being" that new taxonomies threaten and disrupting "the universalizing presumptions of the taxonomical method from within by generating idiosyncratic interpretations and translations that explode the epistemological and ontological foundations of taxonomy itself" (2023, 104–5). By intervening into my primary source, I play off of and critique the long-standing tradition of philological work and generate an interpretation or trans*lation that unsettles gendered language—gender expression and the linguistic expression of gender. I thank Alan Mikhail for encouraging me to clarify this aspect of my argument.

9. Afsaneh Najmabadi writes on the linguistic slippages between the word *jins* used for "sex" (as in coitus) and "social type" from the Greek *genos* and used to denote sexual and sometimes ethnic difference in late-nineteenth-century Persian and Arabic, and how *jins* in Arabic and Persian became inflected with new meaning over time (2013). I note it here to signal that there is a rich vocabulary and semiotic network to think through race, sex, and sexual difference in Arabic and Persian. In Arabic spoken among gender queer and trans* people and our broader communities, some speakers use a neutral plural "they," others a dual neutral *muthana*, and the general rule is more about good manners than grammar—people ask one another how they would like to be referred to and they respect their interlocutors. I thank Ghenwa Hayek for discussing this and the genius of Najmabadi's piece on *jins* and *genos* with me in September of 2019.

10. The discordance between subjects/pronouns and verbs that I am flagging is informed by C. Riley Snorton's article on the psychic life of passing, in which he theorizes raced/gendered mis/recognition as an aperture that is politically actionable (2009). Fred Moten, in outlining an ethos of study for Black performance and mourning, details what it entails, methodologically, to listen while you look (2003, 192–211).

11. Eva Pensis (2023) describes this as the "fundamental slippage" between gay men who perform in drag and transwomen performers. I refer to her

terminology to signal the ways that work, livelihood, life, and gender are fungible for these transfeminine individuals in Asyut who worked as spiritualists and performers or both.

12. The Orientalist Edward Lane describes these child-rearing practices in detail in chapter 2 of his oft-cited 1860 book, *An Account of the Manners and the Customs of Modern Egyptians* (2003); see pages 57–59. The political scientist Mervat Hatem analyzes child-rearing practices in Egypt by synthesizing Marxist and psychoanalytic approaches. Hatem notes "the cultural rewarding of the birth of a son and the opprobrium associated with the birth of a daughter" and that intimacy between mother and son is seen as leading to effeminacy (1987, 295). I pose my question "Are Upper Egyptians bringing up their kids trans?" ironically and to emphasize that some of the practices that the social scientist Hassan al-Sa`ti flagged were commonplace. In posing it, I am also drawing on Eve Sedgwick's 1991 essay "How to Bring Your Kids Up Gay" and Jules Gill-Peterson's *Histories of the Transgender Child* (2018), specifically the concluding chapter, "How to Bring Your Kids Up Trans," in order to note that the etiological impulses of medical practitioners treating effeminate boys and trans children in the U.S. that they analyze appear, albeit differently, in Egypt at roughly the same time.

13. The Ministry of Tarbiyah wa T`alim translates its own title as "the ministry of general and technical education." The word *tarbiyah* can refer to upbringing more broadly. See https://moe.gov.eg/.

14. Beth Baron's *Egypt as a Woman: Nationalism, Gender and Politics* (2005), Wilson Chacko Jacob's *Working Out Egypt: Effendi Masculinity and Subject Formation in Colonial Modernity* (2011), and Lucie Ryzova's *The Age of the Efendiyya: Passages to Modernity in National-Colonial Egypt* (2014) provide archivally rich analyses that account for classed and gendered anxieties, subject formation, and nationalism. Their studies necessarily rely upon and critically reify the binary logics that this piece problematizes.

Works Cited

Alexander, Jacqui. 2005. *Pedagogies of Crossing: Meditations on Feminism, Sexual Politics, Memory, and the Sacred.* Durham: Duke University Press.

Amin, Kadji. 2022. "We Are All Nonbinary." *Representations* 158 (1): 106–19.

———. 2023. "Taxonomically Queer? Sexology and New Queer, Trans, and Asexual Identities." *GLQ: A Journal of Lesbian and Gay Studies* 29 (1): 91–107.

Arondekar, Anjali, and Geeta Patel. 2016. "Area Impossible: Notes toward an Introduction." *GLQ: A Journal of Lesbian and Gay Studies* 22 (2): 151–71.

Baron, Beth. 2005. *Egypt as a Woman: Nationalism, Gender, and Politics*. Berkeley: University of California Press.

DeVun, Leah, and Zeb Tortorici. 2018. "Trans, Time, and History." *TSQ: Transgender Studies Quarterly* 5 (4): 518–39.

Faksh, Mahmud. 1980. "The Consequences of the Introduction and Spread of Modern Education: Education and National Integration in Egypt." In "Modern Egypt: Studies in Politics and Society," special issue, *Middle Eastern Studies* 16 (2): 42–55.

Fuentes, Marisa J. 2018. *Dispossessed Lives: Enslaved Women, Violence, and the Archive*. Philadelphia: University of Pennsylvania Press.

Gill-Peterson, Jules. 2018. *Histories of the Transgender Child*. Minneapolis: University of Minnesota Press.

Gran, Peter. 2021. "Asyut in Modern Times: The Problem of Invisibility." *International Journal of Middle East Studies* 53 (1): 113–17.

Ḥadidi, Hajir el-. 2016. *Zar: Spirit Possession, Music, and Healing Rituals in Egypt*. Cairo: American University in Cairo Press.

Hatem, Mervat. 1987. "Toward the Study of the Psychodynamics of Mothering and Gender in Egyptian Families." *International Journal of Middle East Studies* 19 (3): 287–305.

Hayward, Eva, and Jami Weinstein. 2015. "Introduction: Tranimalities in the Age of Trans* Life." *TSQ: Transgender Studies Quarterly* 2 (2): 195–208.

Jacob, Wilson Chacko. 2011. *Working Out Egypt: Effendi Masculinity and Subject Formation in Colonial Modernity*. Durham, NC: Duke University Press.

Lane, Edward. 2003. *An Account of the Manners and the Customs of Modern Egyptians*. Cairo: American University in Cairo Press, 2003.

Malatino, Hil. 2020. *Trans Care*. Minneapolis: University of Minnesota Press.

Massad, Joseph. 2007. *Desiring Arabs*. Chicago, IL: University of Chicago Press.

Mitchell, Timothy. 2002. *Rule of Experts: Egypt, Techno-Politics, Modernity*. Berkeley: University of California Press.

Moten, Fred. 2003. *In the Break: The Aesthetics of the Black Radical Tradition*. Minneapolis: University of Minnesota Press.

Najmabadi, Afsaneh. 1999. "Reading—and Enjoying—'Wiles of Women' Stories as a Feminist." *Iranian Studies* 32 (2): 203–22.

———. 2013. "Genus of Sex, or the Sexing of Jins." *International Journal of Middle East Studies* 45 (2): 211–31.

Nanda, Serena, ed. 2014. *Gender Diversity: Crosscultural Variations*. Long Grove, IL: Waveland Press, 2014.

Nash, Jennifer C. 2019. "Writing Black Beauty." *Signs: Journal of Women in Culture and Society* 45 (1): 101–22.

Pensis, Eva. 2023. "'Mighty Real': Trans Femme Embodiment and the Cultural Politics of Transmisogyny." PhD diss., University of Chicago.

Reynolds, Nancy. 2012. *A City Consumed: Urban Commerce, the Cairo Fire, and the Politics of Decolonization in Egypt.* Palo Alto, CA: Stanford University Press.

Rizki, Cole. 2021. "Trans-, Translation, Transnational." *TSQ: Transgender Studies Quarterly* 8 (4): 532–36.

Rowson, Everett. 1991. "The Categorization of Gender and Sexual Irregularity in Medieval Arabic Vice Lists." In *Body Guards: The Cultural Politics of Gender Ambiguity,* ed. Julia Epstein and Kristina Straub, 50–79. New York: Routledge.

Ryzova, Lucie. 2014. *The Age of the Efendiyya: Passages to Modernity in National-Colonial Egypt.* Oxford: Oxford University Press.

Said, Edward W. 1979. *Orientalism.* New York: Vintage Books.

———. 2004. *Humanism and Democratic Criticism.* New York: Columbia University Press.

Sanders, Paula. 1991. "Gendering the Ungendered Body: Hermaphrodites in Medieval Islamic Law." In *Women in Middle Eastern History: Shifting Boundaries in Sex and Gender,* ed. Nikki Keddie and Beth Baron. New Haven, CT: Yale University Press.

Shakry, Omnia el-. 2007. *The Great Social Laboratory: Subjects of Knowledge in Colonial and Postcolonial Egypt.* Palo Alto, CA: Stanford University Press.

———. 2020. *The Arabic Freud: Psychoanalysis and Islam in Modern Egypt.* New Brunswick, NJ: Princeton University Press.

Snorton, C. Riley. 2009. "'A New Hope': The Psychic Life of Passing." *Hypatia* 24 (3): 77–92.

Tortorici, Zeb. 2018. *Sins against Nature: Sex and Archives in Colonial New Spain.* Durham, NC: Duke University Press.

Primary Source

Ākhir Sāʿah, April 9, 1958, no. 1224.

Wondrous Bodies:
Trans Epistemology and Nonbinary Saints

C. Libby

Abstract: This article places Marcella Althaus-Reid's theological reflection on popular devotion to the figure of Santa Librada in Argentina in
conversation with scholarship on androgyny, nonbinary identity, and medieval gender-crossing saints. Tying together strands of medieval writing on
wondrous bodies and contemporary articulations of nonbinary identity
foregrounds how nonbinary embodiments destabilize modern conceptions of binary gender. Although I am not suggesting a return to premodern
conceptions of the body, medieval texts are instructive insofar as they offer
an epistemology of embodiment that evades the consolidation of binary
categories of sex and gender. **Keywords:** nonbinary; transgender studies;
medieval Europe; hagiography; liberation theology

From debates about the validity of neopronouns, to *Euphoria* star Hunter
Schafer's "like" of an Instagram post scapegoating nonbinary people as
the linchpin in Florida's recent spate of trans-antagonistic legislation, to
Kadji Amin's scholarly consideration of the genealogy and limitations of
the category of nonbinary, questions surrounding nonbinary identity are
everywhere these days (Murphy 2016; Amin 2022; Blair 2022). This article responds to these questions by placing contemporary understandings
of nonbinary identity in a broader historical and transnational context.
I argue for a reexamination of modern categories of gender through the
lens of a transgender epistemology of embodiment with particular attention to the category of wonder. Foregrounding how wonder appears as an
affective constellation around nonbinary bodies, I examine how wonder
can destabilize the sedimented terrain of binary sex and gender. Turning
first to 1970s-era feminist writing on androgyny, I trace how the concept

WSQ: Women's Studies Quarterly 51: 3 & 4 (Fall/Winter 2023) © 2023 by C. Libby. All rights reserved.

transformed from a utopian critique of hegemonic sex roles to a key metaphor in trans-antagonistic writing. Although enthusiasm for androgyny waned in the following decade, the burgeoning fields of queer studies and transgender studies revivified related questions about sex and gender. Next, I look at how an interest in androgynous embodiment resurfaced in queer theologian Marcella Althaus-Reid's formulation of a *transvestite epistemology* based on popular devotion to Santa Librada. Looking back to the historical origins of this bearded saint in the medieval figure of Wilgefortis, I conclude that wonder can disrupt binary epistemologies of gender. Today, conversations about nonbinary identity have shifted away from idealized conceptions of androgyny. Nonetheless, revisiting these early histories demonstrates how the terms *androgynous* and *nonbinary* often act as imaginative concepts whose functions shift according to the discourses they are embedded in. These concepts can take many forms: a feeling, a sexological diagnosis, the embodiment of an identity, a psychic ideal, or a rejection of stultifying gender roles. When confronted with such variation, it is worth mentioning that many of these imaginative formulations elide the material reality and violence faced by nonbinary subjects. Furthermore, it is important to note that intersex embodiments are not coterminous with nonbinary identity even though there may be overlap in some instances. Careful attention to these differences is evident in contemporary scholarship on nonbinary identity and embodiment.

For instance, recent medieval scholarship grapples with the historical appearance of bodies that fit uneasily into a binary division of sex or gender. Leah DeVun's monograph *The Shape of Sex: Nonbinary Gender from Genesis to the Renaissance* introduces readers to the complexity of premodern thinking about nonbinary gender (2021). This text highlights how nonbinary bodies were interpreted in a variety of ways during the medieval period, at times understood as exemplars of "fluidity and metamorphosis" and at other times interpreted as "hybrids that constrict and police categories" (6). In a more contemporary context, Mo Moulton develops a nonbinary methodology to reinterpret the life of Muriel St. Clare Byrne (1895–1984) in their article "'Both Your Sexes': A Non-binary Approach to Gender History, Trans Studies, and the Making of the Self in Modern Britain" (2023). Moulton explores what the turn to the analytic category of gender might obscure in texts written before the consolidation of sex/gender/sexuality, ultimately arguing that gender "has come to function too smoothly as a category of analysis across time and space" (21).

Likewise, trans studies scholars have grappled with the implications and significance of nonbinary gender. Hil Malatino's 2019 text *Queer Embodiment* examines medical, scientific, and philosophical discourse on intersexuality to argue for an understanding of gender as a process of becoming that exceeds restrictive binary logic. Kadji Amin's 2022 article "We Are All Nonbinary: A Brief History of Accidents" maps a critical genealogy of nonbinary identity routed through the modern cisgender/transgender binary. And P. J. DiPietro's 2020 "Ni humanos, ni animales, ni monstruos: La decolonización del cuerpo transgénero" (Neither Humans, nor Animals, nor Monsters: Decolonizing Transgender Embodiments) offers a decolonial reexamination of transgender and nonbinary embodiment among *travesti* activist groups in Argentina. Despite this expansive field of scholarship, there has been little attention paid to the ways that affect emerges and coheres around nonbinary identity and imaginaries.

The Ambiguity of Wonder

Throughout this article, wonder acts as a ballast to stabilize the temporal and theoretical variations that appear. Although the meaning, interpretation, and response to wonder shifts across time, premodern conceptions of wonder continue to have contemporary affective resonance. Wonder in the Middle Ages was organized around two distinct yet related poles. On the one hand, wonder might be prompted by an unfamiliar yet natural phenomenon like an eclipse or a volcanic eruption. Alternatively, wonder could stem from something that was believed to go against or beyond nature. As Lorraine Daston and Katharine Park's expansive text *Wonders and the Order of Nature* attests, these two sources of wonder are respectively translated with the terms *mirabilia* (marvel) and *miracula* (miracle) (1998, 16). Daston and Park's text traces the ways European naturalists from the High Middle Ages through the Enlightenment understood wonder and wonders, and their primary interest is in how natural phenomena, *mirabilia*, produced wonder in observers and readers alike. These forms of wonder are linked directly to knowledge, or as Daston and Park put it, "wonder as a passion registered the line between the known and the unknown" (1998, 13). It was precisely this type of wonder that Early Modern scientists attempted to eradicate through the accumulation of scientific information and rare specimens. However, in addition to these natural phenomena, medieval thinkers were also concerned with miraculous forms of wonder.

Medieval writing on Christian saints is filled with wonder-inducing descriptions of supernatural phenomena. Bodies exceed their natural capacities, becoming impervious to the elements (untouched by rain, fire, snow), exempt from natural laws (levitation, incorruptibility), and insensitive to somatic pain (nails are pushed through skin, boiling metal is poured over feet). Likewise, souls undergo indescribable ecstatic raptures, heavenly visions, and unitive encounters with the divine. Despite the appeal of such miracles, during the Middle Ages ecclesiastical authorities were quick to remind readers that such texts must cautiously navigate the uneasy slippage between divine inspiration and demonic perversion. In her expansive discussion of medieval wonder, feminist historian Caroline Walker Bynum (2001, 51) explains how the boundary between the divine and the diabolical was policed according to the distinction between *admiratio* (wonder or admiration) and *imitatio* (imitation). Citing the much-used ecclesiastical phrase *non imitandum sed admirandum* (not to be imitated but to be marveled at), she argues that this injunction is replicated in the work of medieval male clerics who recorded the exemplary and extraordinary lives of mystics and saints while simultaneously evidencing a suspicious discouragement of such marvels among observant women (2001, 51). In contrast to Bynum's reading, I turn my attention to how medieval hagiography prompts a desire to participate in the affective circuits of wonder, leading to an integration of *admiratio* and *imitatio*. The wonder evoked through relics, pilgrimages to holy sites, and collections of saints' lives provoked behavioral transformations that undermined clerical protestations against imitation.

Shifting to a more contemporary context, trans studies philosopher Perry Zurn has written extensively on the relationship between curiosity, wonder, and trans subjectivity. He suggests that a turning back to the premodern might offer new ways of conceptualizing wonder and trans bodies when he writes, "Beginning with Western history in the ancient and medieval periods, this might require greater attention to the figures of the hermaphrodite and the cross-dresser, the trickster, and the shapeshifter in the construction of wonder, especially across the developing genre of travel narratives" (2021, 194). As Zurn points out, gender-crossing and nonbinary figures can function as sites from which to theorize complex conceptions of wonder. However, in addition to his focus on the unique potential of such historical investigations, Zurn is also keenly aware of the dangers faced by bodies perceived as a locus of wonder. Balancing the dehumanizing practice of situating trans bodies as sites of curiosity with the innovative potential of wonder, he writes, "While pigeonholed as curios, and feared for the onto-logical fluidity their transgressive curiosity proved, trans people also seized upon curiosity as a technique of self-fashioning and gender legitimation" (2021, 195).

Such trans reclamations of wonder and curiosity are further attested to by media studies scholar Eliza Steinbock, who explains, "Curiosity must be turned away from stultifying relations that mark out a curious object, toward a trans*feminist curiosity about the mechanisms for differencing and how they might work otherwise" (2019, 141). This turn is facilitated by an attention to trans worldmaking. For Steinbock, this is a crucial inter-vention, as they propose that "through curiosity one accesses the ability to break through habituated perceptual circuits, in short, to think other-wise" and that "a resituated curiosity responds to the rage of being made a mute curio or, perhaps worse, made vulnerable to transphobia that excludes monstrous trans bodies from the perceptual schemata for the human" (2019, 24–25). These writers attest to the possibilities inherent in practices of curi-osity and wonder and make a compelling case for understanding wonder as a catalyst for imagining different futures and alternative ways of being in the world. Prior to these contemporary discussions about wonder, nonbi-nary identity, and trans subjectivity, the figure of the androgyne served as a locus of wonder for the feminist imagination in the early 1970s.

Androgyny: From Utopia to Trans Antagonism

Foregrounding the wondrous potential of androgyny to remake social hierarchies, '70s-era feminist writing returned to this historical category of embodiment, drawing heavily on classical, medieval, and Early Modern formulations of the concept. The myth of the primal androgyne, which depicts the first human as an androgynous and often incorporeal being, was used to contest hierarchical and patriarchal configurations of sex differ-ence. Likewise, the Greco-Roman god Hermaphroditus, best known from Ovid's first-century poem *Metamorphoses*, describes a figure who embodies both male and female characteristics (Ovid 2022, 105–8). Hermaphrodi-tus served as a key metaphor for a liberatory model of hybridity. Despite this initially positive spin, these figures appear ambiguously throughout the medieval period as exemplars of category confusion, hybridity, transforma-tion, negation, and monstrosity. Although they are not necessarily linked to understandings of sex differentiation in humans, they play a foundational role as exemplars of difference and sites of wonder and are easily translated to the human.

The variations in meaning that medieval scholars encounter when studying these figures is likewise apparent in medieval understandings of sex. Long-standing debates regarding how sex difference was conceptualized range from Thomas Laqueur's (1990) one-sex model to Joan Cadden's (1993) rebuttal of the concept in favor of a more diverse understanding. Historian Leah DeVun offers a succinct summary of the shifting terrain of medieval thinking, explaining:

> The traditional Hippocratic/Galenic model of sexual difference—popularized by the late antique physician Galen and the ascendant theory for much of the Middle Ages—viewed sex as a spectrum that encompassed masculine men, feminine women, and many shades in between, including hermaphrodites, a perfect balance of male and female. The "Aristotelian" model challenged this view in the thirteenth century by arguing that hermaphrodites were not an intermediate sex but a case of doubled or superfluous genitals. Hermaphroditism, it argued, was not one of a variety of legitimate sexes to which humans might belong; it was a cosmetic defect that obscured an underlying male or female sex. (2018, 140)

This broad overview highlights the hegemonic consolidation of sex difference in the late Middle Ages, but as DeVun points out, there were always exceptions to this rule. The wide array of feminist opinions about androgyny are directly related to these premodern variations.

Despite a lack of consensus about what androgyny meant or how it should be understood, what is clear is that during the early 1970s androgyny was becoming increasingly popular among feminist thinkers. Some radical feminist writers embraced androgyny as a site of wonder, possibility, and transcendence, while others rejected the concept as masculinist and patriarchal. In 1973, the Modern Language Association sponsored a forum titled "Androgyny: Fact or Fiction." The papers presented were then gathered and published as "The Androgyny Papers" in a special issue of the journal *Women's Studies* (Secor 1974). This collection included writing that praised androgyny as the new frontier in gender parity, as well as several cautionary articles that linked androgyny to patriarchal forms of being that prioritized masculinity over femininity. Feminist theologian Mary Daly initially embraced the notion of psychic androgyny, which she described as the commingling of masculine and feminine characteristics to achieve reconciliation in the subject. Daly incorporated psychic androgyny into her utopian vision, where it served as the catalyst that would move people, mostly women, into a new form of consciousness. This formulation was clearly present in *Beyond God the Father*, where she writes, "The healing process demands a reaching out toward completeness of human being in the members of both sexes—that is, movement toward androgynous being" (1973, 150). This vision was integrated with her critique of sex stereotyping and patriarchy. She goes on to say, effusively, "We are breaking the dam of sex stereotyping that stops the flow of being, that stops women and men from being integrated, androgynous personalities" (1973, 158). For Daly, androgyny offered a wondrous opportunity to shift the patriarchal imbalance.

Considering her early enthusiasm, it may be surprising to learn that Daly and her student Janice Raymond had completely abandoned this positive conception of androgyny by 1974. They describe this decision as a response to sexologist John Money's writing on biological and psychosocial androgenization. From this point forward, Daly and Raymond interpret androgyny as an incomplete form of hybridity that glorifies the masculine. As Raymond states, "androgen becomes normative for androgyne" (1975, 60). This new focus on a hybrid model of androgyny is exemplified in Daly's depiction of androgyny as the scotch-taping together of Farrah Fawcett-Majors and John Travolta (1973, xxiv).[1] In her time-traveling utopian book *Quintessence*, she goes even further by reinterpreting the myth of the primal androgyne as a patriarchal capture of motherhood through reproductive technology. She writes:

> It is clear that patriarchal males are attempting to act out the myth of the preexisting divine male giving birth to himself, while simultaneously working to eliminate Divine Female Creative and Procreative Power. The recent developments in cloning coupled with the new reproductive technologies, which are leaping toward their catastrophic conclusions as the twentieth century comes to an end, are manifestations of this megadestructive pattern. (1998, 172–73)

Within this interpretation of androgyny, Raymond and Daly discover a powerful tool for transphobic theorizing from a post-Catholic perspective. By claiming that John Money is simply reiterating an Aristotelian-Thomistic biology that places men above women in the hierarchy of sex difference, they conclude that the figure of the androgyne is inextricably linked to theologically inflected patriarchal forms of oppression.

This logic is subsequently deployed in the service of the denigration and rejection of transgender subjects. In her infamous text *The Transsexual Empire*, Raymond reiterates this argument, stating, "In its emphasis on integration, much of the recent psychological, medical, and medical-ethical literature on transsexualism, and the solutions they propose, resemble theories of androgyny. . . . Transsexualism is comparable to the theme of androgyny that represents biological hermaphroditism, because ultimately the transsexual becomes a surgically constructed androgyne, and thus a synthetic hybrid" (1979, 154–55). This depiction of the constructedness of the androgyne foregrounds an understanding of androgyny that harnesses the medieval distaste for hybridity by associating it with falseness, deception, and monstrosity. Focusing on this truncated understanding of androgyny, Daly and Raymond push this logic to its extreme and offer a potent framework for gender-critical writers today, who continue to portray transgender individuals as monstrously unnatural hybrid bodies.

Queer Theory and Transvestite Epistemology

Despite the vehement rejection of trans subjects by Daly and Raymond, other feminist theologians endeavored to promote a more capacious vision of the possibilities engendered by trans embodiment, nonbinary identity, and androgyny. Queer theologian Marcella Althaus-Reid's 2010 text *Indecent Theology* exemplifies a different approach to nonbinary embodiment, grounded in popular devotion to the figure of Santa Librada. In her chapter "The Indecent Virgin," Althaus-Reid turns her attention to the holy figure Santa Librada, who she describes as the "popular ambiguous divine crossdresser of the poor, the unstable image of Christ dressed as Mary" (2010, 80). Santa Librada appears in statues, prayer cards, and icons as a figure that mixes and blends aspects of Christ and the Virgin Mary (2010, 80). For Althaus-Reid, Santa Librada represents both an untapped resource for indecent theology and a critical point of insight into what she terms *transvestite epistemology*. This religiously inflected articulation of trans epistemology is grounded in a critique of binary logic designed to facilitate an upheaval of the Catholic theological gender system. Santa Librada disrupts the binary gender system by unsettling expectations and offering a theology "on the move" (2010, 82). As Althaus-Reid reflects on the figure of Santa Librada, she endeavors to rethink Christian doctrine by drawing on insights from liberation theology, feminism, and queer theory. She grapples with the entrenched forms of heteronormativity, so prevalent in Catholic theology, by foregrounding the economic and political realities faced by marginalized groups in Argentina and Latin America more broadly. According to Althaus-Reid, "indecent theology is the opposite to a sexual canonical theology, concerned with the regulation of amatory practices justified as normative by economic infrastructural models where anything outside hegemonic patriarchal heterosexuality is devalued and spiritually alienated" (2010, 9). Althaus-Reid offers a new theological vision by foregrounding the revolutionary and creative potential of these typically devalued forms of being and knowing.

Her reflection on the devotional figure Santa Librada emphasizes the productive capacity this gender-ambiguous saint has for those who likewise find themselves devalued and alienated. She links the popularity of the saint to the repressive regime in Argentina in the 1970s that violently regulated behavior, including the enforcement of gendered dress codes. In this context, Santa Librada offers a wonder-inducing vision of gender and embodiment liberated from the confines of restrictive gender roles. Santa Librada models transgression and disruption while promising liberation. As Althaus-Reid notes, this saint is particularly popular among petty thieves, another group that transgresses social boundaries to improve their quality of life. She writes, "The point of this popular transvestite theology is that it is a theology on the move, or on the run (as the people protected by Librada seem to be, escaping from poverty, and/or the police) from one place to another, and without settling" (2010, 82). This attention to movement and escape cultivates both an admiration for and imitation of Librada's transgression of rigid social boundaries.

The trans epistemology Althaus-Reid maps out creates a space of relationality and affective resonance between the saint and her devotees that makes room for different iterations of nonbinary embodiment. However, in her attempt to articulate an epistemology drawn from the legend of the saint, Althaus-Reid's reliance on Marjorie B. Garber's *Vested Interests: Cross-Dressing and Cultural Anxiety* prioritizes an understanding of gender, transgender subjectivity, and transvestism embedded in the work of twentieth-century sexologists and psychoanalysts (Garber 1992; Althaus-Reid 2010, 78–82). In her text, Garber investigates how transvestism might function as a third gender category that disrupts the hegemonic logic of binary gender.

According to Garber, "the 'third' is that which questions binary thinking and introduces crisis—a crisis which is symptomatized by *both* the overestimation *and* the underestimation of crossdressing" (1992, 11). She clarifies that this third is not to be understood as a term, a sex, or a blurred sex but rather as a "way of describing a space of possibility" (1992, 11). Despite the seemingly promising horizon of possibility enabled by this notion of the third, contemporary trans scholarship has demonstrated the limits of the concepts of gender and trans identity articulated by such scholarship, highlighting its complicity in sexological and colonial legacies of pathology and degeneracy.

Although Althaus-Reid is uninterested in the medieval origins of Santa Librada, which as she notes most people simply ignore, I return to the historical record to offer a counterpoint to Althaus-Reid's assumption that the "destabilization produced by Librada is done at the gender level, which is the surface level of names and dresses" (2010, 81). Looking briefly at the fourteenth-century legend of Wilgefortis (also known as Librada, Liberata, Uncumber, or Kümmernis), I highlight how the saint's status as a disfigured (bearded) bride of Christ and as a saint who is fungible with Christ himself enables a radical rethinking of embodiment that goes well beyond the surface level (Société des Bollandistes 2012). Situated within the larger tradition of gender-crossing saints, Wilgefortis's gender ambiguity occurs after she prays to be delivered from the mandates of marriage and reproduction. Although many Christian saints and mystics desired to exempt themselves from the marriage bed, few achieved this goal by enacting the type of embodied transformation seen in this legend. When the saint prays to be disfigured to evade an arranged marriage, this desire is fulfilled by the miraculous appearance of a full beard. Unfortunately, Wilgefortis's father becomes enraged by this turn of events and immediately has Wilgefortis crucified. After death, Wilgefortis's legend circulates across Europe, and they are venerated with several unique cult practices that highlight their status as an ambiguously gendered bride of Christ who is often mistaken for Christ himself.

On one hand, Wilgefortis's legend has been used to demonstrate the power of nonbinary embodiment as a site of veneration and liberation. As historian Lewis Wallace notes, "the saint's gendered transformations were central to her power as a religious symbol" (2014, 44). Wilgefortis's miraculous somatic transformation excises them from the sexual economies of desire, marriage, and reproduction. Remembered for unflinching resistance to an unwanted marriage, Wilgefortis became renowned for helping women with their bad husbands. The appearance of a beard can be interpreted as a marker of gender ambiguity designed to provide the saint with protection from unwanted advances by moving the saint into a liminal somatic reality. Wilgefortis's ambiguous embodiment also demonstrates that it is possible to become an exemplar because of, rather than despite, gender nonconforming characteristics. This rupture in dominant social and political expectations acts as a site of wonder both for the saint and for their devotees.

Although looking back to the medieval origins doesn't fundamentally change Althaus-Reid's interpretation of the specific site of veneration she investigates, it does expand the time line of interest in and admiration of nonbinary embodiment. It also alerts readers to the fact that gender transgression is not just a modern phenomenon. Furthermore, it demonstrates that recent claims by trans-antagonistic groups that modern conceptions of sex and gender require a fundamental break from a long and uninterrupted history of binary sex difference in the Western Christian tradition are inaccurate. What Althaus-Reid invariably gets right in her analysis of Santa Librada is her focus on how the saint can foreground transformation and offer an alternative to stultifying sexual, political, and social realities. However, contemporary trans studies might guide her interpretation of transvestite epistemology away from its focus on the surface level of names and dresses, and even away from a focus on the disruption of binary conceptions of gender, towards a more radical reimagining of gender categories.

On the other hand, many historians have expressed discomfort at the prospect of fitting Wilgefortis's story into contemporary understandings of sex or gender. Robert Mills, for example, in his examination of Hieronymus Bosch's artistic rendering of the saint, concludes that "it might be worth giving up on the project of settling, once and for all, the identity—gendered or otherwise—of Bosch's crucified saint" (2021, 152). Instead, he suggests, "we might be better off accepting the enduring provisionality of such pronouncements and the limits of our taxonomic impulses" (2021, 152). Mills's reticence to make any definitive proclamations about Wilgefortis's gender resonates with a similar reluctance to utilize modern conceptual language to interpret historical texts. Nonetheless, I am interested in thinking with Mills and others about how gender-transgressive medieval subjects can inform current debates around identity and nonbinary embodiment without reinscribing modern categories of sex and gender.

For example, medieval abbess Hildegard of Bingen's text *Cause and Cure* describes several bodies that do not align with the normative patterns of medieval masculinity or femininity (Berger 1999). Françoise Charmaille's recent article "Intersex between Sex and Gender in *Cause et Cure*" suggests a return to the body through the introduction of the analytic category of inter-sex (2021). Here, Charmaille contests both Laqueur's one-sex model and Joan Cadden's articulation of sex difference, critiquing Cadden for remaining beholden to model of sex and gender that interprets these categories as signaling the biological and social respectively. This reading troubles any easy distinction between sex and gender and challenges interpretive prac-tices that reinscribe these categories back onto medieval texts and figures. Charmaille explains, "To expose these concepts as contingent is essential in order to do justice to the people they marginalize and harm—in our case, people with atypical sex" (2021, 340). By introducing the catego-ries of the phlegmatic man and phlegmatic woman as well as the sanguine man into the constellation of embodiment, Charmaille expands how schol-ars might understand the complexity of embodiment both in the Middle Ages and today.

When turning to gender-crossing saints and nonbinary subjects in search of wondrous possibility, it is useful to foreground their position as bodies on the move. Typically, we encounter these figures transgressing bound-aries in hopes of escaping from their current situation, whether that be gendered restrictions or social and political constraints. As a bearded saint who captures viewers' attention through the discontinuity of gendered symbols, Wilgefortis challenges devotees and viewers alike to shift their own expectations about how bodies can appear in the world. Revisiting the wide range of writing on androgyny and nonbinary embodiment high-lights the limitations of trans-antagonistic writing on androgyny and offers an abundance of alternative visions of nonbinary identity.

C. Libby is an assistant professor in women's, gender, and sexuality studies at Penn State University. They can be reached at clibby@psu.edu.

Notes
1. For an excellent discussion of Daly's articulation of androgyny as hybridity, see Partridge 2018.

Works Cited

Althaus-Reid, Marcella. 2010. *Indecent Theology: Theological Perversions in Sex, Gender and Politics*. London: Routledge.

Amin, Kadji. 2022. "We Are All Nonbinary: A Brief History of Accidents." *Representations* 158 (1): 106–19.

Berger, Margret, ed. and trans. 1999. *Hildegard of Bingen on Natural Philosophy and Medicine: Selections from* Cause et Cure. Cambridge: D. S. Brewer.

Blair, Caroline. 2022. "Hunter Schafer Gets Backlash for Seemingly Endorsing Anti-non-binary Post." *Page Six*, August 24, 2022. https://pagesix.com/2022/08/24/hunter-schafer-gets-backlash-for-endorsing-anti-non-binary-post/.

Bynum, Caroline Walker. 2001. *Metamorphosis and Identity*. New York: Zone Books.

Cadden, Joan. 1993. *Meaning of Sex Difference in the Middle Ages*. Cambridge: Cambridge University Press.

Charmaille, Françoise. 2021. "Intersex between Sex and Gender in *Cause et Cure*." *Exemplaria* 33 (4): 327–43.

Daly, Mary. 1973. *Beyond God the Father: Toward a Philosophy of Women's Liberation*. Boston, MA: Beacon Press.

———. 1998. *Quintessence—Realizing the Archaic Future: A Radical Elemental Feminist Manifesto*. Boston, MA: Beacon Press.

Daston, Lorraine, and Katharine Park. 1998. *Wonders and the Order of Nature 1150–1750*. New York: Zone Books.

DeVun, Leah. 2018. "Heavenly Hermaphrodites: Sexual Difference at the Beginning and End of Time." *Postmedieval* 9 (2): 132–46.

———. 2021. *The Shape of Sex: Nonbinary Gender from Genesis to the Renaissance*. New York: Columbia University Press.

DiPietro, P. J. 2016. "Decolonizing *Travesti* Space in Buenos Aires: Race, Sexuality, and Sideways Relationality." *Gender, Place and Culture* 23 (5): 677–93.

———. 2020. "Ni humanos, ni animales, ni monstruos: la decolonización del cuerpo transgénero." *Eidos: A Journal for Philosophy of Culture*, no. 34: 254–91.

Garber, Marjorie B. 1992. *Vested Interests: Cross-dressing and Cultural Anxiety*. London: Routledge.

Laqueur, Thomas. 1990. *Making Sex: Body and Gender from the Greeks to Freud*. Cambridge, MA: Harvard University Press.

Malatino, Hil. 2019. *Queer Embodiment: Monstrosity, Medical Violence, and Intersex Experience*. Lincoln: University of Nebraska Press.

Mills, Robert. 2021. "Recognizing Wilgefortis." In *Trans Historical: Gender*

Plurality before the Modern, ed. Greta LaFleur, Masha Raskolnikov, and Anna Klosowski, 133–59. Ithaca, NY: Cornell University Press.

Moulton, Mo. 2023. "'Both Your Sexes': A Non-binary Approach to Gender History, Trans Studies, and the Making of the Self in Modern Britain." *History Workshop Journal,* no. 95: 2–26.

Murphy, Jessica. 2016. "Toronto Professor Jordan Peterson Takes on Gender-Neutral Pronouns." *BBC News,* November 4, 2016. https://www.bbc.com/news/world-us-canada-37875695.

Ovid. 2022. *Metamorphoses.* Translated by Stephanie McCarter. New York: Penguin Books.

Partridge, Cameron. 2018. "Scotch-Taped Together: Anti-'Androgyny' Rhetoric, Transmisogyny, and the Transing of Religious Studies." *Journal of Feminist Studies in Religion* 34 (1): 68–75.

Raymond, Janice. 1975. "The Illusion of Androgyny." *Quest: A Feminist Quarterly* 2 (1): 57–66.

———. 1979. *The Transsexual Empire: The Making of the She-male.* Boston, MA: Beacon Press.

Secor, Cynthia, ed. 1974. "The Androgyny Papers." *Women's Studies* 2 (2): 139–271.

Société des Bollandistes, ed. 2012. "De S. Liberata alias Wilgeforte virgine et martyre." *Acta SS.,* vol. 5: 50–70. https://archive.org/details/actasanctorum32unse/page/n99/mode/2up.

Steinbock, Eliza. 2019. *Shimmering Images: Trans Cinema, Embodiment, and the Aesthetics of Change.* Durham, NC: Duke University Press.

Wallace, Lewis. 2014. "Bearded Woman, Female Christ: Gendered Transformations in the Legends and Cult of Saint Wilgefortis." *Journal of Feminist Studies in Religion* 30 (1): 43–63.

Zurn, Perry. 2021. *Curiosity and Power: The Politics of Inquiry.* Minneapolis: University of Minnesota Press.

The Resistant Body

Abby C. Emerson

This visual text was co-created with a nonbinary child. At the center is an outline of their body with quotes from their own moments of self-definition. They also contributed to the design and artistic choices of the piece. On my end, it is a form of literature review exploring the historicized creation of the gender binary and the deep ties that political project has to white supremacy (Bederman 1995; Schiebinger 2004; Schuller 2018). Surrounding their body are quotes from my reviewed texts arranged haphazardly in layers of white paint and black marker. These narratives are visible but somewhat difficult to read, similar to how these discourses are around us all the time, impressing upon young bodies and forcing them into constrained ways of being. They're hard to see, read, and most importantly, resist. In addition to text drawn from academic sources about the ties between the gender binary and white supremacy, some of the text fragments are quotes from adults that question children's capacities to define themselves as nonbinary. The artwork incorporates not just macro social narratives, but also the micronarratives from transphobic teachers, family members, and friends. The yellow halo reads as an exertion against all those narratives; a visual representation of the force nonbinary children are emanating in their resistance. Fluidity and movement that young children demonstrate as they move amongst genders and pronouns is often read as confusion when really it is a resistance to the sex-based paradigmatic narrative laid out for them.

Abby C. Emerson is an assistant professor in elementary special education at Providence College. Her research and teaching centers on anti-racist and abolitionist teacher education, a critique of whiteness in education spaces, parenting as a site of social change, and arts-based research methodologies. Previously, she was an elementary school teacher for ten years in NYC public schools. During that time she was named the 2018

WSQ: Women's Studies Quarterly 51: 3 & 4 (Fall/Winter 2023) © 2023 by Abby C. Emerson. All rights reserved.

Abby C. Emerson. *The Resistant Body*. Acrylic and ink on paper.

National Association for Multicultural Education's Critical Teacher of the Year. Her writing about teaching and learning can be found in *Radical Teacher, Whiteness and Education, Review of Research in Education*, and *Bank Street Occasional Paper Series*. She can be reached at aemerso1@providence.edu.

Works Cited

Bederman, Gail. 1995. *Manliness and Civilization: A Cultural History of Gender and Race in the United States, 1880–1917*. Chicago: University of Chicago Press.

Schiebinger, Londa L. 2004. *Nature's Body: Gender in the Making of Modern Science*. New Brunswick, NJ: Rutgers University Press.

Schuller, Kyla. 2018. *The Biopolitics of Feeling: Race, Sex, and Science in the Nineteenth Century*. Durham, NC: Duke University Press.

Desi Genderqueerness:
The Mystery and History of Gender Diversity in India

Raagini Bora

Abstract: The goal of this article is to conceptualize a decolonial understanding of an Indian genderqueerness, trying to contest the false temporal binaries of coloniality and postcoloniality. Tracing India's complex and rich queer and genderqueer history preceding British colonization, I dissect the impact of colonization on postcolonial transphobia and understandings of trans. Through a historical literature review and media content analysis of the controversial film *The Pink Mirror* (2003), I apply a decolonial lens to reimagine locally produced narratives of queerness and genderqueerness through local genderqueer communities, such as Hijras and Kothis.
Keywords: queer theory; decolonization; Indian history; Hijras; genderqueerness; Hindi cinema

Once Upon a Time in Genderqueer India

Forms of art such as music have always been of importance in gauging India's rich culture and heritage. The Hijra community, for instance, has historically been considered outcast and abject yet sacred and spiritually gifted, all of which mostly derives from their ambiguous gender identity (Sherinian and Nyong'o 2019). With mythological roots to their significance, the traditional occupation of Hijras has been performing—singing and dancing at baby showers, weddings, and other auspicious events—rituals of cultural importance. Hijras are said to embody the Mother Goddess in Hindu mythology, where their impotency is linked conversely to the power of generativity. They also link to Lord Shiva, who embodies both the ascetic and the erotic and has various gender nonconforming forms of existence (Nanda 1990; Lal 1999).

WSQ: Women's Studies Quarterly 51: 3 & 4 (Fall/Winter 2023) © 2023 by Raagini Bora. All rights reserved.

Hijras are mostly people assigned male at birth or intersex people, trans-women, and people who undergo ritual practices such as castration to enter the community. A stigmatization that is placed upon the Hijras for being perceived as "effeminate" and "emasculated" men circulates simultaneously with esteem for embodying spiritual divinity beyond the ordinary (Nanda 1990). Individual experiences of Hijras in relation to their gender identities, sexual orientations, and (non)sexualities combined with cultural defini-tions of their roles holistically construct the Hijra identity (Nanda 1990). However, Hijras transgress social norms of embodied and performative queerness over and over again, which excludes them from "normal" zones of social participation by tying them down to their "designated" traditional occupation almost by compulsion (Lal 1999). This same transgression manifested in religious respect or fear of being cursed by them has been what pins them within social tolerance or acceptability. The idea of India as one homogenous queer-regressive social space is challenged by such nuanced and overt existence of queerness (though India has had its own queerphobic mechanisms, of course).

Evidence of queer and genderqueer identities, relationships, and expe-riences have been a part of Indian history, but without the ease of being expressed within the language and conceptual categories characteristic of the West. Hindu deities displayed homoerotic desires in various forms, including male, female, and even nonhuman (Dasgupta 2011). Though heteronormative expression and desire were normalized, associations with divinity and rebirth legitimized and "excused" queer and genderqueer prac-tices to some degree (Dasgupta 2011).

An Indian Flag Band-Aid to Heal Colonial Scars?

Rooted in the creation and maintenance of a hierarchy between the rulers and the ruled, regulation of sexuality and queerness were significant in Brit-ish colonial projects (Bhaskaran 2002). The British government disallowed legal support for Hijras to discourage "breach of public decency," which further marginalized their social capital, position, and unstable incomes (Nanda 1990, 51). The British goal to "understand their subjects better" came with making lists and categories that excluded everything that did not fit within their framework. Understandings of queerness within the frame-work of Western modes of knowledge production have been reproduced by "our epistemological obedience to them" (Bakshi 2016, 2). In a conscious attempt to distance Indian nationalism from its colonial past, the ways of the colonizers are ironically replicated in reclaiming the nation through cleansing it of nonnormative and transgressive identities (Dasgupta 2011). The "naturalness"—of heterosexuality, cisnormativity, compulsory sexuality, monogamous practices—that is constructed through a routinization of cultural performativity becomes a precondition of how we understand our social world. It works to send out to the peripheries any forms of "deviance" that do not seem to comply with the norm, especially within India's postindependence nation-(re)building (Dasgupta 2011). If genderqueerness in India is so "unnatural," then why has it existed so vividly throughout Indian history?

Terms and Conditions for Unqueer Cinema

The short 2003 film *The Pink Mirror* (*Gulaabi Aaina*, dir. Sridhar Rangayan), which depicts two Indian drag queens as protagonists, was completely denied approval to be screened in India, on the grounds of "vulgarity, obscenity and depravity" (Smith 2004). The film engages with two drag queens, Shabbo and Bibbo, who translate their local term of identification— *Kothi*—to the anglicized term "drag queens." Kothis are a group of gender nonconforming people assigned male at birth who are often characterized as embodying a "feminized masculinity" and as "male-desiring" in their sexual orientation (Kumar 2018). It becomes interesting, then, to see how Shabbo and Bibbo find the translation of *Kothis* to "drag queens" as the closest way to capture their identities and experiences. It is interesting to see that their identification with femininity goes beyond their drag performances, indicating an assumed alignment with a Western understanding of drag in the first place (Kavoori and Punathambekar 2009). Even when they are "out of character," they mention their "mother-daughter"-style kinship, use feminine pronouns, and identify with the desires of a cis and gay man in the film. A local Kothi culture is the backdrop of this narrative, where gender, sexuality, and their performativity are not seen as rigidly bound, breaking binaries of masculine/feminine.

Decolonizing Desi Queerness

When using terms such as *lesbian, gay, bisexual, transgender,* or *nonbinary,* we need to actively recognize that the formulation of that vocabulary did not occur within a South Asian context. Usage of those terms in contemporary conceptualizations of queerness implies an approximation of meaning within this context, an effort to get as close to that understanding as possible (Vanita 2002). However, this usage also comes with the assumption that these terms meant something in the first place, which may be an inaccurate presumption in itself (Vanita 2002). Hijras "are referred to as a people who are intersexed, emasculated, impotent, transgendered, castrated, effeminate, or somehow sexually anomalous or dysfunctional" (Lal 1999, 120). These labels, which are often used interchangeably, make it hard to see how these identities can all belong to describe the same community. This conflates the meaning of the word *Hijra* and what it signifies to be able to understand it within a Western globalized template of queerness. Kumar (2018) brings into focus "the absence of any 'pure' indigenous term to describe and capture the powerlessness as well as the subversive potentials of non-heterosexual erotic subjects in South Asia or in the non-western contexts" (65).

Initiation and ritualistic participation within the community is significant in Hijra and Kothi communities in the construction of their identities, which occurs within a complex network of kinship ties. For instance, in the film *The Pink Mirror*, Shabbo refers to Bibbo as "mother," with an emotional expression of gratitude, community, and family in accepting her as her own and guiding her through her performance journey. It "re-appropriates the gender of the term *mother* by making it trans-inclusive, third-gender inclusive, and non-binary inclusive" (Hussain 2021, 5). Claiming motherhood and legitimacy of kinship ties within such communities challenges oppressive institutions of family, motherhood, and gender performativity. Identities such as Hijra and Kothi are far removed from essentialist understandings of gender and cannot be captured through Western categorical understandings but rather through local contextualization of intersectionality. A decolonial understanding of such genderqueerness necessitates the acknowledgment that Indigenous identifications of nonconformity do not fit into neat categorizations (Kumar 2018). With categorization a prime reflector of white western colonial projects, it becomes important to aggressively reject a false rigidity between temporal binaries of colonial and postcolonial. As Halberstam states, colonialism and nationalism cannot be seen as two separate binaries of temporality and ideology; decolonization involves a recurring disruption to colonial modes of production and reproduction (2011).

Conclusion

Evidence of genderqueerness has been a part of Indian history, appearing in complex forms that were conflated with British colonial legal structuring. In postindependence India, an understanding of trans and genderqueer emerged that is not aligned with local experiences. Local genderqueer communities such as Hijras and Kothis messily combine aspects of gender, sexuality, class, and socialization of queer identities, all of which need to be understood in a more decolonial vein. Breaking gender binaries and temporal boundaries of colonial/postcolonial is essential to understanding genderqueerness in India.

Raagini Bora is a social science researcher focusing on gender and queer studies and decolonial theory. With a strong affinity towards activism through the arts, she finds expression through music, performance, and public speaking. Her involvement in grassroots organising and activism is fueled by a rageful passion and sustained by joy created through community care and love. She can be reached at bora.raagini@gmail. com.

Works Cited

Bakshi, Sandeep. 2016. "Decoloniality, Queerness and Giddha." In *Decolonizing Sexualities: Transnational Perspectives, Critical Interventions*, ed. Sandeep Bakshi, Suhraiya Jivraj, and Silvia Posocco, 81–99. Oxford: Counterpress.

Bhaskaran, Suparna. 2002. "The Politics of Penetration: Section 377 of the Indian Penal Code." In *Queering India: Same-Sex Love and Eroticism in Indian Culture and Society*, ed. Ruth Vanita, 30–46. New York: Routledge.

Dasgupta, Rohit K. 2011. "Queer Sexuality: A Cultural Narrative of India's Historical Archive." *Rupkatha Journal on Interdisciplinary Studies in Humanities* 3 (4): 651–70.

Halberstam, Jack. 2011. *The Queer Art of Failure*. Durham, NC: Duke University Press.

Hussain, Rukhsar. 2021. "Hijra Representations in Bollywood: Adoption and Legal Discourses." *Adoption and Culture* 9 (2): 276–97. https://doi.org/10.1353/ado.2021.0026.

Kavoori, Anandam P., and Aswin Punathambekar. 2009. *Global Bollywood*. New Delhi: Oxford University Press.

Kumar, Pushpesh. 2018. "Queering Indian Sociology: A Critical Engagement." *E-journal of the Indian Sociological Society*, no. 2: 60–85.

Lal, Vinay. 1999. "Not This, Not That: The Hijras of India and the Cultural Politics of Sexuality." *Social Text*, no. 61: 119–40. http://www.jstor.org/stable/488683.

Nanda, Serena. 1990. *Neither Man nor Woman: The Hijras of India*. Belmont, CA: Wadsworth.

Sherinian, Zoe, and Tavia Nyong'o. 2019. "Interdisciplinary Enqueeries from India." In *The Oxford Handbook of Music and Queerness*, ed. Fred Everett Maus and Sheila Whiteley, 524–38. New York: Oxford University Press.

Smith, Neil. 2004. "Entertainment: UK Premiere for Indian Drag Film." *BBC News*, May 6, 2004.

Vanita, Ruth. 2002. *Queering India: Same-Sex Love and Eroticism in Indian Culture and Society*. New York: Routledge.

Queerly Comprehensible: The Nonbinary Art of Kris Grey

Chris Straayer

Abstract: This essay argues that nonbinary artist Kris Grey deploys a genderqueer aesthetic to undo taxonomy. Their ceramic sculpture and performance art cross and diffuse binaries through reversals, implosions, conversations, and invitations. I contextualize Grey's art within the work of other contemporary artists who have creatively investigated and engineered gender, sex, and sexuality. Following Vittorio Gallese, I argue that Grey's embodied images haptically share nonbinary physicality with audiences. Through centrifugal and centripetal reconfigurations, they make new experiences visible, imaginable, and available. Following Caroline Walker Bynum, I argue that by queerly foregrounding the nonbinary underpinning of a master aesthetic discourse, Grey shows the seemingly unfamiliar nonbinary body to be affectively comprehensible. **Keywords:** Kris Grey; art; performance art; nonbinary; transgender; trans*; queer; feminist

Mingled Sex

What does it mean to be a nonbinary artist when "nonbinary" instantiates not only one's gender but also one's aesthetic? What is a genderqueer mentality, and what is its relation to a nonbinary art practice? What generates what? Reflects? Instructs? Critiques? This article maps some of the strategies that genderqueer artist Kris Grey takes up in order to "irritate gender" and some of the binaries that Grey thus undoes. I argue that Grey's art-making pushes for gender beyond taxonomy and that their reference in *Homage* to the doubting apostle Thomas radically links their nonbinary art to religious iconography, thus queering a master discourse.

Kris Grey embraces all pronouns. This meaningful choice is consequential in their art. For the most part, this article will use the nonbinary

WSQ: Women's Studies Quarterly 51: 3 & 4 (Fall/Winter 2023) © 2023 by Chris Straayer. All rights reserved.

pronouns *they/their/them*, but I begin by deploying *he*, *she*, and *they* inter-changeably in order to foreground Grey's genderqueer disposition. By expanding rather than transitioning their pronouns, Grey enacts an identity that does not issue "she" to deadnaming, nor "he" to a fait accompli. Grey has not changed his pronouns on legal documents, thus producing conster-nation among law enforcers and border guards, who must contemplate her masculine presentation while they perform legitimizing and corral-ling roles. Grey's top surgery and testosterone intake have so sufficiently undone his female body markers that the F on their driver's license can only fail at denoting cis female. At the same time, the upsetting of that F insinu-ates Grey's transgender living as stealth. Grey's explanation is that F stands for "feminist." By purposefully sliding their pronominal signification, Grey simultaneously risks retribution for fraud and puts gender taxonomy to the test of nonbinary dialectics.

Grey is both ceramicist and performance artist. From porcelain, they make exquisite objects: smooth, delicate, ornate, and precious. In perfor-mance, their body serves as raw material: ductile, vulnerable, flowing, and carnal. These very different strands of art practice nevertheless intersect symbiotically through aesthetic reversals. Basically, as performance artist, Grey positions their sentient body as an object, and as ceramicist, they endow objects with corporeal propensities.

Grey's porcelain objects are sculptures of innovative genitals or sex toys. They recombine organic forms, asserting biology and imploding gender, with haptic effects that ebb and flow, penetrate and ooze, bounce and screw, slide and twirl. *Pink Bits* (2008) is a group of pink-colored compound organs (figure 1). Each consists of a pair of heart-shaped bulbs at the base of a long curved protuberance. Is it testicles and penis? Or is it a sexual instrument in which the protuberance presents a vaginal cavity? Such "ambivalent deno-tation" recalls the pre-eighteenth-century, one-sex conceptualization of genitals recounted by Thomas Laqueur, in which the vagina was understood to be an internal penis (Laqueur 1990). In its hard curvaceousness, *Pink Bits* is reminiscent of Louise Bourgeois's late 1960s sculptures of indeter-minable organic forms in bronze and marble, condensing testicles, breasts, penis, glans, nipples, and eggs in twisting, generative flesh, for example, *Janus Fleuri* (1968) and *Cumul I* (1969). Displayed as a set, *Pink Bits* reminds the viewer that its objects are cast, molded to allow replication, thus demoting assumptions of the original art object as well as original genitals. These are morsels on the table of sexual consumption.

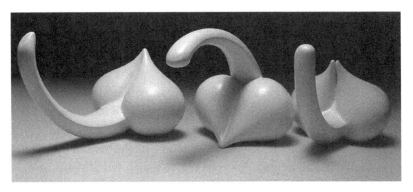

FIGURE 1: Kris Grey, *Pink Bits* (2008). Porcelain, paint. 12 × 14 × 6 in. each.
Courtesy of the artist.

Grey's ceramic art throbs with sexual vitality. It interpellates viewers as sexed beings and beckons them to sexual activities. *Bottoms Up* (2009) is a porcelain dinner plate with a matching butt plug positioned at one corner, where a drinking glass might have sat (figure 2). It is glazed, with an ivory background decorated with decals of a gold curling vine and a pink flower on the butt plug. Sex toy as art object infiltrates a good family's best china, couching anal sex in civility for the unsuspecting guest. While its kitschy aesthetic points to gay male taste, the activity that *Bottoms Up* serves up does not discriminate on the basis of either sex or sexual orientation.

Bottoms Up recalls the porcelain plates in Judy Chicago's *The Dinner Party* (1974–79), a triangular table with thirty-nine place settings honoring mythical and historical women (Chicago 2007). Although Chicago was addressing a different aspect of binary gender, that is, the patriarchal erasure of "herstory," her intervention, like Grey's, boldly acknowledged bodily sex. Each china plate in *The Dinner Party* displays a fleshy vulva or undulating flower-like imagery suggestive of genitalia. Also evocative of *The Dinner Party* is Grey's *Memoria* (2019–), a project that includes making a porcelain plate to commemorate every person killed in the U.S. since 1970 for being transgender.

In their artwork, Grey spurns many demarcations: fine art/craft, beauty/kitsch, food/sex, propriety/obscenity, private/public, male/female, gay/straight, inside/outside, presence/absence, strength/vulnerability, person/object, and art/life. These centripetal executions catalyze an implosion of binary gender. At the same time, Grey's creativity is nourished by a sophisticated engagement in art discourse and trans and gender diverse (TGD)

FIGURE 2: Kris Grey, *Bottoms Up* (2009). Porcelain, glaze, decal. 6 × 6 × 3 in.
Courtesy of the artist.

subculture, and their work reaches outward through reference, homage, and extension. Turning now to Grey's performance art, I describe how centripetal collapse and centrifugal intertextuality render Grey's nonbinary body comprehensible.

Declarative Sex

Kris Grey's body is not unlike that of many trans men, nor is their appearance on the street. The difference between their body and those of most trans men is its didactic exposure in performance art, by which Grey wraps together vulnerability, intervention, and relationality to achieve nonbinary comprehensibility.

Within the context of their performance art, Grey's use of testosterone matches that of certain nonbinary people who, as Rillark Bolton describes, "re-form testosterone as a substance that can unmake, rather than confirm gender" (2013, 15). Sufficient testosterone intake by almost anyone produces masculine secondary sex characteristics. Grey's beard, lowered voice, and developed upper body, alongside nonfeminine attire, result in their being read as male in the public arena. However, male recognition is not generally the goal of nonbinary-identified persons, including those on the masculine end of a gender spectrum. Some may feel more comfortable in either a male or female aspect, but neither aspect represents their gender. As Michel Foucault asked rhetorically when introducing the memoir of nineteenth-century hermaphrodite Herculine Barbin, "Do we really need a true sex?" (Foucault 1980, vii).

A nonbinary person who was assigned female at birth (AFAB) has a different relation to testosterone than does a trans man (also AFAB). Testosterone not only augments male signification but also truncates female signification. Rather than absorbing testosterone to summon a true (trans) sex, some nonbinary persons utilize testosterone to weaken the autonomy of (assigned at birth) "true sex." In the latter case, testosterone-induced appearance does not equal male gender expression. Bolton elaborates, "How non-binary people reposition testosterone in relation to their use yields altered ways of conceiving of testosterone and the gendered body, and crucially opens up possibilities of non-binary futures that may allow for a body altered by testosterone" (Bolton 2013, 15).

Kris Grey's artistic practice frequently reflects that of other contemporary performance artists who challenge the boundary between life and art. For example, Linda Montano, a trailblazer of art/life practice, performs "creative schizophrenia" through personas (Maloney 2014; Roth 2015). In her 2010 doppelgänger performance of Mother Teresa at the Empire State Building (ESB), Montano enacted her reconnection to Catholicism (which came about through care taking of her dying father) as well as a tremor she has developed from cervical dystonia. Montano's description of her performance offers surprising osmotic connections:

> At the performance, Catholic and non-Catholic visitors/protestors came to me for "blessings" and the ecstasy of incorporating her holiness into ME and sharing that faux-holiness with the Catholics at the ESB was both overwhelming and radically questioning of the theological politics of the church which does not allow for womenpriests let alone performance art recreations of Saints. (Montano 2017)

For Grey, challenging the art/life binary facilitates an intervention in binary sex along with an intention to create connections. Living one's nonbinary gender as art calls upon this testosterone-taking artist to make legible their nonbinary body. Within the social hegemony of binary sex, nonbinary

FIGURE 3: Kris Grey, *Ask A Tranny* (2011). Performance, Newark. Courtesy of the artist.

gender requires marking. When their masculinity trumps their femininity in everyday views, a nonbinary artist must either countersignify visually or repeatedly come out verbally.

Different coming-out acts communicate different information, producing different knowledge effects. Coming out in earnest changes the relation between self and others, testing one's own expectations, inviting others' questions, and altering knowledge on both sides. In their performance of *Ask a Tranny* (2012), Grey stands in a public site holding a poster board displaying the words "Ask a Tranny" (figure 3). The message invites strangers to engage in a discussion about transgenderism while also outing Grey as transgender. That is, it announces that the man they see is not cis, despite appearing so.

Talia Mae Bettcher has shown how clothes do not just cover over sexed bodies but rather re-present them: "Gender presentation isn't merely a euphemism for restricted discourse about genitalia, it's a euphemistic stand-in for genitals *per se*" (2012, 329). Grey's performance instructs the audience that their passing is inadvertent—the result of having masculine secondary characteristics and wearing masculine-coded clothes—which their verbal sincerity corrects. This performance no doubt depends on a preexisting curiosity about transgenderism often exemplified by intrusive staring, but it also instigates a specific curiosity about Grey, about what viewers want firsthand information about, including their genitals. Of course, they cannot and will not see Grey's naked body on the street, because public nudity is censored. Returning to Bettcher, she states the following:

> A gap exists between signifier and signified—a barrier between private and public presentations. In this way, the referential structure and the restrictions/allowances on self-presentation are co-constituting within this system of intimacy: it's through being the referent of clothed-presentation that genitalia become morally private. (2012, 230)

In a sense, Grey's personal uptake of the term "tranny" both pays allegiance to public trans visibility and references (perhaps to neutralize) an abusive normative gaze. Imperatively addressing strangers in public space, Grey offers personal conversation about what the public cannot see, about their more private content. One effect of this is the prying apart of stealth appearance from stealth living. When not carrying the "Ask a Tranny" poster board, Grey reads as cis male, and "his" male clothing, for all intents and purposes, covers cis male genitals. By displaying the "Ask a Tranny" poster board, Grey produces a cis-to-trans transition within the viewers' conceptual framework that provides them both de-signification and curiosity, both knowledge and invitation to knowledge—an opportunity to acknowledge "moral genitals," that is, rightful genitals, including those of nonbinary people. By imploding private and public, Grey attempts not only to reveal an inadvertently private dimension but also to contextualize through conversation the knowledge produced by that information. Partly, they do this by individualizing strangers through conversation's promise of reciprocal listening. As Grey states,

> The result, when I appear in public and make myself vulnerable, is that strangers meet me there with their own care and vulnerability. We exchange stories and create empathetic connections. Gender and my transness is the place we start but the conversations are as varied as the participants. (Credible 2015)

Graceful Sex

In *Homage* (2013–15), Kris Grey pursues emotional and physical exchange by opening their body to the gallery audience (figure 4). Firstly, their body is displayed in open sight. Secondly, their body surface is opened. Grey

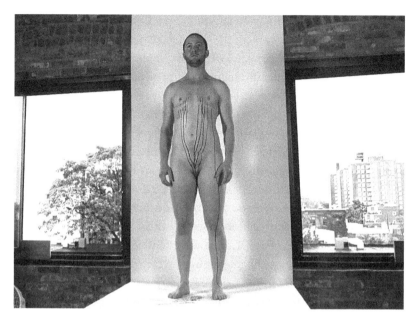

FIGURE 4: Kris Grey, *Homage* (2013). Performance, Pioneer Works, Brooklyn. Courtesy of the artist.

states their goal: "I'm aiming for a place when the audience almost feels like they can go right into me—the space where we might eradicate the boundaries between us" (DeBrincat 2013). When performing *Homage*, Grey stands naked on a plinth with long needles piercing each side of their chest. Their chest resembles that of many trans men, with slightly curving scars of reconstruction running horizontally along the pectoral muscles. The needles enter Grey's body below the scars, travel upward behind them, and exit the skin above to finally be held in place by scar tissue, like a row of vertical spikes. They form a double row of metal bars, framing the surgical lines. Over a period of approximately forty-five minutes, Grey proceeds to pull out these needles and drop them on the floor. Blood begins coursing down their body from chest to feet.

Homage literally pays homage to performance artist Ron Athey, known for bloodletting in his HIV-activist performance art (Abraham 2014). Athey helped prepare Grey for the performance, including inserting the needles. In addition to Athey, *Homage* is inspired by performance artists such as Bob Flanagan, who translated his lifetime struggle with cystic fibrosis into performance art via his persona Supermasochist (Flanagan 1993), and Annie Sprinkle, who, with speculum and flashlight at hand, invited audience members to view her cervix during her performance of *Post-porn Modernist* (1989–95) (Sprinkle 1991). Grey explicitly offers vulnerability and seeks empathy by literally opening their body.

As Grey slowly pulls one needle after another out of their chest, several thin streams of blood run down each side of their torso. Some continue straight down the legs to splash onto feet and floor; others curve centrally and meet at the groin. These inward-curving lines, drawn by slow-moving blood upon Grey's body, direct the audience's visual attention from chest to mons pubis and testosterone-nurtured genitals. Reemerging from this second site, a thin line of blood then begins trickling down Grey's inner thigh, suggesting menstrual blood. But must that image of genital blood bring to mind a vagina? For performance art enthusiasts, it may also recall Bob Flanagan's bleeding penis after he hammers it to a board and then pulls out the nail (Dick 1997).

In her study of the role of skin in body art, Kathy O'Dell describes a masochistic contract between artist and audience that reduces the distance among differences: "Artists who stage performances of any sort necessarily foreground the body, risking a simplistic reading of the human form as the ultimate emblem of nature" (1989, 16). Notably, in many cases, Grey's included, the risk is, furthermore, a reading of the *white* human body as nature: "By meddling with the apparent seamlessness of that emblem in visual and haptic ways, they can temporarily restore for the observer proof of the 'it's me' sameness of the body and provide access to experiences of the body that are culturally specific but suppressed. In doing so, they challenge the stereotyped fixity of those differences" (O'Dell 1989, 16). Grey's goal is not to connect with "like" bodies but rather to open their particular ambiguous body to the entire audience.

One might contrast the image of Grey's naked body in *Homage* to that of trans man Loren Cameron's nude body on the cover of his book, *Body Alchemy* (Cameron 1996). Both Cameron and Grey use testosterone to alter their bodies. Indeed, Cameron depicts himself injecting testosterone. Cameron's photographic self-portrait adopts the classically posed, phallic masculinity of physique culture, thus asserting trans men's place within cis men's masculinity. By contrast, Grey's sublime performance reveals a body in flux, with needles inserted for a more ambiguous gendering effect.

When considering the genesis of *Homage,* Grey recalls a postsurgery dream in which they watched their chest weeping (DeBrincat 2013). One cannot help but hear ambivalence. Does this framing and reopening of scars also pay homage to Grey's breasts? When considering intention, Grey explains that *Homage* provided a means to (re)enact agency over their chest reconstruction (DeBrincat 2013). Even when one chooses surgery, anesthesia (usually) elides consciousness.

Kris Grey is intentionally crafting a body that is more complex than what a shirt worn over a flat chest in public euphemizes. As Grey explains, "I use hormones and surgeries as a way to craft a queer form outside the binary of male and female" (Credible 2015). By exposing their nonbinary body in a semipublic art space and in published visual documentation, Grey not only shares complexity but also makes allowances for it. Grey is not proselytizing nonbinary body modification. Like Annie Sprinkle, they are hinging edification to curiosity. Grey is urging viewers to undertake new conceptualizations.

Psychoanalyst Griffin Hansbury advocates a "transgender edge," a place both psychic and transitional "in which body parts and gendered bits bump up against each other and merge" (2017, 1010). Within this space, gay, straight, cis, and trans men can not only desire and envy but also psychically obtain vaginas. Hansbury proffers "the Vaginal" as a counterpoint to the symbolic "Phallic." Just as the phallus is culturally available to people of all sexes, an empowered male vagina is available to all: "It is to this edge that we can help our male-identified patients go, in order to grieve and reclaim precious lost and castrated parts of themselves" (Hansbury 2017, 1019). Extending Hansbury, we can ask if, in *Homage*, Grey's chest is not only weeping for lost breasts but also psychically claiming them. Erotic and nurturing, breasts are attractive and generous to others, comforting. Grey's open chest is not exactly comforting, but it offers generosity and vulnerability to audience members as an invitation to be generous and vulnerable themselves. Hansbury states, "In fantasy, for bodies with or without a material vagina, the Vaginal may offer an access point to interiority, receptivity, openness, and expressiveness" (2017, 1010). This aptly describes the bodily conduit that Grey seeks to be for their audience.

Homage is not just gender deconstruction. It is also construction. A naked nonbinary body may lend to an audience's experience and beliefs, but it cannot alone determine potentiality. It cannot "eradicate boundaries" between performer and artist. And it cannot generate a new conceptualization of gender capable of being cognitively shared, regardless of whether one occupies a binary or nonbinary gender. In Grey's body art, these goals are sought via aesthetics. Grey's art pressures binaries, enter-tains combinations, engages symbols, follows slippages, and reaches out to references. In *Homage*, their aestheticized exhibition of a crafted body creates queer ambiguity as the trace and residue of artistic actions on and of the body.

For Vittorio Gallese, aesthetic responses to works of art emerge from mechanisms of mirroring. The same neural networks that one would use to perform an action are also stimulated when one instead watches or imagines another person performing that action. Such mirroring has been proposed as a basis for social empathy. Here, we might look back on the butt plug protruding from Grey's *Bottoms Up* and feel a redolent corporeality. Vision is thus multimodal, engaging not only image perception but also motor activ-ity and affect. Gallese terms this "embodied simulation" and proposes that "mirroring mechanisms and embodied simulation can empirically ground the fundamental role of empathy in aesthetic experience" (2011).

Empathetic viewers of *Homage* simultaneously watch Grey's naked body and its aestheticized nudity, and they consciously or unconsciously expe-rience corporeal sensations by mirroring both. The coexistence of naked body and nude body in Grey's performance extends their art-life practice to allow viewers a double-layered embodied simulation. They may them-selves experience the coolness of air touching a naked body, as well as the tightness of manipulated scar tissue. Their neurons might invisibly mirror Grey's deliberately modeled arm movement in pulling out a needle, while their chest might "share" Grey's breath as the needle moves through their skin. As numerous audience members have told Grey, *Homage* creates an empathic bridge between Grey's trauma and their own. As they watch blood spill out of Grey's body, they might experience not only queasiness but also an outsized physical condition in their own body. Finally, when the trick-ling blood reaches Grey's genitals, viewers might suddenly feel exposed and embarrassed. Or vitalized. Their genital soma might even undergo a new capability for gender. As Gallese explains:

> Very often artistic fiction is more powerful than real life in evoking our emotional engagement and empathic involvement. . . . We liberate new ener-gies and put them into the service of a new dimension that, paradoxically, can be more vivid than prosaic reality. Aesthetic experience of artworks, more than exclusively being a cognitive suspension of disbelief, can be thus interpreted as a sort of "liberated embodied simulation." (2011)

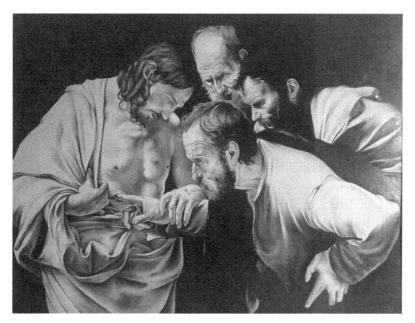

FIGURE 5: Michelangelo Merisi Caravaggio (1571–1610), *The Incredulity of St. Thomas* (1601). Oil on canvas. 107 cm (42.1 in) × 146 cm (57.4 in). Bildergalarie (Sanssouci), Prussian Palaces and Gardens Foundation Berlin-Brandenburg, Potsdam, Germany.

What new capacity for gender can a nonbinary body offer? Is it possible for nonbinary gender to exist and express itself without continually reconstituting binary gender via negation? How can nonbinary gender avoid the opposition between binary and nonbinary gender? I contend that a capacity for new gender requires a queering of the taxonomic project. The task is to locate a territory where "opposites" are not mutually exclusive.

While discussing *Homage*, Grey refers to the figure of Doubting Thomas (DeBrincat 2013). For me, this is a salient reference. It points to the story of Jesus Christ's crucifixion and resurrection, specifically to when Thomas could not believe that Jesus was resurrected, without first verifying crucifixion wounds on his body. Caravaggio's *The Incredulity of Saint Thomas* (1602) portrays the apostle Thomas looking intently at Jesus's wound as Jesus pulls cloth aside to expose his open chest. Jesus's hand lies upon Thomas's hand, insistently guiding its inquiry, as the tip of Thomas's outstretched finger enters Jesus's body (figure 5).

For Grey, this scene of Doubting Thomas is uppermost an image of body boundary crossing (DeBrincat 2013). In *Homage*, Grey similarly invites the audience across the body boundary by creating new body orifices on their chest. For me, Jesus's opened body and its exhibition for penetration render a phenomenology of gender outside the relevance of binary gender. Grey's reference to this historically distant but aesthetically near scene provides the impetus for me to elaborate on Jesus's body as an open-to-appropriation instance of gender that transcends taxonomy.

Doubting Thomas's scrutiny of Jesus's open body brings us to what Caroline Bynum terms "symbolic reversals" in later medieval religious practice. Men's writing of the time dichotomized male/female differences such as authority/nurture, spirit/flesh, law/mercy, divinity/humanity, and food receiver/food preparer and generator. These dichotomies that elevated men over women, however, created a religious problem for men, because the Holy Scripture made clear that the lowly would be welcomed into heaven and rewarded therein (Bynum 1987). Normativity was not the way to transcendence—hence the symbolic reversals enacted by saints and other pious males, who abruptly gave up their status and possessions or donned women's or beggars' clothing. These symbolic reversals were also informed by a God that became man and by a Jesus depicted during this time less often as the king of men than as humble caretaker and food provider. Jesus was mother, as priests giving Holy Communion also needed to be (Bynum 1987). In the Eucharist, Christ symbolically feeds his own body to humanity. Bynum points to numerous medieval images of Christ projecting a stream of blood from his chest wound into a chalice or communion cup and notes a parallelism between these and images of Mary projecting a stream of milk from her breast into open mouths. Describing these images, Bynum refers to Christ's chest as breast. She notes that in Quirizio da Murano's (fl. 1460–78) *The Savior*, Christ's wound is positioned where a nipple would be (1987, plates 12, 18–19, 25–30). According to Bynum, "God's dying body was female" (1987, 285). Of course, God exceeds that dying body, and that body's death exceeds the life/death binary.

In medieval European Catholicism, the gender of Christ and the men who modeled themselves after him through symbolic reversal cannot be understood through male/female dichotomous thought. As Bynum notes, to explain dichotomy is not to explain reversal (1987, 286). Within this religious practice, we find a reversal that can lend a new capacity to gender. Outside dichotomy, (nonbinary) gender requires a different comprehensibility. The roots of the word "comprehend" suggest "grasp together." Like Caravaggio's painting, Grey's *Homage* engages viewers haptically. Christ guides Doubting Thomas's touch to their womb in order to nurture belief. Kris Grey draws a doubting audience to their weeping chest for empathic comprehensibility. As Kris Grey opens their chest and blood streams from their wounds down a nonbinary body, their reference to the doubting apostle Thomas foregrounds the aesthetic component of symbolic reversal in *Homage*. By allowing Thomas to reach into their crucifixion wound, a nonbinary Christ shows him life and death not as two separate states but grasped together. Given Bynum's gendering of Christ's death, perhaps Thomas is also exploring Christ's vagina-inclusive body? I have dwelled upon Grey's reference to the doubting apostle Thomas because it summons nonbinary expression within a master discourse—and Christianity is only one of many religious master discourses in which opposites are not mutually exclusive. Without falling into the authoritative claims of master discourses, Grey's reference reminds us of a long-standing and widespread abundance of nonbinary living and art-making.

Kris Grey's genderqueer aesthetic intervenes in binary gender, binary sex, and binary sexuality. *Pink Bits* joyfully gifts us innovative genitals. *Ask a Tranny* cooperatively reroutes visual objectification into verbal sharing. *Bottoms Up* and *Homage* haptically inspire interpenetration of artist, art, and audience. Finally, Grey's commentary on personal and intertextual influences creates a textual art supplement to these objects and performances. My analysis of Grey's genderqueer aesthetic has described centripetal strategies resulting in imploded binaries (e.g., vagina/penis, beauty/kitsch, presence/absence, blood/tears) and centrifugal strategies that proliferate capacities (e.g., multifarious pronouns, empathic mirroring). Especially, Grey's supplemental reference to Doubting Thomas spurred my reading of *Homage* as an act of nonbinary inclusion rather than negation. By referencing the iconography of a master discourse, Kris Grey presents a nonbinary body as unexceptional, relatable, and queerly comprehensible.

Chris Straayer, associate professor of cinema studies at New York University, is the author of *Deviant Eyes, Deviant Bodies* (Columbia University Press, 1996) and numerous articles in queer and trans studies, and is coeditor (with Eric Plemons) of *TSQ: Transgender Studies Quarterly 5.2, The Surgery Issue*. Straayer can be reached at chris. straayer@nyu.edu.

Works Cited

Abraham, Amelia. 2014. "Ron Athey Literally Bleeds for His Art." *Vice*, September 23, 2014. https://www.vice.com/en_us/article/vdpx8y/ron-athey-performance-art-amelia-abraham-121.

Bettcher, Talia Mae. 2012. "Full-Frontal Morality: The Naked Truth about Gender." *Hypatia* 27 (2): 319–37.

Bolton, Rillark M. 2013. "Reworking Testosterone as a Man's Hormone: Nonbinary People Using Testosterone within a Binary Gender System." *Somatechnics* 9 (1): 13–31.

Bynum, Caroline Walker. 1987. *Holy Feast and Holy Fast: The Religious Signification of Food to Medieval Women*. Berkeley: University of California Press.

Cameron, Loren. 1996. *Body Alchemy: Transsexual Portraits*. Berkeley, CA: Cleis Press.

Chicago, Judy. 2007. *The Dinner Party: From Creation to Preservation*. London: Merrell.

Credible, Justin. 2015. "OtherPeoplesPixels Interviews Kris Grey." *OtherPeoplesPixels* (blog), March 19, 2015. https://blog.otherpeoplespixels.com/otherpeoplespixels-interviews-kris-grey-slash-justin-credible.

DeBrincat, A. M. 2013. "Empowered Vulnerability." *ArtFile Magazine*, October 8, 2013. https://www.artfilemagazine.com/Kris-Grey.

Dick, Kirby. 1997. *Sick: The Life and Death of Bob Flanagan, Supermasochist*. Video (90 minutes).

Flanagan, Bob. 1993. *Bob Flanagan: Supermasochist*. San Francisco, CA: RE/SEARCH Publications.

Foucault, Michel. 1980. *Herculine Barbin: Being the Recently Discovered Memoirs of a Nineteenth-Century French Hermaphrodite*. Translated by Richard McDougall. New York: Pantheon.

Gallese, Vittorio. 2011. "Seeing Art . . . Beyond Vision: Liberated Embodied Simulation in Aesthetic Experience." In *Seeing with Eyes Closed*, ed. Alexander Abbushi, Ivana Franke, and Ida Mommenejad, 62–65. Berlin: Association of Neuroesthetics.

Hansbury, Griffin. 2017. "The Masculine Vaginal: Working with Queer Men's Embodiment at the Transgender Edge." *Journal of the American Psychoanalytic Association* 65 (6): 1009–31.

Laqueur, Thomas. 1990. *Making Sex: Body and Gender from Greeks to Freud*. Cambridge, MA: Harvard University Press.

Maloney, Patricia. 2015. "Women in Performance: The New Endurance of Linda Mary Montano, Part 1." *Art Practical*, January 19, 2015. https://www.artpractical.com/column/

women-in-performance-the-new-endurance-of-linda-mary-montano-part-1/.

Montano, Linda Mary. 2017. "Mother Teresa Bio." *Linda Mary Montano* (blog), May 5, 2017. http://lindamarymontano.blogspot.com/2017/05/mother-teresa-bio.html.

O'Dell, Kathy. 1989. *Contract with the Skin: Masochism, Performance Art, and the 1970s*. Minneapolis: University of Minnesota Press.

Roth, Moira. 2015. "Women in Performance: The New Endurance of Linda Mary Montano, Part 2." *Art Practical*, January 21, 2015. https://www.artpractical.com/column/women-in-performance-the-new-endurance-of-linda-mary-montano-part-2/.

Sprinkle, Annie. 1991. *Annie Sprinkle: Post Porn Modernist*. Amsterdam: Torch Books.

Trans* Lives of Jadzia Dax: A Queer Ecology Reading of Symbiosis in *Star Trek: Deep Space Nine*

Gizem Senturk

Abstract: This article explores the symbiotic relationship of the Trill species in *Star Trek* from nonbinary, trans*, and queer ecological perspectives. The Trill's unique physiology allows them to enter into a symbiotic relationship with a symbiont, leading to nonheterosexual, nonbinary, and androgynous features. By examining the trans metaphor represented by Jadzia Dax, a Trill character in *Star Trek: Deep Space Nine*, the article highlights the ways in which the Trill challenge traditional notions of gender, biology, and symbiosis by introducing queerness. Furthermore, the article argues that symbiosis, when viewed through the lens of queer ecology, posthumanism, and more-than-humanisms, reveals that all living beings engage in queering, emphasizing the interconnectedness of life and the absence of living without symbiosis. **Keywords**: *Star Trek*; Trill; symbiosis; trans*; nonbinary; queer ecology; more-than-humanisms

Introduction

Star Trek (1966–) is one of the biggest franchises to imagine and speculate on the possibility of a utopia. Following the captains, lieutenants, and ensigns of the United Federation of Planets, *Star Trek* brings extraterrestrial adventures with an emphasis on diplomacy, peace, and equality. Regardless of the conflicts and hardships, the basic premise of the franchise lies in the possibility of a peaceful existence between humans and nonhumans. On the more critical side of the franchise lies *Star Trek: Deep Space Nine* (1993–1999), produced in a transitioning and turbulent era for politics and civil rights movements, which often impacts the stories *Star Trek* depicts onscreen. This series, unlike the others, does not follow a starship crew in their adventures in deep space. Instead, Deep Space Nine is a static space station that holds a strategic position in the galaxy due to its proximity to

WSQ: Women's Studies Quarterly 51: 3 & 4 (Fall/Winter 2023) © 2023 by Gizem Senturk. All rights reserved.

a wormhole. A science officer with excellent academic and professional success, Jadzia Dax is unusual among the officers to arrive at this station now under the Federation rule. Dax comes from a planet called Trill, inhabited by a species with the same name. What makes the Trill unique is their ability to enter into a symbiotic relationship with another species, referred to as a symbiont. Jadzia Dax hosts the Dax symbiont, therefore taking the last name Dax. Her symbiont companion lives inside her body and merges with her personality completely. Moreover, the symbiont can change hosts. While carrying the memories of previous hosts intact, symbionts can change bodies, genders, professions, partners, and every other detail about their life, except that they require a symbiotic relationship.

This article explores the Trill's symbiotic relationship from nonbinary, trans*, and ecological perspectives. Presented as a role model for the trans community due to their changed bodies and genders, the Trill showed up on fans' radar as early as the '90s, when the discourses of transness were distinguishing themselves from those of cisgender. The trans metaphor Jadzia Dax represents is one of the ways her character is immortalized in the significant amount of content in the *Star Trek* universe. On the other side, however, a queer ecological point of view reveals that the trans metaphor is not the only reason the Trill are considered queer and beyond the binaries of gender. Instead, their unique physiology enables them to engage in symbiotic relationships with the symbiont, already positioning them as a species with nonheterosexual, nonbinary, and androgynous features. Moreover, this queering via symbiosis has consequences for humans beyond the fictive worlds of science fiction. By blurring the lines between science fiction and science fact, symbiosis becomes a central theme for this article to question whether trans and nonbinary experience can be opened to all living beings. This article claims that when symbiosis is centered in the imaginaries of queer ecology, posthumanism, and more-than-humanisms, it reveals that *all living is queering*, as there is no living without symbiosis. It comes to this conclusion while rediscovering what has been missed in the scholarship of *Star Trek*, namely environmental humanities and trans studies, all of which cross paths with Jadzia Dax.

Nonbinary Imaginaries in *Star Trek: Deep Space Nine*

Among other things, science fiction enables a wild imagination that engages with metaphors in both literal and literary form. For example, the questions of trans reproduction and the embodiment of and symbiotic relations with the other all find representation in *Star Trek,* making space for a nonbinary investigation through metaphors. Here, I would like to go back to feminist science fiction writer Ursula K. Le Guin, who suggests, "All science fiction is a metaphor. . . . The future is a metaphor" (Barclay and Tidwell 2019, xi). Once again, the potential of science fiction, through metaphors of transness, nonbinary futures, dystopias, and utopias, is revealed with the help of creative academic engagement, especially with related theories of queer ecology, posthumanism, and gender studies. I also find it essential to refer to Michel Foucault's *History of Sexuality* (1976), where he defines gendered and sexual identities as "fiction" (Halberstam 2018, 7). Fiction, with its power to generate a common imagination, is a crucial part of constructing gender. This common imaginary can be a critical tool to dismantle the fictive identity that was created under the exact mechanisms of fiction. The same fiction, especially science fiction, can disrupt mainstream narratives of gender or, as in the case of Jadzia Dax, create nonbinary alterations, diverging from the mainstream perspectives of cisheteronormativity. It should come as no surprise that *Star Trek* can be used as a tool for trans* and queer ecological discussions.

Star Trek: Deep Space Nine and the Trill's symbiotic relationships allow a rediscovery of an overlooked phenomenon of ecology: symbiosis. The series and characters lead the discussion to a queer ecological reading of becoming with and living with others. With their symbiotic relationships with another species, aptly called "the symbiont," the Trill presents a unique opportunity to speculate about the trans* readings in *Star Trek*. As the Trill imagery throughout the series is carefully read through, it becomes clear that the Trill as a species can be read as a metaphor for transness. Moreover, symbiosis, the central metaphor as well as a biological event that enables life, is what makes ecology queer in its fluidity. There are no binaries for biology, symbiosis, the Trill, humans, fungi, or living beings at large. By moving forward from the arguments of trans* towards an ecological reading, without compromising the queer aspects, I will expand the focus towards symbiosis as a phenomenon that encapsulates, creates, enables, and encourages trans*, nonbinary and more-than-human ecologies.

Being the first Trill character to have a recurring role, and one of only a few that appeared in the franchise overall, Jadzia Dax holds crucial importance in the discussions around the species. Through her experiences, psyche, and character, the audience is introduced to the species. Jadzia Dax, taking her last name from the symbiont with whom she is joined (called the Dax symbiont), is a close friend to the captain of Deep Space Nine, Benjamin Sisko, and a science officer of the transitioning space station. The friendship between Captain Sisko and Jadzia Dax already signals and reveals the multitemporal, multipersona character of the Trill. To understand precisely how these multidimensional people are represented throughout the series, I determine two important subjects that reveal how the trans* metaphor operates. The first subject is the general similarities between trans* and the Trill, including the intensive gatekeeping and medical interventions. The second subject revolves around the pronouns and naming practices of the Trill, making an argument for trans as nonbinary species.

Dax Symbiont and the Trans Metaphor

The gatekeeping surrounding medical interventions, name changes, hormone access, and many other trans issues is a common problem faced by many people under the trans umbrella. With repeated doctor visits and therapy sessions, trans individuals must qualify with the appropriate medical authorities to gain approval for the medical interventions they require, positing the individual under, or over and under, institutionalized powers that determine whether one's subjective sense of self conforms to and meets preestablished scientific standards. Understood in the context of Foucault's concept of biopower, the trans experience inevitably involves confirmation, before confirmation of one's subjective sense of self in relation to a set of preexisting definitions and criteria; if qualified, one is identified as both distinguished and yet entirely the same as others with whom one has no relation. Thereby, any perceived threat of trans embodiment is subdued by having universal categories applied to each trans individual, who in turn is charged with the responsibility of having to demonstrate their own subjective experience, not as an authentic experience, but as an experience already recognized and deemed to be safe, predefined, known about, and on record. While such diagnostic procedures may be apt when dealing with diseases and illnesses, the trans experience cannot and should not be aligned alongside such parameters, as it can have detrimental effects for the individual's psychological well-being while also impeding (as opposed to facilitating) medical and scientific understandings of such conditions and experiences.

Similar to trans communities' experience with transitioning or gender reaffirmation surgeries, the Trill who desire to join with a symbiont must go through similar gatekeeping processes with the Trill Symbiosis Committee. In the process of joining, the host candidates (also known as "Trill initiates") get tested constantly by this committee for their "strength of character," "academics," and "psychological stability" ("Dax"; "Playing God"). Moreover, Jadzia Dax confesses that the process requires competition with many other young people as well as winning scholarships. As illustrated by Jadzia's four different types of academic education, the orientation to science and intellect of Trill society is shown in the parameters they require from those who want to be joined ("Dax"). The process is so heavily controlled that one Trill, Verad, decides to steal the Dax symbiont after being rejected by the committee even though he "constantly studied, every day, every waking hour" and "sacrificed everything" ("Invasive Procedures"). He tells the story of how the symbiosis evaluation board "reduced [his] entire life to one word: *unsuitable*" ("Invasive Procedures"). These gatekeeping practices do not fall far from the many reasons for rejection given to trans people today, which range from showing examples of detransitioning to claiming that their mental health needs to be on a level deemed healthy by the medical community for them to be able to decide on a gender reaffirmation surgery. In "Invasive Procedures," upon hearing Jadzia's defense of the validity of gatekeeping practices, the denied Verad rightfully answers that "he will not spend his life dreaming about what he could have been." The similarities between trans communities and the Trill are close, evoking art projects by trans artists who engage in guerrilla science projects to teach people to make the hormones they need so much gender reaffirmation, in order to circumnavigate impractical and laborious institutional demands and expectations.

Moving towards my second subject, defining how the trans* metaphor works in *Star Trek: Deep Space Nine*, I turn to discussions of naming and pronouns, as well as considering the Trill as a nonbinary species. In his explanation of *trans** as a term going beyond the binaries of gender, trans* scholar Halberstam mentions one of the most important defining characteristics of the term: a refusal of "situating transition in relation to a destination, a final form, a specific shape, or an established configuration of desire and identity" (2018, 4). The interpretation of the Trill in this article is also based on this definition: while the symbiont carries the memories of previous hosts, its future is in flux, with endless possibilities. Moreover, each host brings a different personality that can interact with the symbiont as well as other hosts, creating a new persona each time. This refusal of destination also makes it impossible to assign an "established configuration of desire and identity," including gender and sexual identities (4). Therefore, Halberstam's definition and the refusal of destination describes the experience of the Dax or any other symbiont, as their existence revolves around constant change without progressing towards any specific shape, gender, or other "configuration" or teleology (4). In their discussion of pronouns in trans* communities, Jack Halberstam describes an interview with Jill Soloway, the creator of the trans* TV show *Transparent*, and the journalist Ariel Levy. There, Soloway refers to the queer poet Eileen Myles and how she struggled with the pronoun *they*. The connection to the many personalities and the gender of the Trill lies in Myles's description of a Bible story in which Jesus sees a person possessed by demons; though the poet struggled to "refer to an individual person as they. . . . She liked the idea of a person containing more than one self, more than one gender" (11). More importantly, Myles declares that "whatever is not normative is many" (qtd. in Halberstam 2018, 11). The poet recognized the refusal of static, singular existence even when her singularity made it difficult to use *they/them* pronouns. Containing more than oneself becomes more than a metaphor, a reassuring theme throughout this article, as the Trill embodies many selves within the symbiont. This refusal of destination and striving for constant change is recognized and signaled from the beginning of the series. For example, the friendship between Jadzia Dax and Captain Benjamin Sisko represents one of the first signals toward a unique "past" of Trills who are joined with a symbiont. The Dax body Captain Sisko knows and befriends is the past host of the Dax symbiont Curzon Dax. This past friendship with another body, another gender, and another personality is carried through the body of Jadzia Dax, with all of its new attributes. However, the old friendship is not forgotten. While the relationship between Jadzia Dax and Captain Sisko takes a new shape, with added dynamics of differing ranks among them as well as gender expressions, the captain keeps the nickname "Old Man" for his new friend. This cross-gender naming signals and acknowledges the existence of the joined experience of the Dax symbiont and the hosts. Another critical aspect of names is how Jadzia Dax calls Sisko "Captain," for he is known and called as such to almost everyone on the station. However, due to their past together, which comes from the symbiont's older host, Curzon Dax, Jadzia Dax calls Captain Sisko by his first name, Benjamin. The closeness arising from their past relationship subdues the hierarchical nature of the relationship Starfleet officers normally would have.

The terms under the trans* umbrella, such as *nonbinary, genderqueer,* *gender nonconforming*, and many more, describe the specifics of the relation between the self and gender. Many of those definitions stem from a refusal of static, unchanging identity. If nonbinary is a refusal of being placed on a binary scale, then the Trill symbionts can and should be considered nonbinary characters. As my usage of *they/them/their* pronouns for the symbiont suggests, the plurality of the Trill symbiont, regardless of their hosts' body and gender, can be read as a refusal of statically occupying one gender of the binary. The pronoun discussion is not overlooked by the Trill experience either. After the current host, Jadzia, loses her life after a political attack, the Dax symbiont is carried over to a new host: Ezri. While the characters never openly use nonbinary pronouns, the struggles of the newly joined Ezri Dax reflect the more-than-one nature of their existence. In the episode "After Image," Ezri Dax struggles with what kinds of pronouns they can use, declaring: "These pronouns are going to drive me crazy!" Although nonbinary existence is not bounded by physical appearance, the fact that Ezri Dax had less traditionally feminine features, with her shortened "boyish" hair and masculine mannerisms, should be considered as an attempt to break away from the gendered body and memory of Jadzia, which lingers on the Deep Space Nine station as the crew grieves.

Finally, in addition to the two major focal points of the Trill-trans* metaphor outlined thus far, I would like to weave connections between the Trill and their implications on symbiosis-as-queering. One of the most crucial reasons why the symbiont and the hosts are joined reveals the adaptability of the Trill metaphor to referring to the environment and human relationships. Although this reason does not have a significant screen presence within the franchise, it is known that the symbionts and the hosts joined for survival (Berman and Piller 1992, 10). It is suggested that the symbionts, who still mainly inhabit caves, used to "live underground" on the Trill planet, while the humanoid hosts were on land (Berman and Piller 1992, 10). They had to go through symbiosis after an environmental disaster on the planet left them no choice but to combine their existence (Berman and Piller 1992, 10). This storyline illustrates a lesson that many environmental humanities scholars, activists, and other stakeholders try to convey: the environmental disaster that lingers around the planet, affecting many on differing scales, can only be survived via either literal or metaphorical symbiosis that equalizes humans and nonhumans alike. Considering this traumatic experience that shaped the lives of the Trill species as well as the planet Trill, it is only expected that the spiritual aspects of the Trill society value the symbiont highly, to the extent that the society itself often attempts to control who has access to it. "We're all part of something that is bigger than us," declares Julian Bashir, who embodies one of Jadzia Dax's previous hosts, Tobias. Died too young, the host mourns his memories while being "revived" through a telepathic ritual called "zhian'tara" ("Facets"). This ritual allows the joined Trill to talk to previous hosts through bodies that project the symbiont's memories. Talking to Jadzia Dax, Tobias Dax concludes that all of them are connected, both to each other and to the symbiont, much like the circular understandings of ecology, or "the mesh," as Timothy Morton describes it in his article regarding queer ecology (Morton 2009, 278). The mesh assumes that things, beings, objects, and subjects are all connected in a messy, complex way—not unlike Tobias Dax with the other hosts, his memories, and the personalities that came after his death. Considering the similarities between the Trill and humans can be a tool to discover how living is already a queering act. The symbiosis the Trill go through in their lifetime can be likened to the human symbiotic relationships of many more-than-human organisms. In fact, if the Trill are understood as trans through the symbiotic relationship, which opens up the questions of species' individuality, self, and borders, humans as species could be trans with the same logic. For example, a close look at bacteria enables a reframing of the human symbiotic relationships in light of the Trill and symbiont entanglement. Just as the symbiont exists in the belly of a Trill host, many bacteria live in the human body's guts. When considering the bacteria as kin and looking into their gender-bending capabilities, it is easier to imagine the human species as trans.

Symbiosis: A Queering Life Force

Life cannot be imagined without symbiosis, which is a fact accepted across natural science disciplines. For example, evolutionary biologists Scaringe and Wildman state that "biological data suggests an alternative" to the idea of individuality. Instead, this data suggests that "all life can be understood as contingently existent or mutually constituted" (Scaringe and Wildman 2020, 2). Taking their "suggestion" further, I claim that symbiosis is the process that enables life, making living organisms possible across the planet. Considering the amount of data, insight, and interpretation that biology and its subfields gather, as well as environmental humanities scholars' discussions, it is not absurd to suggest that living is *living with*. As environmental humanities scholars van Dooren, Kirksey, and Münster observe, the new research in biology and its subdisciplines, such as evolutionary biology and ontogeny (the study of the entire lifespan of an organism), shows that the division between the life spans of a single organism and a species could be more related than previously was known. Accepting this closer connection between different scales of life span requires "scientists and allies to rethink inheritances (genetic, epigenetic, behavioral, and cultural) as part of larger developmental processes" (van Dooren, Kirksey, and Münster 2016, 2). In other words, evolution is shaped by a contemporary species' behavior, as much as that behavior is shaped by evolution. In other words, the relationships that keep us alive affect our becoming, as "becoming is always *becoming with*" (van Dooren, Kirksey, and Münster 2016, 2; emphasis mine).

Symbiosis is not only an occurrence of the present moment, benefiting some or all members that are participating. The reinterpretation of symbiosis as a force of life leads to the consideration that it is also an evolutionary force. However, this attention to symbiosis in the evolutionary processes of all species has not found acceptance, perhaps due to the implications of anti-essentialist and anti-individualist concepts. Nancy A. Moran describes the "appreciation of symbiosis as a source of evolutionary novelty" as a recent development (Moran 2006, 866). According to the theory of "symbiogenesis," first argued by renowned scientist Lynn Margulis in her influential book *The Symbiotic Planet* (1998), the cells that are the building blocks of all complex life result from a symbiotic relationship. These building-block cells are called "eukaryotic," meaning they have a nucleus containing DNA and other crucial components, as opposed to "prokaryotic" cells that have no distinct nucleus (Martin and Hine 2008). Considering that there are no prokaryotic beings except bacteria, eukaryotic cells are critical in understanding biology. Margulis defines symbiogenesis as "an evolutionary term" that "refers to the origin of new tissues, organs, organisms—even species— by the establishment of long-term or permanent symbiosis" (Margulis 1998, 14). In other words, bacterial cells that became important components of cells had first formed a symbiotic relationship that enabled life to flourish. This means that from plants to humans to other animals, "associations with fungi and bacteria were key innovations" (Moran 2006, 866). Symbiosis does not change across scales either. From macro-organisms, meaning anything that can be observed with the naked human eye, to micro-organisms, all participate in some level of symbiosis. This participation is at such a level that scientists are unable to "culture 99% of microorganisms," as the exact components of their symbiotic relationships are not known and are incredibly complex to replicate (Moran 2006, 866). Symbiosis not only impacts the notions of the individual and the human but also the associations living beings form with each other. Interestingly, just as Jadzia Dax's relationship connotes pregnancy, so does symbiosis research. In her article, Moran also describes how the offspring is fed by the pregnant host, as an example of transmitting microbes, bacteria, and the overall transfer of the microbiome in a symbiotic relationship (Moran 2006, R867). Consequently, as is implied, pregnancy is a form of symbiosis. Not only is the host-symbiont relationship reproduced through pregnancy, but it is also used as a means to enable other symbiotic relationships to occur. For example, much like in the case of Dax hosting the symbiont, many symbioses that are crucial for the survival of the young are transmitted during embodied symbiotic relationships.

One of the essential realities that is taken into consideration in the conceptualization of queer ecology is evolution, seen as a continuation of one species to another. The biological data points out new insights regarding evolution, disabling the idea of any species' solitary existence (Scaringe and Wildman 2020, 3). In his article defining queer ecology, environmental humanities scholar and object-oriented ontology philosopher Timothy Morton argues for a field that is not a comparison of "literary-critical apples and oranges" but is more of an acknowledgment that "fully and properly, ecology is queer theory and queer theory is ecology: queer ecology" (Morton 2010, 273, 281). Morton also marks this inability to separate one species from another when he states that "evolution theory is anti-essentialist in that it abolishes rigid boundaries between and within species" (Morton 2010, 275). Moreover, he introduces the term "strange stranger" as a deliberate mistranslation of deconstructionist philosopher Jacques Derrida's *arrivant*. Though the topic of queer ecology's deconstructionist roots deserves an article of its own, it should be underlined that Derrida's *arrivant* is a crucial term offering similar flexibility and openness, as "trans*" does for nonhuman animals. The intentional mistranslation to "strange stranger" magnifies the openness of the other without creating boundaries of self, animal, or human (Morton 2010, 274). This term then becomes vital to denote the process of speciation undergone by many living beings, including strange strangers, by stating that strange strangers are uncanny, familiar and strange simultaneously. Their familiarity is strange, their strangeness familiar. They cannot be thought of as part of a series (such as species or genus) without violence. However, their uniqueness is not such that they are independent. They are composites of other strange strangers. Every life form is familiar since we are related to it. We share its DNA, its cell structure, and the subroutines in the software of its brain. Its unicity implies its capacity to participate in a collective. Queer ecology may espouse something very different from individualism, rugged or otherwise. (Morton 2010, 277)

Going further from the idea of "species ambiguity," biology scientists also point out the fact that "no life form has yet been found to exist in nature completely on its own without connections to other life forms" (Scaringe and Wildman 2020, 3). In addition, there have not been any complex eukaryote organisms that do not have a microbiome, that is, a surrounding of microbes, bacteria, and more that accompany them (Scaringe and Wildman 2020, 3). This could also be connected to the fact that in the specific case of bacteria accompanying other species, it is known that without the bacteria that enable many functions such as digestion and immune system activation, many species cannot live for very long (Scaringe and Wildman 2020, 4). While the relationship between queer theories and ecology can be found in layers of complexity, some examples illustrate this link more directly. One such example is the symbiotic relationship between spiroplasmas and the Bacteroidetes symbiont *Cardinium hertigii*. Often cited by scientists and other scholars alike, this symbiotic relationship ends up impacting "reproductive compatibility" among the hosts (Moran 2006, 867). Some symbiotic relationships impact the sex ratio of their hosts, making the symbiont a sexual determinant, a third (or more) component in the sexual relationships found in nature that are far from heterosexual (Moran 2006, 867).

What does this shift in biological sciences towards symbiosis and entanglements between different species mean for human species? What happens when humans are imagined less as individuals and more "as a superorganism, composed of and kept alive by diverse microbial kin" (Lorimer 2016, 57)? By centering symbiosis in readings of ecology, environment, and nonhuman relationships, *Homo sapiens* are destabilized as a singular, hierarchical, and static category. Similarly, this destabilization and flux foreground trans*-ness of humans as much as for all life. Another destabilizing example is the comparison between human DNA and other types of DNA. Human

DNA comprises only 1 percent of the DNA that is found in the human body (Lorimer 2016, 57). Moreover, in the human gut alone, there are "persistent partnerships with over 150 species of bacteria," with more than "1000 major bacteria groups" present (Gilbert et al. 2012, 327). The gene set that includes all these symbiotic relationships would equal a "150 times larger gene set than the human eukaryotic genome" (Gilbert et al. 2012, 327). This is undoubtedly destabilizing the concept of the human as it is imagined in modern Western thinking, as a dominant power that over-comes animals, nature, and all of those who are not human (or not "human enough"). However, biology suggests that besides our small percentage of human DNA, human bodies comprise bacteria, fungi, archaea, and a few animals invisible to the naked eye.

As apparent from the discussions so far, symbiosis is not a subject free from ideological discussions. In this regard, it is not surprising to attach metaphors of trans* onto symbiosis, all while attempting to move beyond that metaphor toward empirical life. As Donna Haraway's reading of biol-ogy also suggests, biology itself "is an inexhaustible source of troping. It is certainly full of metaphor, but it is more than a metaphor" (Haraway and Goodeve 2001, 81). Moreover, upon being asked what it means to have more than metaphors in biology, she replies:

> I mean not only the physiological and discursive metaphors that can be found in biology, but the stories. For instance, all the various ironic, almost funny, incongruities. The sheer wiliness and complexity of it all. So that biology is not merely a metaphor that illuminates something else, but an inexhaustible source of getting at the nonliteralness of the world. (Haraway and Goodeve 2001, 81–82)

As in the case of the Trill's trans* experience of living (and becoming) with their symbionts, the facts and fiction complement each other through the phenomenon of symbiosis. Symbiosis provides a unique opportunity to study political and social issues of living with others, of regenerative cultures, and of the climate crisis, all while allowing the biological facts to be consid-ered again from a different perspective of inclusivity. Moreover, even devoid of its political implications, it questions the integrity of Western philosophy by destabilizing the notion of individuality and thus, identity. One of the "faces" of symbiosis is the *Mixotricha paradoxa*,[1] a microorganism that has been brought to the attention of scientists and humanities scholars alike by Donna Haraway's "Cyborgs and Symbionts: Living Together in the New

World Order" from *The Cyborg Handbook* (Haraway 2009, 81–83). The microorganism is also an ambassador of symbiosis because it embodies an exaggerated level of symbiosis, just like the Trill with their symbionts. It is exaggerated from the perspective of those who are not familiar with symbiotic relationships, as the "microscopic single-celled organism that lives in the hind gut of the South Australian termite . . . lives in obligatory symbiosis with five other kinds of entities" (Haraway 2009, 82). However, it should not be taken as a unique example—while observing this number of beings involved in a symbiotic relationship is uncommon, the phenomenon of symbiosis is undoubtedly not. The more scientists explore biology, the more metaphors and more-than-metaphors one can discover, as "biology is an endless resource" (Haraway 2009, 82).

By focusing towards symbiosis and the human as a species, this article sees the human as a new, plural, and trans* entity. While the aim is not to center humans in the discussions of multispecies becoming and more-than-humanisms, it is helpful for humans to reflect on the knowledge and insights gained from studies of "others." Moreover, this new reading of the human can enable "a new understanding" that sees humanity "co-constituted inside dense webs of lively exchange" (van Dooren, Kirksey, and Münster 2016, 14). In the context of the close attention both ecology and queer theory are giving to intimacies among multiple parties (Morton 2010, 281), symbiosis offers an example of an evergreen, open flux of change and queerness that happens in, on, and around humans. An interesting reading of the Trill is that they are a representation of humans as a species, with their symbiotic relationship made more visible to the human eye. Symbiosis shows that even "DNA is performative" (Morton 2010, 276) by "blurring the lines of the organism" and "obscuring the notion of essential identity" (Gilbert et al. 2012, 326). Given the social, political, ethical, and biological importance of the implications of symbiosis, it is of the utmost importance that scholars across disciplines revise the ideas adjacent to essentialism, with a radical queer ecological take. When living is "living with" and becoming is "becoming with," there is no way of seeing ecology other than as queer ecology.

Conclusion

In many ways, it is safe to say that there is a search for an alternative understanding for ideas and concepts that are deemed unchangeable. With the looming catastrophes of climate crisis approaching, many scholars, thinkers, philosophers, and artists speculate on how to reimagine life as it is known to make the future a place fundamentally different from the present. In this article, one concept among the many "essentials" of life, symbiosis, was analyzed and reinterpreted as a queer and binary-breaking phenomenon, with the help of science fiction. More specifically, the Trill from *Star Trek: Deep Space Nine* allowed this reinterpretation, as the characters are often considered a metaphor of transness, with their changing bodies and genders beyond binaries. While depicting the trans* metaphor, the show also highlighted symbiosis as a phenomenon that challenges the ideas of cisheteronormativity.

Overall, the article analyzed, investigated, and answered questions about queer ecology, posthumanism, more-than-humanisms, and environmental humanities. While this particular work was concerned with the metaphors of trans* experience in *Star Trek: Deep Space Nine*, other subjects point to the fact that more research is needed on symbiosis. Symbiosis brings together the issues of many different disciplines willing to search for a nonbinary future. As the discussions of trans* studies, the Trill, and symbiosis are concluding, it is crucial to underline the political ramifications of the ideas and ideologies discussed throughout this article. While the academic ambition of this work has been to analyze the discourses of trans* and queer studies and point out symbiosis as a phenomenon of interest, the article is not free from social and political concepts. Essentially, this article argued that with a radical change in how nature, the human, the nonhuman, and life are imagined, a chance of *living and becoming with* through symbiotic relationships is born.

Gizem Senturk is an independent researcher and artist working with queer ecology, more-than-humanisms, and symbiosis. They have an interdisciplinary background in comparative literature and visual arts from Koc University and hold a research MA in environmental humanities from VU Amsterdam. They are currently completing an MA in fine arts and design at St. Joost School of Art and Design, under the Ecology Futures programme. Previously, they have been published in Fiber Festival, *NOIA Magazine*, and Field Arts Docket with their academic and artistic work. They can be reached at g.sent@hotmail.com.

Notes

1. Donna Haraway also points out that "mixotricha" means "mixed threads," making a very apt name for the species as well as the entangled condition humans and all other beings are in (Haraway 2009, 81–83).

Works Cited

"After Image." 1998. *Star Trek: Deep Space Nine*, season 7, episode 3.

Barclay, Bridgitte, and Christy Tidwell. 2019. *Gender and Environment in Science Fiction*. Lanham, MD: Lexington Books.

Berman, Rick, and Michael Piller. 1992. *Star Trek: Deep Space Nine Bible*.

"Dax." 1993. *Star Trek: Deep Space Nine*, season 1, episode 8.

"Facets." 1995. *Star Trek: Deep Space Nine*, season 3, episode 25.

Foucault, Michel. 1976. *The History of Sexuality*. New York: Penguin Books.

Gilbert, Scott F., Jan Sapp, Alfred I. Tauber, James D. Thomson, and Stephen C. Stearns. 2012. "A Symbiotic View of Life: We Have Never Been Individuals." *Quarterly Review of Biology* 87 (4): 325–41.

Halberstam, Jack. 2018. *Trans**. Berkeley: University of California Press.

Haraway, Donna J. 2009. "Cyborgs and Symbionts: Living Together in the New World Order." In *The Cyborg Handbook*, ed. Chris Hables Gray, xi–xx. New York: Routledge.

Haraway, Donna J., and Thyrza Nichols Goodeve. 2001. "More than Metaphor." In *Feminist Science Studies: A New Generation*, ed. Maralee Mayberry, Banu Subramaniam, and Lisa H. Weasel, 81–86. New York: Routledge.

"Invasive Procedures." 1993. *Star Trek: Deep Space Nine*, season 2, episode 4.

Lorimer, Jamie. 2016. "Gut Buddies." *Environmental Humanities* 8 (1): 57–76. https://doi.org/10.1215/22011919-3527722.

Margulis, Lynn. 1998. *Symbiotic Planet: A New Look at Evolution*. New York: Basic Books.

Martin, Elizabeth, and Robert Hine. 2008. "Symbiosis." In *A Dictionary of Biology*. Oxford: Oxford University Press. https://www.oxfordreference.com/view/10.1093/acref/9780199204625.001.0001/acref-9780199204625-e-4314.

Moran, Nancy A. 2006. "Symbiosis." *Current Biology* 16 (20): 866–71. https://doi.org/10.1016/j.cub.2006.09.019.

Morton, Timothy. 2010. "Guest Column: Queer Ecology." *PMLA* 125 (2): 273–82.

"Playing God." 1994. *Star Trek: Deep Space Nine*, season 2, episode 17.

Scaringe, Stephen A., and Wesley J. Wildman. 2020. "Biological Symbiosis and Mutualism: Notable Advances, and More to Come." *Theology and Science* 18 (2): 211–25. https://doi.org/10.1080/14746700.2020.1755535.

van Dooren, Thom, Even Kirksey, and Ursula Münster. 2016. "Multispecies Studies." *Environmental Humanities* 8 (1): 1–23. https://doi.org/10.1215/22011919-3527695.

The Nonbinary Blackness of Pauli Murray and Ornette Coleman: Constraint and Freedom within the Glandular Imaginary

Susan Stryker

Abstract: This short essay reflects on desires for body modification expressed by civil rights activist Pauli Murray and jazz innovator Ornette Coleman to offer some preliminary thoughts on the concept of "nonbinary Blackness." It compares the different ways Murray and Coleman negotiated the "glandular imaginary" that informed mid-twentieth-century ideas about sex, gender, and identity, and influenced decisions they made about their own bodies. The transmasculine Murray reconciled to living as a woman once medical examinations determined that there was no hormonal or gonadal cause for her/their masculine identifications, while Coleman, a seemingly cisgender man, drew creative insight from his decision to undergo the genital surgery of circumcision. **Keywords:** nonbinary; Blackness; endocrinology; surgery; jazz; Ornette Coleman; Pauli Murray

In "Becoming Glandular: Endocrinology, Mass Culture, and Experimental Lives in the Interwar Age", historian Michael Pettit explores how, in his words, "the human sciences work to refigure what counts as selfhood" (2013). He focuses specifically on the rise of endocrinology as a medical specialty in the late nineteenth century, and the eventual emergence in popular culture of beliefs in, and discourses about, the power of hormones to alter the conditions of embodied being-in-the-world. Against the historical backdrop of this "glandular age", Western embodiment and subjectivity increasingly came be seen as sites of bio-medical and technological intervention, capable of transformation according to ideological programs. People, in other words, became imaginable as designable and engineerable through endocrinological manipulation.

As Kyla Schuller argues so persuasively in *The Biopolitics of Feeling*, cultural fantasies of the body's actual transformability have never been

WSQ: Women's Studies Quarterly 51: 3 & 4 (Fall/Winter 2023) © 2023 by Susan Stryker. All rights reserved.

equally distributed. Particularly in the United States—where Lamarckian evolutionary theory held greater sway than Darwinian ideas well into the twentieth century, and legacies of chattel slavery positioned people of African descent as biologically distinct from and inferior to people of western European heritage—a proto-eugenic and explicitly racialist medical science in the late nineteenth and early twentieth centuries conceived of bodies of colour as more primitive and less "plastic" than white bodies, less able to receive sensory impressions from the environment, and therefore less able to respond and evolve (Schuller 2018).[1] Jules Gill-Peterson, in *Histories of the Transgender Child*, extends this insight into racially inflected cultural beliefs about somatic plasticity to argue that part of what has produced the dominant trope of the transsexual as implicitly white has been the historical exclusion of gender-variant subjects of colour from medical treatment protocols that always-already imagine them less capable of transformability (2018). Given that whiteness is the privileged locus of imagined plasticity—an insight lucidly delineated in Deleuzian ethnographer Arun Saldhana's *Psychedelic White*, a study of the rave scene in Goa, India (2007)—the figure of the white transsexual has been positioned as the hypervisible site of a diffuse, racially differentiated cultural imaginary that informs practices of bodily transformation for everyone.

   This short article showcases two suggestive episodes in the lives of two celebrated people of colour in the U.S.—legal scholar Pauli Murray and jazz musician Ornette Coleman—to suggest how, on the one hand, an endocrinological framework informed and influenced some of their life-choices and, on the other hand, how their non-whiteness and ostensible non-transness has rendered their clearly expressed desire for somatic transformation through hormonal and glandular manipulation illegible. Ultimately, I suggest, their lives can help orient us toward a new conceptual framework of "nonbinary blackness" as another way to imagine the constraints and possibilities of somatic transformation that lies beyond the implicit whiteness that informs the transgender framework as it has been developed over the past thirty years.

   Though little-known, Pauli Murray was one of the most influential figures of twentieth-century U.S. history. A former assistant Attorney General for the state of California, as well as an ordained Episcopal minister and graduate of Yale Divinity School, Murray was the person who introduced Bayard Rustin to Gandhi's practice of non-violent mass civil disobedience, who in turn introduced it to Rev. Martin Luther King, Jr., who in turn made it a linchpin of the African American Civil Rights Movement. Murray led a bus desegregation protest a decade before Rosa Parks. As a lawyer and legal theorist, Murray's research into the history of racial segregation provided the foundation for Thurgood Marshall's argument in the *Brown v. Board of Education* Supreme Court case that outlawed the "separate but equal" doctrine, and Murray's articulation of the concept of "Jane Crow"—the double-oppression of black women through both race and gender under the U.S. apartheid regime commonly known as "Jim Crow"—was the inspiration for Kimberlé Crenshaw's concept of "intersectionality" and a point of departure for what has come to be called Critical Race Theory.[2]

Murray, a black-identified person of mixed racial heritage was, arguably, also a gender-nonbinary person *avant la lettre*. Although Murray was assigned female at birth and tacitly agreed to be called "she", they thought of themselves as a "boy-girl", formally adopted a gender-ambiguous version of their given name "Pauline", resisted the imposition of femininity, preferred masculine attire, felt erotically and romantically attracted to feminine heterosexual women and wrote for the African American press using the pseudonym "Peter Panic"—a cheeky double-entendre that implied being like the fictional boy who would never grow up to be a man, as well as a person in a panic over a slang term for a penis. Until quite recently, their gender-nonbinary status has been trivialised in the black and feminist scholarship on Murray's life, as well as ignored as part of transgender history.

Both omissions are, in part, consequences of Murray's own understanding of how endocrinology, glands and gonads undergird gendered personhood. They struggled with acute anxiety over their masculinity and their attraction to women, often to the point of being emotionally paralyzed and incapacitated. As a young adult in the 1930s, they read widely in the endocrinological and sexological literature and accepted the prevailing notion that their desires and identifications could be explained by a glandular imbalance, possibly due to an undiagnosed intersex condition leading to "pseudo-hermaphroditism". Murray repeatedly requested masculinizing hormone treatments to correct the perceived imbalance but—for all the reasons Gill-Peterson outlines—was repeatedly denied access to this form of treatment. Before undergoing an emergency appendectomy, Murray requested that the surgeon also perform exploratory surgery to look for gonadal irregularities. They found none, and Murray reconciled to the idea that there was no underlying physiological cause of their masculinity. Because they accepted that they were unambiguously female, they decided that they must therefore actually be a woman, however unconventional a one they might be. The glandular imaginary, in other words, becomes the means of Murray's disappearance into a cisgender norm.

This same rootedness in a glandular imaginary informed jazz musician Ornette Coleman's similarly unsuccessful attempt to alter his body in pursuit of musical innovation, an act similarly obscured in Coleman's constitutive influence in the development of "free jazz" as well as in the history of gender and sexuality. In contrast to Murray, who seems to have found in their beliefs about glands and gonads a check or limit to a perceived sense of self, Coleman found unrecognized and unexpected potentials for creative expression.

Influential avant-garde filmmaker Shirley Clark's last film, *Ornette: Made in America* (1985),[3] contains the following remarkable exchange:

> **Clark (off-camera):** Tell us the castration story.
> **Ornette:** [W]hen I played music I always got a different kind of relationship to girls. And then I started wondering . . . if playing music has anything to do with these girls liking me, and if I wasn't playing music how would they respond to me? . . . I never got over the feeling of knowing whether some girl would like me because of me just being a person and not just a performer. And so after having been married and having a kid, I was thinking about eliminating any sexual feeling I could have in my body. So I was told that was called castration.
>
> So I went to the doctor and told him that's what I thought I was interested in him doing. . . . So you know, he looked at me very strange and said, "Well are you sure that's what you really want?" I said, "Yeah, that's what I want." And so he said, "Well, I'll tell you what. Before you try that, why don't you try circumcision first?" I said I didn't have any idea what he was talking about because, you know, it's just something I hadn't thought about. And I said, "Is that a kind of form of castrating?" And he said, "Well, not exactly, but it's symbolic."
>
> So I had the operation of being circumcised, and finally after I got well I still didn't feel any change. I mean, it didn't improve. I didn't solve that problem by having that particular operation.
>
> But one thing that I did solve was the fact that I realized that being physical or sexual has nothing to do with what you think or believe. It has more to do with who you think you're affecting and what you think you're affecting. And so from then—from that day to this day—I have decided there's two kinds of human beings—one female and one male, and one man and one woman. So I decided to join what I thought the categories would be. I would rather be a man than a male.

Coleman, like Murray—and, indeed, like his culture at large—imagined glands and gonads as foundational sites of sexuality and subjectivity, and saw altering them as a practice of self-elaboration. What is so striking about Coleman's efforts to find agency and creative potential within the psychical topography of the glandular imaginary, especially given his medical service providers steering him away from his own expressed desires and intention, is his sense that even without a successful gonadal transformation, pursuing what might be called a "sex-change" procedure (the symbolic castration of circumcision) could function as an experimental artistic method.

Although Coleman was not a transgender person and didn't have access to currently preferred terminology and concepts, his remarks neverthe-less make a distinction between his physical body and his subjective sense of self, which is of course central to contemporary articulations of trans identity. But there's another root for that distinction—one more related to blackness than transness—of not being defined by one's physicality, and of fugitivity, of escaping toward freedom elsewhere whether in the physical or immaterial realm. That the freeform improvisation signposted by the "free" of Coleman's "free jazz" can be indexed to the act of living and making art in the afterlife of slavery has long been recognized by musicologists;[4] that it can also be indexed to the sense of emancipating embodiment from the sex/gender binary has heretofore gone unremarked.

Coleman doesn't explicitly think past the gender binary—for him, there's male/female and man/woman—but he suggests that maleness and manhood as well as femaleness and womanhood are distinct from one another. And he imagines some way of subjectively identifying as a man and socially being perceived as a man as a space of freedom that is not grounded in biological maleness. In this regard, he could be regarded as a cisgender male-to-man trans person. He conceptualizes gender identity and expression (that is, "what you think" not "what you are physically") as being essentially a mode of connection with others: it has to do with affecting and being affected. Gender for Coleman thus becomes something uplifted from the body. It is an affective technology for relating to others according to a certain style, whose abstraction from the biological depends on recognis-ing and moving in a trans-dimensional gap between physicality and a sense of self that is the wellspring of creative freedom.

In offering these brief but hopefully generative observations, my goal is to suggest new ways in which we might understand the legacy of the glan-dular imaginary that emerged in the late nineteenth and early twentieth centuries: as a terrain differentially accessible based on racialized notions of somatic plasticity, one that can function as a site of constraint while nevertheless harboring possibilities of agency. In decentering "transgender" as the privileged and implicitly white site of somatic plasticity rooted in gonadal or glandular manipulation, examples of negotiating the glandular imaginary drawn from the lives of Pauli Murray and Ornette Coleman can help reframe potentials for becoming otherwise through reimagining the flesh through a nonbinary lens drawn from histories of black fugitivity and freedom-seeking.

Susan Stryker, Professor Emerita of Gender, Women's, and Sexuality Studies at the University of Arizona, will join the faculty of the University of Southern California as Dean's Professor of Gender and Sexuality Studies in 2024. She is the author of *Transgender History*, codirector of the Emmy-winning documentary film *Screaming Queens: The Riot at Compton's Cafeteria*, cofounder of the academic journal *TSQ: Transgender Studies Quarterly*, and coeditor of the Duke University Press book series *ASTERISK: gender, trans-, and all that comes after*. She can be reached at susan@susanstryker. net.

Notes

1. See in particular chapter 3, "Vaginal Impressions: Gyno-Neurology and the Racial Origins of Sexual Difference," 100–132.
2. On Pauli Murray, see Rosenberg 2020 for a note on pronouns (xvii) and a synopsis of Murray's biography and thoughts on "hormonal imbalance" (1–6). A good recent documentary film on Murray is *My Name Is Pauli Murray* (dir. Betsy West and Julie Cohen, Amazon Studios, 2021). For Crenshaw and intersectionality, see Crenshaw 2017.
3. For the "castration story," see 1:06–1:10.
4. On Coleman, free jazz, and its relation to African American history and the afterlives of slavery, see Baskerville 1994; Hersch 1995; Rustin 2003; Carles and Comolli 2008; Carlisle 2014; and Rush 2017.

Works Cited

Baskerville, John D. 1994. "Free Jazz." *Journal of Black Studies* 24 (4): 484–97.
Carles, Phillipe, and Jean-Louis Comolli. 2008. *Free Jazz, Black Power*. Paris: Gallimard.
Carlisle, Crystal BlackCreek. 2014. *Free Jazz Improvisation: A Continuum, from Africa to Congo Square, from Early Jazz to Bebop, and the Return to Mysticism for Communal Healing and Transcendence*. West Hollywood, CA: Urspirit.

Crenshaw, Kimberlé. 2017. *On Intersectionality: Essential Writings*. New York: New Press.

Fisher, Simon D. 2016. "Pauli Murray's Peter Panic." *TSQ: Transgender Studies Quarterly* 3 (1/2): 95–103.

Gill-Peterson, Jules. 2018. *Histories of the Transgender Child*. Minneapolis: University of Minnesota Press.

Hersch, Charles. 1995. "'Let Freedom Ring!': Free Jazz and African-American Politics." *Cultural Critique*, no. 32: 97–123.

Ornette: Made in America. 1985. Dir. Shirley Clark. Milestone.

Pettit, Michael. 2013. "Becoming Glandular: Endocrinology, Mass Culture, and Experimental Lives in the Interwar Age." *American Historical Review* 118 (4): 1052–76.

Rosenberg, Rosalind. 2020. *Jane Crow: The Life Of Pauli Murray*. New York: Oxford University Press.

Rush, Stephen. 2017. *Free Jazz, Harmolodics, and Ornette Coleman*. New York: Routledge.

Rustin, Nichole T. 2003. Review of *Going for Jazz: Musical Practices and American Ideology*, by Nicholas Gebhardt. *Journal of American History* 90 (1): 300.

Saldhana, Arun. 2007. *Psychedelic White: Goa Trance and the Viscosity of Race*. Minneapolis: University of Minnesota Press.

Schuller, Kyla. 2018. *The Biopolitics of Feeling: Race, Sex, and Science in the Nineteenth Century*. Durham, NC: Duke University Press.

PART II. **CLASSICS REVISITED**

Not to Be Dramatic But

Kyra Gregory

My work is rooted in an existential search for self and community, and driven by my personal experiences with queerness, mental illness, and spirituality. As a transmasc/genderfluid/nonbinary person, I am drawn to self-portraiture as an attempt to externalize my varied self-perceptions and visualize my constantly morphing gendered self-states. These prints are physical expressions of my experiences and are manifestations of myself that are untranslatable into written or verbal language.

Kyra Gregory (they/them) is a printmaker, painter, and collage artist born in Richmond, Virginia, and currently living and working in Queens, New York. They graduated from Princeton University in 2019 with a major in visual arts and a certificate in gender and sexuality studies. They can be reached at kmgregory16@gmail.com.

WSQ: Women's Studies Quarterly 51: 3 & 4 (Fall/Winter 2023) © 2023 by Kyra Gregory. All rights reserved.

Kyra Gregory. *Not to Be Dramatic But*, 2022. Woodblock relief print on paper.

Dear Theresa, from *Stone Butch Blues*

Leslie Feinberg

Dear Theresa:

I'm lying on my bed tonight missing you, my eyes all swollen, hot tears running down my face. There's a fierce summer lightning storm raging outside. Tonight I walked down streets looking for you in every woman's face, as I have each night of this lonely exile. I'm afraid I'll never see your laughing, teasing eyes again.

I had coffee in Greenwich Village earlier with a woman. A mutual friend fixed us up, sure we'd have a lot in common since we're both "into politics." Well, we sat in a coffee shop and she talked about Democratic politics and seminars and photography and problems with her co-op and how she's so opposed to rent control. Small wonder—Daddy is a real estate developer.

I was looking at her while she was talking, thinking to myself that I'm a stranger in this woman's eyes. She's looking at me but she doesn't see me. Then she finally said how she hates this society for what it's done to "women like me" who hate themselves so much they have to look and act like men. I felt myself getting flushed and my face twitched a little and I started telling her, all cool and calm, about how women like me existed since the dawn of time, before there was oppression, and how those societies respected them, and she got her very interested expression on—and besides it was time to leave.

So we walked by a corner where these cops were laying into a homeless man and I stopped and mouthed off to the cops and they started coming at me with their clubs raised and she tugged my belt to pull me back. I just looked at her, and suddenly I felt things well up in me I thought I had buried. I stood there remembering you like I didn't see cops about to hit me, like I was falling back into another world, a place I wanted to go again.

And suddenly my heart hurt so bad and I realized how long it's been since my heart felt—anything.

I need to go home to you tonight, Theresa. I can't. So I'm writing you this letter.

I remember years ago, the day I started working at the cannery in Buffalo and you had already been there a few months, and how your eyes caught mine and played with me before you set me free. I was supposed to be following the foreman to fill out some forms but I was so busy wondering what color your hair was under that white paper net and how it would look and feel in my fingers, down loose and free. And I remember how you laughed gently when the foreman came back and said, "You comin' or not?"

All of us he-shes were mad as hell when we heard you got fired because you wouldn't let the superintendent touch your breasts. I still unloaded on the docks for another couple of days, but I was kind of mopey. It just wasn't the same after your light went out.

I couldn't believe it the night I went to the club on the West Side. There you were, leaning up against the bar, your jeans too tight for words and your hair, your hair all loose and free.

And I remember that look in your eyes again. You didn't just know me, you liked what you saw. And this time, ooh woman, we were on our own turf. I could move the way you wanted me to, and I was glad I'd gotten all dressed up.

Our own turf . . . "Would you dance with me?"

You didn't say yes or no, just teased me with your eyes, straightened my tie, smoothed my collar, and took me by the hand. You had my heart before you moved against me like you did. Tammy was singing "Stand By Your Man," and we were changing all the he's to she's inside our heads to make it right. After you moved that way, you had more than my heart. You made me ache and you liked that. So did I.

The older butches warned me: if you wanted to keep your marriage, don't go to the bars. But I've always been a one-woman butch. Besides, this was our community, the only one we belonged to, so we went every weekend.

There were two kinds of fights in the bars. Most weekends had one kind or the other, some weekends both. There were the fights between the butch women—full of booze, shame, jealous insecurity. Sometimes the fights were awful and spread like a web to trap everyone in the bar, like the night Heddy lost her eye when she got hit upside the head with a bar stool.

I was real proud that in all those years I never hit another butch woman.

See, I loved them too, and I understood their pain and their shame because I was so much like them. I loved the lines etched in their faces and hands and the curves of their work-weary shoulders. Sometimes I looked in the mirror and wondered what I would look like when I was their age. Now I know!

In their own way, they loved me too. They protected me because they knew I wasn't a "Saturday-night butch." The weekend butches were scared of me because I was a stone he-she. If only they had known how power-less I really felt inside! But the older butches, they knew the whole road that lay ahead of me and they wished I didn't have to go down it because it hurt so much.

When I came into the bar in drag, kind of hunched over, they told me, "Be proud of what you are," and then they adjusted my tie sort of like you did. I was like them; they knew I didn't have a choice. So I never fought them with my fists. We clapped each other on the back in the bars and watched each other's backs at the factory.

But then there were the times our real enemies came in the front door: drunken gangs of sailors, Klan-type thugs, sociopaths and cops. You always knew when they walked in because someone thought to pull the plug on the jukebox. No matter how many times it happened, we all still went "Aw . . . " when the music stopped and then realized it was time to get down to business.

When the bigots came in, it was time to fight, and fight we did. Fought hard—femme and butch, women and men together.

If the music stopped and it was the cops at the door, someone plugged the music back in and we switched dance partners. Us in our suits and ties paired off with our drag queen sisters in their dresses and pumps. Hard to remember that it was illegal then for two women or two men to sway to music together. When the music ended, the butches bowed, our femme partners curtsied, and we returned to our seats, our lovers, and our drinks to await our fates.

That's when I remember your hand on my belt, up under my suit jacket. That's where your hand stayed the whole time the cops were there. "Take it easy, honey. Stay with me baby, cool off," you'd be cooing in my ear like a special lover's song sung to warriors who need to pick and choose their battles in order to survive.

We learned fast that the cops always pulled the police van right up to the bar door and left snarling dogs inside so we couldn't get out. We were trapped, alright.

Remember the night you stayed home with me when I was so sick? That was the night—you remember. The cops picked out the most stone butch of them all to destroy with humiliation, a woman everyone said "wore a raincoat in the shower." We heard they stripped her, slow, in front of everyone in the bar, and laughed at her trying to cover up her nakedness. Later she went mad, they said. Later she hung herself.

What would I have done if I had been there that night?

I'm remembering the busts in the bars in Canada. Packed in the police vans, all the Saturday-night butches giggled and tried to fluff up their hair and switch clothing so they could get thrown in the tank with the femme women—said it would be like "dyin' and goin' to heaven." The law said we had to be wearing three pieces of women's clothing.

We never switched clothing. Neither did our drag queen sisters. We knew, and so did you, what was coming. We needed our sleeves rolled up, our hair slicked back, in order to live through it. Our hands were cuffed tight behind our backs. Yours were cuffed in front. You loosened my tie, unbuttoned my collar, and touched my face. I saw the pain and fear for me in your face, and I whispered it would be alright. We knew it wouldn't be.

I never told you what they did to us down there—queens in one tank, stone butches in the next—but you knew. One at a time they would drag our brothers out of the cells, slapping and punching them, locking the bars behind them fast in case we lost control and tried to stop them, as if we could. They'd handcuff a brother's wrists to his ankles or chain his face against the bars. They made us watch. Sometimes we'd catch the eyes of the terrorized victim, or the soon-to-be, caught in the vise of torture, and we'd say gently, "I'm with you, honey, look at me, it's OK, we'll take you home."

We never cried in front of the cops. We knew we were next.

The next time the cell door opens it will be me they drag out and chain spread-eagle to the bars.

Did I survive? I guess I did. But only because I knew I might get home to you.

They let us out last, one at a time, on Monday morning. No charges. Too late to call in sick to work, no money, hitchhiking, crossing the border on foot, rumpled clothes, bloody, needing a shower, hurt, scared.

I knew you'd be home if I could get there.

You ran a bath for me with sweet-smelling bubbles. You laid out a fresh pair of white BVDs and a T-shirt for me and left me alone to wash off the worst layer of shame.

I remember, it was always the same. I would put on the briefs, and then I'd just get the T-shirt over my head and you would find some reason to come into the bathroom, to get something or put something away. In a glance you would memorize the wounds on my body like a road map— the gashes, bruises, cigarette burns.

Later, in bed, you held me gently, caressing me everywhere, the tenderest touches reserved for the places I was hurt, knowing each and every sore place—inside and out. You didn't flirt with me right away, knowing I wasn't confident enough to feel sexy. But slowly you coaxed my pride back out again by showing me how much you wanted me. You knew it would take you weeks again to melt the stone.

Lately I've read these stories by women who are so angry with stone lovers, even mocking their passion when they finally give way to trust, to being touched. And I'm wondering: did it hurt you the times I couldn't let you touch me? I hope it didn't. You never showed it if it did. I think you knew it wasn't you I was keeping myself safe from. You treated my stone self as a wound that needed loving healing. Thank you. No one's ever done that since. If you were here tonight . . . well, it's hypothetical, isn't it?

I never said these things to you.

Tonight I remember the time I got busted alone, on strange turf. You're probably wincing already, but I have to say this to you. It was the night we drove ninety miles to a bar to meet friends who never showed up. When the police raided the club we were "alone," and the cop with gold bars on his uniform came right over to me and told me to stand up. No wonder, I was the only he-she in the place that night.

He put his hands all over me, pulled up the band of my Jockeys and told his men to cuff me—I didn't have three pieces of women's clothing on.

I wanted to fight right then and there because I knew the chance would be lost in a moment. But I also knew that everyone would be beaten that night if I fought back, so I just stood there. I saw they had pinned your arms behind your back and cuffed your hands. One cop had his arm across your throat. I remember the look in your eyes. It hurts me even now.

They cuffed my hands so tight behind my back I almost cried out. Then the cop unzipped his pants real slow, with a smirk on his face, and ordered me down on my knees. First I thought to myself, *I can't!* Then I said out loud to myself and to you and to him, "*I won't!*" I never told you this before, but something changed inside of me at that moment. I learned the difference between what I can't do and what I refuse to do.

I paid the price for that lesson. Do I have to tell you every detail? Of course not.

When I got out of the tank the next morning you were there. You bailed me out. No charges, they just kept your money. You had waited all night long in that police station. Only I knew how hard it was for you to withstand their leers, their taunts, their threats. I knew you cringed with every sound you strained to hear from back in the cells. You prayed you wouldn't hear me scream. I didn't.

I remember when we got outside to the parking lot you stopped and put your hands lightly on my shoulders and avoided my eyes. You gently rubbed the bloody places on my shirt and said, "I'll never get these stains out."

Damn anyone who thinks that means you were relegated in life to worrying about my ring-around-the-collar.

I knew exactly what you meant. It was such an oddly sweet way of saying, or not saying, what you were feeling. Sort of the way I shut down emotionally when I feel scared and hurt and helpless and say funny little things that seem so out of context.

You drove us home with my head in your lap all the way, stroking my face. You ran the bath. Set out my fresh underwear. Put me to bed. Caressed me carefully. Held me gently.

Later that night I woke up and found myself alone in bed. You were drinking at the kitchen table, head in your hands. You were crying. I took you firmly in my arms and held you, and you struggled and hit my chest with your fists because the enemy wasn't there to fight. Moments later you recalled the bruises on my chest and cried even harder, sobbing, "It's my fault, I couldn't stop them."

I've always wanted to tell you this. In that one moment I knew you really did understand how I felt in life. Choking on anger, feeling so powerless, unable to protect myself or those I loved most, yet fighting back again and again, unwilling to give up. I didn't have the words to tell you this then. I just said, "It'll be OK, it'll be alright." And then we smiled ironically at what I'd said, and I took you back to our bed and made the best love to you I could, considering the shape I was in. You knew not to try to touch me that night. You just ran your fingers through my hair and cried and cried.

When did we get separated in life, sweet warrior woman? We thought we'd won the war of liberation when we embraced the word gay. Then suddenly there were professors and doctors and lawyers coming out of the woodwork telling us that meetings should be run with Robert's Rules of Order. (Who died and left Robert god?)

They drove us out, made us feel ashamed of how we looked. They said we were male chauvinist pigs, the enemy. It was women's hearts they broke. We were not hard to send away, we went quietly.

The plants closed. Something we never could have imagined.

That's when I began passing as a man. Strange to be exiled from your own sex to borders that will never be home.

You were banished too, to another land with your own sex, and yet forcibly apart from the women you loved as much as you tried to love yourself.

For more than twenty years I have lived on this lonely shore, wondering what became of you. Did you wash off your Saturday night makeup in shame? Did you burn in anger when women said, "If I wanted a man I'd be with a real one?"

Are you turning tricks today? Are you waiting tables or learning Word Perfect 5.1?

Are you in a lesbian bar looking out of the corner of your eye for the butchest woman in the room? Do the women there talk about Democratic politics and seminars and co-ops? Are you with women who only bleed monthly on their cycles?

Or are you married in another blue-collar town, lying with an unemployed auto worker who is much more like me than they are, listening for the even breathing of your sleeping children? Do you bind his emotional wounds the way you tried to heal mine?

Do you ever think of me in the cool night?

I've been writing this letter to you for hours. My ribs hurt bad from a recent beating. You know.

I never could have survived this long if I'd never known your love. Yet still I ache with missing you and need you so.

Only you could melt this stone. Are you ever coming back?

The storm has passed now. There is a pink glow of light on the horizon outside my window. I am remembering the nights I fucked you deep and slow until the sky was just this color.

I can't think about you anymore, the pain is swallowing me up. I have to put your memory away, like a precious sepia photograph. There are still so many things I want to tell you, to share with you.

Since I can't mail you this letter, I'll send it to a place where they keep women's memories safe. Maybe someday, passing through this big city, you will stop and read it. Maybe you won't.

Good night, my love.

The Old Days, from *S/HE*

Minnie Bruce Pratt

The Old Days

Standing in the pit of the auditorium, you are someone I don't know yet, handsome in silky shirt and tie, hair clipped close almost as skin on your fine-boned head. You read a story about bar raids in the 50s, a dawn scene on the street between a butch just released from jail and the woman who has waited for her and now smooths her shirt, mourns the indelible blood-stains that will never wash out. As you read, I am the woman who touches the shirt, startled to be so translated to a place I think I've never been.

Yet later I remember that when I got to the trailer she had already show-ered and changed out of her overalls. The plaid shirt, her favorite shirt he had slashed with his knife, was a heap on the bathroom floor. I thought then he had raped her because she was a lesbian. But he had raped her because she was a butch, her cropped hair, her walk, three o'clock in the afternoon, taking out the garbage to the dumpster behind the 7-11, finishing up her shift. I smoothed her shirt over my knees, I pinned the frayed plaid together. I hand-sewed with exquisite care until the colors matched again, trying to keep us together.

In the dim light of the auditorium, you see me standing in your past. Your message on my phone machine the next morning says, "So glad to see a femme from the old days." I write to correct you, to explain about my lesbian-feminist political coming-out. In return, your letter says, of me listen-ing in the auditorium, "While I was reading, it was as if you were moving emotionally with me in the symmetry of a slow dance." I don't understand what you mean, me who begins to wander off in my own direction halfway through every dance with a lover, my attention and my confidence failing. I reply, dubiously, hopefully, "I have so much trouble following—perhaps

WSQ: Women's Studies Quarterly 51: 3 & 4 (Fall/Winter 2023) © 2023 by Minnie Bruce Pratt. All rights reserved.

I haven't had a skillful enough partner?"

When we dance at the Phase, you have a pocketful of quarters and arrange for three slow Anita Bakers in a row. I am nervous and tentative for the first song and a half, you murmur endearments and instructions. Then suddenly I lean back in your arms, look into your eyes, and begin to move as if the dance is air I am flying into, or water I am finning through, finally moving in my element.

When we sit to drink Calistogas and lime with friends, you say, "I never thought I'd dance again with a femme lover in a bar like this, like the ones I came out into." Behind us the jukebox glows like a neon dream, and dykes at the green baize table are clunking their pool cues.

I tell you about my first bar, in North Carolina, almost ten years after the Stonewall Rebellion in New York City, an uprising of lesbian and gay liberation that I had not yet heard of. At that bar we parked around the corner so the police wouldn't photograph our license plates. We had to sign a roster at the door because it was a "private club." Rumor was that the lists got handed over to the police. My friends taught me to give a fake name; sometimes I signed in as Susan B. Anthony.

Everyone always turned around to see who was coming in when the door opened. Everyone knew about the second exit in the dance room, double doors onto the street just in case of a raid, which never came while I was there. You lean toward me, tie loosened, shirt sleeves rolled up in the heat. You pull me into the hard circle of your arm and say, "Baby, no one knows about the second exit except someone from the old days."

Sugar Tit

You say, "I've wondered how you'd explain what it's like to be lovers with someone seen as woman and man." I think of the dance we went to at a friend's house, the whisper about you repeated to me, "Well, it must be a woman, it's with you. But she's wearing men's pants and men's shoes." I don't point out to the whisperer that I am the only woman at the party wearing a skirt. Of the other women, all with short hair and jeans and slacks, some are femmes, some butches with their legs spread apart and their hands in their pockets, some are kiki or androgynous. But no one pushes masculine and feminine to the edge of woman as we do.

We slow-dance, even to the fast songs. Every so often, the same woman, drunk, walks by and says loudly, "They're still doing it. Did you only learn one step at Arthur Murray's?" Whispers, sidelong glances from a group of younger white dykes. We decide to keep dancing, we don't know what else to do. An older crowd arrives, more African-American; a femme friend comes over to us to laugh and joke. When you fast-dance with her, the same drunken woman says, "You can do that—why didn't you?" And you reply, "But this friend isn't the woman I love." I move with you and against you, slipping back and forth, grinding, shifting the earth under our feet.

Later you say to me, "You gave me everything in front of them." How they stared as you pulled me to you, hand in the small of my back, as we danced, your thigh between mine, grinding gently. Your grip on me inexorable and sure, my counter-point crossing you with my hips. How you began to sweat with desire, and the effort of working against my desire, your arms and legs the channel I flowed between, surging like a river released from underground.

You held me as we danced, your shirt wringing wet, and the other women stared and stared at us writhing in and out of womanhood. My skirt swung around my hips. The last man I'd danced with was my husband, whose hands longed for me to hold him like a mother. The last woman wanted me to follow, but her hands weren't strong enough to hold me.

You know that when you hold me, I will follow. You know I will give you my breast, but not as sugar tit. You long to see how much pleasure I will let flow through my nipples like milk, gushing and falling on the ground, perhaps in your mouth, perhaps on my own hands for me to lick off.

Husband

At the March on Washington, the man sitting next to me on the grass asks "Is he your husband?" as I return from kissing you, as you step down from the microphone. On stage Peggy DuPont in beaded white chiffon is ferociously lip-synching and tail-switching a drag queen's answer to the introduction you have given her, praise from a drag king resplendent in your black-on-black suit.

In the audience I hesitate over my answer. Do I change the pronoun and the designation of "husband"? Finally I reply, "Yes, she is."

He hesitates in his turn: "He hasn't gone through the operation?" The complexity of your history crowds around me as I mentally juggle your female birth sex, male gender expression. I say, "She's transgendered, not transsexual."

Up on stage Miss Liberty is reading, with sexy histrionics and flour-
ishes of her enormous torch, a proclamation from a woman who is a U.S.
Senator, a speech that trumpets and drums with the cadences of civil rights.

The man blinks his eyelashes flirtatiously, leans toward me, whiskey on
his breath, waves his hand at his companions, "We're up from North Carolina." Then, femme to femme, he begins to talk of your beauty: "He is perfect.
If I ever wanted a woman it would be someone just like her."

With innuendo and arch look he gives truthful ambiguity to what he
sees in me, in you, something not simply about "gay rights." The queen
whispers in my ear with his sharp steaming breath, "Don't let her get away.
Hang onto him."

Making Pictures:
Disabled Nonbinary Praxis in Leslie Feinberg's *screened-in* Photography Series

Joy Ellison

Abstract: This paper expands historical and theoretical engagements with Leslie Feinberg's life by analyzing the nonbinary and disability politics of hir *screened-in* photography series. Through a consent-based method called "making" photographs, Feinberg challenged the conventions of photographic representation of disabled and transgender people. The *screened-in* series provides a nonbinary political/relational model of gender, sexuality, race, and disability. **Keywords:** Leslie Feinberg; nonbinary; disability; interdependence; photography; transgender

In 2014, as Leslie Feinberg lay dying, zie said, "Remember me as a revolutionary communist" (Feinberg and Pratt 2014). That hir last words were instructions for how zie wished to be remembered highlights the way zie was misrepresented in life. Feinberg is most praised for hir novel *Stone Butch Blues* and often hailed as a lesbian to the exclusion of hir stated transgender identity (Prosser 1998, 171–207). A groundbreaking transgender activist and writer, zie helped to popularize the term "transgender" in its most common usage today: a wide variety of gender non-normative identities that zie hoped would unite in solidarity (Stryker 2017, 153). However, Feinberg's intended meaning for the term "transgender" was more specific than its typical usage. For hir, the category of transgender was comprised of people who (1) experienced state and interpersonal violence because of their gender and (2) chose to organize as transgender (Feinberg 1992). Through this vision of solidarity, Feinberg's conception of gender liberation exceeded and challenged the narrower concept of transgender identity that dominates today.

Although the word "nonbinary" was not in widespread use until the

WSQ: Women's Studies Quarterly 51: 3 & 4 (Fall/Winter 2023) © 2023 by Joy Ellison. All rights reserved.

very end of Feinberg's life, hir praxis can be claimed as an example of nonbinary living. Feinberg's gender disrupted the boundaries between men and women. Hir embodied experience navigating social systems overlapped with that of trans men and trans women but was also distinct, having much in common with that of nonbinary people today. Further, Feinberg's politics made hir nonbinary analysis distinct from contemporary transgender politics that are increasingly invested in articulating gender categories that can be used to claim rights and protections within a neoliberal system that requires stable identities through which it can administrate. Neoliberal courts have struggled to account for the multiplicative impacts of intersecting systems of oppression and often reject the legal claims of transgender people whose genders are not affirmed by medical authorities.[1] Likewise, mainstream transgender movements have sometimes adopted the same logics (Bassichis, Lee, and Spade 2011). In contrast, Feinberg defiantly insisted on hir "right to be complex" (Feinberg 1998, 70). Hir Marxist-feminist attention to the intersections between gender and other social systems distinguished hir analysis. Feinberg further articulated a version of transgender/nonbinary politics that was at home in feminist and queer circles. Zie was unwilling to disavow hir deep roots within lesbian communities, calling hirself a transgender lesbian. Zie insisted that transgender women and gender nonnormative people had long been integral parts of queer women's communities. Zie remained committed to fighting for the inclusion of transgender women in feminist circles, playing an important role in protests at the Michigan Womyn's Music Festival (Feinberg 1997, 109–19). Feinberg was assuredly transgender, but zie can be more specifically described as both nonbinary and feminist.

Feinberg's thinking provides a useful starting point for developing a nonbinary politic that serves today's radical movements. Hir theory and praxis address tensions and limitations in today's mainstream conception of transgender/nonbinary identity: Feinberg's analysis does not rest on a binary between transgender and cisgender, which has been criticized for its failure to account for the ways the gendered oppression of Black people challenges the category of cisgender (Bey 2022). Instead, zie emphasized the social position of gender nonnormative people, rather than explicating identity categories. This creates an opportunity for solidarity among gender nonnormative people that does not obscure differences between them. Further, Feinberg's attention to structural oppression draws awareness to the ways that gender is always embedded in other social categories. Thus, hir nonbinary politics lays the groundwork for a gender liberation movement that arises out of an awareness of intersectionality and interdependence.

To explicate Feinberg's nonbinary politics, I analyze hir final major creative project: the *screened-in* photography series. Feinberg created the series while disabled by Lyme/+ disease. Through a consent-based technique that zie called "making" photographs, Feinberg challenged the dominant visual rhetoric aimed at disabled and transgender/nonbinary people. Hir photographs emphasize hir structural and affective relationships and blur the boundaries between hirself and the wider world. Themes of interdependence and solidarity enliven hir unique visual art. Drawing theory from Feinberg's art allows me to better describe the unique ways of living and struggling that hir analysis allows.

I call the analysis expressed by the *screened-in* series a nonbinary political/relational politic. I draw the term *political/relational* from Alison Kafer's discussion of disability, a choice justified by Feinberg's emphasis on disability in hir photography and which opens new connections between disability studies and transgender/nonbinary studies. Kafer proposes the political/relational model of disability as an alternative to both the medical and social models (2013, 4). A political/relational model of disability rejects pathologization but affirms disabled people who seek medical care, much as Feinberg rejected medical authority while affirming gender-related medical services. Kafer's political/relational model draws on queer and feminist critiques of identity to describe disability as a complex experience that evades easy binaries (2013, 9). She notes that the experience of requiring assistance in the activities of daily living provides a unique standpoint from which disabled people can rethink cultural ideas of independence and self-sufficiency. Thus, disability is a valuable form of difference that can provide insight into intimacy and relationships, not just among communities of people but with the other-than-human natural world as well (Kafer 2013, 83). Feinberg's photography expands this insight. Hir work engages gender, disability, sexuality, and race through a political/relational model that troubles binaries between pain and pleasure, separation and solidarity, and socially created barriers and physical limitations. Feinberg's work resists analyses that take up singular aspects of identity without engaging the interlocking nature of oppressive systems. The *screened-in* series presents a complex understanding of embodiment that extends Kafer's political/relational model of disability into a political/relational model of gender and sexuality that can be a basis for a revitalized nonbinary politic.

Through the *screened-in* series, Feinberg used hir camera to document hir life and community, the Hawley-Green neighborhood of Syracuse, New York. Zie created the *screened-in* series at a time when Lyme/+ disease caused hir "physical agony" (Feinberg n.d.). Photography provided a means for hir to continue communicating after writing and speaking became too painful (Feinberg 2011c). The *screened-in* series is hir most formal photo project within hir larger practice. It included 556 photographs posted to hir Flickr account, an online photography-sharing platform, in albums with titles ranging from "gender thru my lens" to "Palestine will be free!" (Feinberg n.d.).

Feinberg's photography reflects the Marxist-feminist analysis that animated all hir work. Zie wrote, "I decided right away that I wasn't going to 'take' pictures, I was going to make them"(Feinberg 2011c). In contrast to profit-driven, voyeuristic photography, Feinberg's photography centered community. Making photographs was a collaborative, consent-based practice. This was evident throughout hir process, from the subjects zie chose, to hir decision to release hir photographs under a Creative Commons license (Feinberg n.d.). Zie wrote, "I would ask permission before making a photo . . . and then show them the photo and delete it if they didn't like it for any reason" (Feinberg 2011c). Feinberg's commitment to making photographs was challenged when hir disability kept hir at home, making it impossible to ask permission (Feinberg 2011c). Feinberg adjusted to this limitation by adapting hir photography technique. Zie wrote, "I've paid conscious attention to distance, angle, composition, time of day, shadow, blur, manipulation of pixels and other techniques to protect the anonymity of my neighbors" (Feinberg 2011c). The resulting photographs document unique forms of beauty that arise from Feinberg's disabled, nonbinary embodiment.

Feinberg's method of "making pictures" created a disabled, nonbinary counternarrative to dominant visual rhetorics. Both transgender and disabled communities have been photographed without their consent and in a manner that others them. Photography has often been used as documentation of physical evidence of disabled and gendered embodiment for outside authorities to evaluate. Rosemarie Garland-Thomson writes that photography of disability "invoke[s] the extraordinariness of the disabled body in order to secure the ordinariness of the viewer" (2001, 341). In the nineteenth and twentieth centuries, most of the photography of disabled people were medical photographs, which were used toward the goal of curing and controlling disabled people (Garland-Thomson 2001, 336). New photography conventions have emerged in the contemporary era, but their effects on disabled people are much the same. The same is true of photographs of transgender people. Julian Carter, David Getsy, and Trish Salah argue that for trans people, "photography's indexical function places the trans body in a double bind: it must declare its visibility, but in doing so, it initiates the diagnostic gaze that demands that the temporal process of transition be legible on the body"(2014, 471). In contrast, Feinberg refuses to make hir disabled and nonbinary body extraordinary, nor does zie portray it as proof of hir disabled, transgender experience. Instead, Feinberg uses the method of "making pictures" to depict and foster interdependent relationships with hir larger communities.

Political/Relational Critiques of Photography in the Art of Disabled Transgender People

While Feinberg's method of "making pictures" is unique, hir critique of photography is rooted in feminist visual rhetorics, such as that of lesbian feminist photographer Joan E. Biren (Manders 2019). It is also in harmony with emerging thought developed by disabled transgender artists, particularly those who are nonbinary, genderqueer, or otherwise resistant to binary gender categories. These artists critique photographic conventions by calling attention to the structural relationships that hinder transgender and disabled people's ability to evade the lenses aimed at them. For example, Eli Clare, a white genderqueer trans man with cerebral palsy, wrote a poem entitled "Photographs," inspired by the photographs of able-bodied and able-minded artist Abraham Menashe. Menashe photographed what he called "the multi-handicapped institutionalized individual"(1980, 1). In the fourth stanza of his poem, Clare describes Menashe's work: "bodies tumble roll / rise *crazy clumsy* arriving / again body against / body *awkward* / *ugly* each inviting / the next tongue to tooth sweet / sweet skin *twisted* /*deformed* a thoughtless /rhythm *freak monster* breath to muscle / to ragged breath grace lives / tangled and strong" (2007, 97). Clare's poem moves between a hegemonic reading of Menashe's work, in which disabled people are inflected with ideas of defect and otherness, and crip counterreadings, which appreciate what disabled cultural worker Mia Mingus would call the "magnificence" of his subjects (Mingus 2011). Clare writes of Menashe, "Tell me: / did that woman in the corridor / invite your camera? . . . when you leave, the door will lock behind you" (2007, 97). In this way, Clare describes the damage done by the nonconsensual photography of oppressed communities and draws attention to unequal relationships that require transformation.

Poet Kay Ulanday Barrett, a disabled queer, transgender, philipinx-amerikan person, also describes the impact of photography in their poem "YOU are SO Brave." This piece takes the form of a series of statements reflecting intertwined ableism, transphobia, queer antagonism, and racism. They write, "Wait (laughs) is that supposed to be a girl? / Awwww, you so cute when you dance. Let me take a picture of you holding your back." By interweaving microaggressions about their gender and race with comments aimed at their body and demands for photographs that present physical evidence of their disability, Barrett describes their experiences of multiple oppressions as simultaneous and interlocking, a key element of political/ relational critique. Barrett's and Clare's poetry about photography provides an important queer, disabled, nonbinary critique of photographic visual rhetoric and is an example of how nonbinary people have used creative modalities to express their personal experiences and systematic analyses simultaneously. Feinberg's work is another part of this emerging creative intervention.

The Political/Relational Model in the *screened-in* Series

While Feinberg's work refuses narratives of hir disability as confining, the *screened-in* series is neither a portrayal of triumph over disability nor an evasion of hir physical pain and the emotional toll of ableism and trans-phobia. The photograph *walled in* typifies the complex representation of disability in the *screened-in* series (Feinberg 2009d). In this photograph, a box of tissues and an alarm clock sit in the foreground, with a window in the middle ground of the image. The composition highlights the bars of the window against the brick wall, showing the overlay of patterns of light and shadow. By finding beauty in the sunshine and shadow, *walled in* refuses narratives of Feinberg's life at home as tragic, also implying a distinction between hir confinement at home as opposed to involuntary confinement in nursing homes or prison. Feinberg also posted *walled in* in a different album titled "dis/able/access." This album contains five photographs about disability that recontextualize the meaning of *walled in*. In the first picture, Feinberg photographed a set of stairs covered in an intricate pattern of shadows. Like many of Feinberg's photographs, this image uses textures, patterns, and symmetry to create interest. However, by entitling this photo *stairs shadow barrier*, Feinberg makes it clear that these stairs prevent the access of many disabled people (Feinberg 2009b). Next, Feinberg photographed a locked fence in front of a green field. On each side of the frame are two signs emblazoned with the wheelchair symbol, with arrows directing disabled people to other entrances. The photograph is titled *no access = disability* (Feinberg 2010d). These two photographs invoke the social model of disability. In the context of the photographs *stairs shadow barrier* and *no access = disability*, the meaning of *walled in* shifts and the physical restriction Feinberg experienced comes to the fore. Hir real pain, both physical and emotional, is brought into relief and placed alongside these other representations of access barriers. Nonetheless, *walled in* presents an experience of disability that cannot be fully explained by the social model of disability. Feinberg's impairments, including physical pain, cannot be ameliorated by access alone and thus require a political/relational response.

Feinberg further extends the political/relational model through photographs that express feelings of connection and solidarity with other disabled people across physical isolation. In *tower conversations*, zie photographed disabled people and elders waiting outside a clinic at a nursing home visible from hir apartment (Feinberg 2011f). The differences between Feinberg's images and dominant visual rhetorics are striking. Thompson notes that photographs of disabled people favor close-ups of faces and bodies, rendering them exceptional and other. Photographs of transgender people often accomplish the same effect through images of dressing and makeup application (Serano 2009, 35–53). In contrast, in Feinberg's photographs it is impossible to surmise details about hir subjects. Instead, their relationships with each other are centered. The patio of the clinic is a lively site of conversation and community. While photographers usually approach disabled and transgender bodies as though they are evidence to be evaluated by outside authorities, Feinberg's photography focuses on relationships between disabled and transgender people and on their social positions.

Screened-In and Out: Subverting Diagnosis and Separation, Creating Solidarity

Feinberg's photographs evade diagnostic gazes leveled at both hir disability and hir gender by using light and shadow to produce ambiguity. In a photograph entitled *self-portrait in dawn light,* Feinberg photographed hir shadow in the darkened hallway of hir home (Feinberg 2011e). This photograph preserves the outline of hir silhouette as zie would have seen it, thus emphasizing hir own perspective. The angle of the wall distorts the outline of Feinberg's body, preventing a diagnostic gaze from gaining information about hir disability or gender. In this way, Feinberg's work is like the documentary work of Kai Green, a Black transgender scholar and activist. Green purposefully creates space for what they call "the unknowable" (Green 2015, 190). Likewise, *self-portrait in dawn light* evades the medicalized gaze, while emphasizing hir own embodied perspective, the starting point for a political-relational critique of gender, ability, and sexuality.

While Feinberg's photographs maintain the unknowability of hir body, they expose disabled and transgender life as pleasurable. *Self-portrait in dawn light* is one of four photographs that document the reflection of light and shadows on hir walls (Feinberg 2011e). These photographs document the beauty Feinberg found while living exclusively within hir apartment. Feinberg wrote, "Illness keeps me home, much of the time in a darkened room. Dawn, dusk and dark are the least painful times for me to make photographs" (Feinberg 2011c). Hir photography presents this limitation both as painful and as a unique opportunity for beauty. By preserving both the pains and pleasures and the knowns and unknowns of hir life, Feinberg's work refuses binary, simplistic understandings of disability, sexuality, and gender. Hir commitment to this complexity underscores the possibility opened by a nonbinary political/relational politic.

The *screened-in* series depicts Feinberg's interdependent relationships with human and nonhuman communities, defying the expectation that disabled and transgender people are separate from the natural world. The majority of *screened-in* photographs show nature as Feinberg saw it from hir home: skylines at dusk, hir neighborhood blanketed in snow, and a community garden. In the photograph *screened out_bat*, a bat perches against the screen of Feinberg's window (Feinberg 2011d). Sixteen of Feinberg's photographs foreground the screen of hir windows against views of the outside world. For example, *crayon houses* uses the texture of the window screen to blur the view of colorful townhouses, creating an image that resembles an impressionist painting (Feinberg 2010a). These photographs present Feinberg's windows as sites through which zie allowed the outside world into hir living space. Like hir photographs of natural light and screens, these photographs show windows as barriers, but permeable ones. They document how, from hir home, Feinberg remained connected to flora, fauna, and the elements. In this way, Feinberg's work takes part in an emerging disability justice movement rooted in the concept of interdependence with both the human and the other-than-human world.

Interdependence is a key component of Feinberg's thinking, manifested most directly in hir production of images showing connections between hir body and the other-than-human natural world. In *tree_me*, Feinberg photographed hir shadow while standing on a street corner (Feinberg 2009c). Feinberg's body casts a shadow that overlaps with the shadow of a bare tree, creating the impression that the tree is shooting through hir. Strikingly, *tree_me* is similar to a painting entitled *Circle Stories / Eli Clare*, painted by disabled artist Riva Lehrer through a collaborative process with Clare. In this painting, Clare crouches on one knee in a forest, in front of a river lined with plants. As in *tree_me*, a sapling emerges from Clare's chest (Kafer 2013, 146–47). Both photographs resist dominant narratives that cast the other-than-human world as opposite to transgender and disabled people (Kafer 2013, 147). While disabled people are assumed to be unable to access the other-than-human natural world, transgender people are often presented as in a conflicted relationship to "nature," in which transition is described as a movement away from a natural state. Dean Spade reminds us that "there is no naturalized gendered body," as all forms of gender include body modification (Spade n.d.). Feinberg's *tree_me* and Lehrer's painting challenge the idea that cisgender and able-bodied people are natural and separate from the larger world, presenting an alternative way to understand the interdependence of all human beings and the other-than-human world.

Marxist-Feminist Interventions in the *screened-in* Series

Feinberg's photographs disrupt understandings of relationships with nature as individualized and as marked by sentimentality or recreation. Instead, Feinberg extends the concept of interdependence into a wider notion of justice that includes a robust political/relational analysis of social systems, through photographs of labor and queer relationships. This subject matter reflects hir love for photographing nature and hir chosen family, but also hir Marxist-feminist commitments. Feinberg photographed humans working the land, refusing a separation between a love of the natural world and the act of laboring on and with it. For example, Feinberg took eleven photographs of hir loved ones working in a community garden (Feinberg 2010b). Not only are these relationships with queer people but their character is nonnormative, reflective of both queer and disabled sociality. In a sequence of four pictures, zie photographed Pratt investigating a construction site (Feinberg 2010c). Feinberg's engagement with the world outside of hir apartment is facilitated by hir relationship with hir loved ones. The celebratory tone of these photographs of working-class people contrasts with Feinberg's presentations of wealth and the ruling classes.

Feinberg's condemnation of the capitalist system is depicted in a diptych about eviction. In the first photograph, *eviction_police*, Feinberg photographs an eviction in progress (Feinberg 2011b). Two police cars are parked in the roadway, and belongings are piled in front of an apartment building. An adult covers their face, appearing to cry. Another adult holds a child in their arms. In keeping with Feinberg's commitment to consent, their faces are not visible. Instead, the naked power of the capitalist system, enforced by police, is on display. In the second image, *after eviction*, Feinberg photographed the apartment building with its door flung open and empty boxes, shelves, mattresses, and a shopping cart cast around the parking lot (Feinberg 2011a). Although Feinberg provided no commentary on the photographs, they are deeply moving, especially viewed in the context of hir photographs of daily life in the same complex. Feinberg's photographs of the workings of capitalism as visible from hir window highlight its racist components and the resilience and labor of hir Black neighbors. In this way, hir work presents an understanding of racism as a part of an interlocking system of oppression.

Nonbinary Political/Relational Approaches to White Anti-racism

In hir photography and written work, Feinberg portrayed relationships between various systems of oppression to foster solidarity and collective action against them. In *"Jerry rescue"_continuing impact*, Feinberg photographed a child standing in front of a monument to an event in Syracuse history that typified hir conception of solidarity (Feinberg 2009a). The "Jerry Rescue" monument marks an 1851 mass action to free William Henry, known as Jerry. Henry escaped from slavery in Missouri in 1843, settling in Syracuse in 1849 or 1850. On October 1, 1851, officials arrested him on a minor offense. He did not resist, unaware that his capture would be the pretext for returning him to bondage under the Fugitive Slave Act. When he realized what was happening, he escaped. When slavecatchers found him, he fought back. At the urging of Black abolitionist Reverend Jermain Loguen, the Syracuse Vigilance Committee stormed the police station and freed Henry (Hunter 1993, 124–26). He brazenly printed in Syracuse newspapers his address and invitations to other runaways seeking freedom. He became infamous for his leadership in the "Jerry Rescue"—one of the very few successful fugitive slave rescues in the country. During his lifetime he was hailed as the "Underground Railroad King" and worked closely with Frederick Douglass, Henry Highland Garnet, Gerrit Smith, Samuel May, and other leading figures in the abolitionist movement. He was ordained in the AME Zion Church and utilized his many church connections to help fugitives and assist the self-emancipated in finding jobs and making the transition to freedom. In 2011 Reverend Jermain Loguen was one of the early inductees into the National Abolition Hall of Fame. This unsung hero held a passionate lifelong stance for freedom, human rights and equality, his dagger-sharp oratory as preacher and writer, and his internal turmoils as someone who, in his own words, would have preferred to have been "a still quiet man, but oppression has made me mad." Following the Jerry Rescue, abolitionists used the phrase "at the Jerry level," to describe direct action supporting Black people and the belief that breaking the law in resistance to slavery was justified (Murphy 2016). It is unsurprising that Feinberg would photograph this memorial, as zie spent hir life seeking out ways to act "at the Jerry level." That practice is documented in Feinberg's picture with incarcerated Black transgender activist CeCe McDonald (Feinberg 2012).

Feinberg photographed McDonald while visiting her as a member of the Free CeCe support community, an organization that Black trans woman activist Tourmaline described as literal in their intention to free McDonald. In 2011, McDonald was arrested and incarcerated in a men's prison after defending herself against an attacker who screamed racist and transphobic slurs at her and her friends (Feinberg 2014, 9). Feinberg was charged with felony property damage for spray painting "Free CeCe" on the wall of the county jail during a noise protest for McDonald. Zie was held without bond for three days in the same Minneapolis jail as McDonald (Hamel 2012). On the first day of McDonald's trial, Feinberg and McDonald made a photograph of themselves touching hands through the glass during a visit. This photo is printed in the introduction of the new edition of *Stone Butch Blues*, along with a link to a photo album of pictures from the Free CeCe campaign entitled "This Is What Solidarity Looks Like" (Feinberg 2014, 10). Feinberg's documentation of this campaign illustrates what solidarity meant to hir: direct, material support and resistance arising from an awareness of the interdependence of oppressed communities.

Feinberg's descriptions of solidarity are instructive for other white disabled and transgender/nonbinary people, because they provide a rare example of white people engaging deeply in anti-racist work. Hir early written work has been justifiably critiqued for using Black and Native experiences to establish the legitimacy of white transgender subjectivity (Somerville 2000, 172–74). However, hir photography raises a fruitful question: if white people understand themselves as interdependent with Black and Indigenous people and communities of color, how might their political struggles transform?

Conclusion

Consistently emphasizing interdependence, Feinberg's *screened-in* series explores themes of gendered embodiment, disability, the other-than-human world, queerness, labor, solidarity, and anti-racism. The *screened-in* series can be claimed as a nonbinary cultural production for two reasons. First, it challenges a range of binaries: disability/impairment, separation/ solidarity, human/other-than-human, and the gender binary. Second, it is rooted in Feinberg's vision of gender liberation for all in a way that challenges the assumed binary between cisgender and transgender identities. Through a queer and feminist critique of identity and a keen attention to how political systems shape embodied experience, Feinberg extends Kafer's political/relational model of disability into a political/relational model of gender and sexuality. Feinberg's political/relational approach to gender and sexuality is a fruitful starting point for a nonbinary theory and praxis. By emphasizing building interdependent relationships and intersectional movements, Feinberg presents a kind of gender liberation that challenges neoliberalism instead of reinforcing it through demands for inclusion. Feinberg's political/relational nonbinary praxis builds on existing feminist and transgender movements, pointing a path toward the anti-racist, anti-ableist, Marxist-feminist revolution zie so desired.

Joy Ellison is an assistant professor of gender and women's studies at the University of Rhode Island. They are the coauthor of *The Afterward: Sylvia Rivera and Marsha P. Johnson in the Medieval Imaginary* (Medieval Feminist Forum, 2019). Their research covers transgender history in the Midwestern United States from 1945 to 2000. They can be reached at joy.ellison@uri.edu.

Notes
1. On intersectionality, see Crenshaw 1991.

Works Cited

Barrett, Kay Ulanday. 2016. "YOU are SO Brave." In *When the Chant Comes*, 62–64. New York: Topside Press.

Bassichis, Morgan, Alexander Lee, and Dean Spade. 2011. "Building an Abolitionist Trans and Queer Movement with Everything We've Got." In *Captive Genders: Trans Embodiment and the Prison Industrial Complex*, ed. Nat Smith and Eric A. Stanley, 15–40. Oakland, CA: AK Press.

Bey, Marquis. 2022. *Cistem Failure: Essays on Blackness and Cisgender*. Durham, NC: Duke University Press Books.

Carter, Julian B., David J. Getsy, and Trish Salah. 2014. "Introduction." *TSQ: Transgender Studies Quarterly* 1 (4): 469–81. https://doi.org/10.1215/23289252-2815183.

Clare, Eli. 2007. *The Marrow's Telling: Words in Motion*. Ypsilanti, MI: Homofactus Press.

Crenshaw, Kimberle. 1991. "Mapping the Margins: Intersectionality, Identity Politics, and Violence against Women of Color." *Stanford Law Review* 43 (6): 1241–99. https://doi.org/10.2307/1229039.

Feinberg, Leslie. 1992. *Transgender Liberation: A Movement Whose Time Has Come*. New York: World View Forum.

———. 1997. *Transgender Warriors: Making History from Joan of Arc to Marsha P. Johnson and Beyond*. Boston, MA: Beacon Press.

———. 1998. *Trans Liberation: Beyond Pink Or Blue*. Boston, MA: Beacon Press.

———. 2009a. *"Jerry rescue"_continuing impact*. Photo. https://www.flickr.com/photos/transgenderwarrior/3285883674/.

———. 2009b. *stairs shadow barrier*. Photo. https://www.flickr.com/photos/transgenderwarrior/3671221839/.

———. 2009c. *tree_me*. Photo. https://www.flickr.com/photos/transgenderwarrior/4919488182/.

———. 2009d. *walled ins*. Photo. https://www.flickr.com/photos/transgenderwarrior/4195159433/.

———. 2010a. *crayon houses*. Photo. https://www.flickr.com/photos/transgenderwarrior/6139588893/.

———. 2010b. *loved ones waving_garden*. Photo. https://www.flickr.com/photos/transgenderwarrior/6162470870/.

———. 2010c. *Minnie Bruce Pratt_curiosity (quartet-1)*. Photo. https://www.flickr.com/photos/transgenderwarrior/6203777655/.

———. 2010d. *no access = disability*. Photo. https://www.flickr.com/photos/transgenderwarrior/4878294301/.

———. 2011a. *after eviction (diptych-2)*. Photo. https://www.flickr.com/photos/transgenderwarrior/6715256973/.

———. 2011b. *eviction_police (diptych-1)*. Photo. https://www.flickr.com/photos/transgenderwarrior/6715255663/.

———. 2011c. "'Screened-in' Series." (album description). Flickr. August 26, 2011. https://www.flickr.com/photos/transgenderwarrior/sets/72157627520720784.

———. 2011d. *screened out_bat*. Photo. https://www.flickr.com/photos/transgenderwarrior/6151366231/.

———. 2011e. *self-portrait in dawn light*. Photo. https://www.flickr.com/photos/transgenderwarrior/6151365139/.

———. 2011f. *tower_conversations*. Photo. https://www.flickr.com/photos/transgenderwarrior/6152017746/.

———. 2012. *CeCe McDonald, introduction, jail*. Photo. https://www.flickr.com/photos/transgenderwarrior/7194732366/.

———. 2014. *Stone Butch Blues: A Novel*. 20th anniv. ed. Self-published by author. https://lesliefeinberg.net/wp-content/uploads/2015/08/Stone-Butch-Blues-by-Leslie-Feinberg.pdf.

———. n.d. "Casualty of an Undeclared War." *Transgender Warrior*. http://www.transgenderwarrior.org/lymeseries.html. Accessed November 16, 2018.

Feinberg, Leslie, and Minnie Bruce Pratt. 2014. "Leslie Feinberg (1949–2014)." *Leslie Feinberg*, March 27, 2014. http://www.lesliefeinberg.net/self/.

Garland-Thomson, Rosemarie. 2001. "Seeing the Disabled: Visual Rhetorics of Disability in Popular Photography." In *The New Disability History: American Perspectives*, ed. Paul K. Longmore and Lauri Umansky, 335. New York: New York University Press.

Green, Kai M. 2015. "The Essential I/Eye in We: A Black TransFeminist Approach to Ethnographic Film." *Black Camera* 6 (2): 187–200.

Hamel, Kris. 2012. "Leslie Feinberg upon Release from Jail: 'Free CeCe McDonald!'" *Worker's World*, June 15, 2012. https://www.workers.org/2012/us/free_cece_mcdonald_0621/.

Hunter, Carol. 1993. *To Set the Captives Free*. New York: Garland.

Kafer, Alison. 2013. *Feminist, Queer, Crip*. Bloomington: Indiana University Press.

Koyama, Emi. 2006. "Whose Feminism Is It Anyway?" In *The Transgender Studies Reader*, ed. Susan Stryker and Stephen Whittle, 698–705. New York: Routledge.

Manders, Kerry. 2019. "Photos of Lesbian Lives Meant to Inspire a Movement." *New York Times*, April 8, 2019. https://www.nytimes.com/2019/04/08/lens/lesbian-lives-movement-jeb.html.

Menashe, Abraham. 1980. *Inner Grace: Photographs*. New York: Knopf.

Mingus. 2011. "Moving toward the Ugly: A Politic beyond Desirability." *Leaving Evidence* (blog), August 22, 2011. https://leavingevidence.wordpress.com/2011/08/22/moving-toward-the-ugly-a-politic-beyond-desirability/.

Murphy, Angela F. 2016. *The Jerry Rescue: The Fugitive Slave Law, Northern Rights, and the American Sectional Crisis.* Oxford: Oxford University Press.

Prosser, Jay. 1998. *Second Skins: The Body Narratives of Transsexuality.* New York: Columbia University Press.

Serano, Julia. 2009. *Whipping Girl: A Transsexual Woman on Sexism and the Scapegoating of Femininity.* New York: Seal Press.

Somerville, Siobhan B. 2000. *Queering the Color Line: Race and the Invention of Homosexuality in American Culture.* Durham, NC: Duke University Press.

Spade, Dean. n.d. "Dress to Kill, Fight to Win." *LTTR.* http://lttr.org/journal/1/dress-to-kill-fight-to-win. Accessed January 17, 2019.

Stryker, Susan. 2017. *Transgender History: The Roots of Today's Revolution.* 2nd ed. Berkeley: Seal Press.

Support CeCe. 2014. "Cece's Release: What a Welcome!" *Support CeCe McDonald!,* January 17, 2014. https://supportcece.wordpress.com/2014/01/17/ceces-release-what-a-welcome/.

PART III. **BOOK REVIEWS**

Generations of Ex-lovers Cannot Fail: Rethinking Lesbian Feminism Today

Cait McKinney's *Information Activism: A Queer History of Lesbian Media Technologies*, Durham, NC: Duke University Press, 2020

Rox Samer's *Lesbian Potentiality and Feminist Media in the 1970s*, Durham, NC: Duke University Press, 2022

Jack Jen Gieseking

Executive Director Sarah Chinn of the (then) Center of Lesbian and Gay Studies (CLAGS)[1] co-organized the Lesbians in the 1970s conference in 2010 to "commemorate, celebrate, and evaluate the diverse contributions of lesbians over the course of the 1970s" (Chinn 2011). In her *CLAGSNews* newsletter retrospective, Chinn delightedly records that hopeful estimates for 250 registrants were surpassed with 450 attendees(!) "filling the halls of the [CUNY] Graduate Center with more lesbians than the building has ever seen and most likely ever will see!" She adds how exciting it was that paper proposals "came from younger women (and a couple of men), who were engaging lesbian experiences in the 1970s as meaningful topics for academic study and political analysis." Over a decade later, academic work about 1970s lesbian feminism has finally begun to accumulate—by an ever more diversely gendered authorship—including the publication of two central, insightful texts: Cait McKinney's *Information Activism: A Queer History of Lesbian Media Technologies* and Rox Samer's *Lesbian Potentiality and Feminist Media in the 1970s*.

These books fit together; they are complementary texts. Both argue against limiting notions of lesbian feminism as any fixed, certain framework or as defined by any one group of people. Both authors write against any claim to lesbian feminism by trans exclusionary radical feminists (TERFs). Instead, lesbian feminism is multitudinous and malleable—in fact, what is lesbian (or the 1970s-style of capitalized Lesbian) is still being constructed and will be constructed again. Both books draw on new archives and texts and rethink previously studied materials in important ways, and both are packed with readable, powerful prose from which to rethink, reimagine, write, and teach about lesbians in the 1970s. While the authors do bring in

WSQ: Women's Studies Quarterly 51: 3 & 4 (Fall/Winter 2023) © 2023 by Jack Jen Gieseking. All rights reserved.

race and disability and provide significant theorizing around both concepts, the most significant shared weakness is the uneven attention both books pay to these positionalities, whereby some areas are stronger than others.

Published in 2020, McKinney's *Information Activism*, a finalist for the Lambda Literary Award, does the profound work of turning lesbian information-making and -sharing into an utterly invigorating read. The book's principal concept, "information activism," is the work of "women who responded to their frustrated desire for information about lesbian history and lesbian life by generating that information themselves" and thus produced "how movement-related information is stored, sorted, searched for, and retrieved by lesbian-feminist activists serving communities they care about" (2, 13). In other words, McKinney traces how this "not-so-sexy shuffling of documents . . . about sex and sexuality" was a practice of information activism (9). This massive effort was a project of survival, connection, and self-understanding and collective insight.

Bridging the emergence of 1970s lesbian feminist media with the shifts to 1980s lesbian database creation and maintenance, computer use, and software selection, McKinney frames their *Information Activism* through the production of lesbian information infrastructure, which also will be of interest to infrastructure studies. The first of the book's four core chapters focuses on that most popular of lesbian documents, newsletters, the "connective tissue that made readers aware of the larger information infrastructure" (35). The following chapters examine phone hotlines, indices, and, finally, the digitization practices of lesbian archival materials. McKinney is especially enthralled with—and good at—making visible the labor of lesbian information-making. Even as an expert in this area, I was repeatedly wowed by how little access lesbians had to the positive, accessible, and organized information that we could so easily rely on by the twenty-first century, even before search engines, thanks to amateur-cum-professional archivists and librarians and activists.

McKinney's book pays homage to the many excellent books that have examined lesbian print culture before it, like Agatha Beins's (2017) *Liberation in Print: Feminist Periodicals and Social Movement Identity*. The first chapter in *Information Activism*, "The Internet That Lesbians Built: Newsletter Networks," dives into not just the arguments and ideas of the newsletters but also how their mutual precarity and interdependence served to turn what seemed like nothing (from people told they were not worthy) into so much infrastructure. The next chapter turns to the nightly call records, including the "trolls," and marginalia ("a treasure trove of doodles, jokes, idiosyncratic handwriting, and notes passed among volunteers") of the Lesbian Switchboard phone hotline, which connected callers with information, people, and places to make sense of their own lives. Here, McKinney aims to unpack "what kinds of media practices are remembered, or *rememberable*, within feminist archives," beyond print practices alone (69, emphasis in the original). Much of the book also tends to the emotional and affective work of producing care through these networking practices, like in the third chapter on *The Lesbian Periodicals Index* (Potter 1986) and *Black Lesbians: An Annotated Bibliography* (Roberts 1981), which relay how "lesbian indexers worked as benevolent infiltrators within conditions of gendered, racialized, and technological exclusion from control over information" (122). Still, McKinney notes, many efforts toward anti-racism failed through the ways the "white lesbian-feminist economy" privileged "middle class ideals of sisterhood without difference" (120).

The final chapter's reveal of the slow and careful archival work of digitizing many of the Lesbian Herstory Archives' materials pays special attention to the way names, genders, and pronouns shift for those recorded in, organizing, and tending these materials. "Making this infrastructure together, bit by bit, materializes a desire for history and gives life to lesbian feminism," because, as McKinney also notes, "these activists needed to be able to easily revise how they were describing political and identity-laden materials in databases in order to be sensitive to shifting community values" (44, 11). The text is a strong contribution to feminist media studies, communication studies, and lesbian feminist queer trans theory more broadly.

Now, let's dish on *Lesbian Potentiality*. The potentiality of what "lesbian" is, was, and yet could be (or vice versa) derives from the dream of the wide range of lesbian feminists: the "potential that gendered and sexual life could and would someday be substantially different, that heteropatriarchy may topple, and that women would be the ones to topple it" (227). "Lesbian potentiality" is a theoretical concept as well as a way of operating in the world that builds from and contributes to queer trans feminist theory. Lesbian potentiality does the work of "connecting potentialities past and present [in a way] that neither obfuscates nor reifies their differences" and illuminates "social movement history that also attends to its privations— the what was *and* the what could have been" (7).

A film scholar, Samer especially draws on audience studies to frame their arguments across the book by placing chapters on film and science fiction side by side, an unusual, energizing pairing. Samer argues that what functions under the "lesbian sign" did its "most robust work in feminist media . . . cultures of the second half of the 1970s" (2). Lesbian potentiality and its counterpart, "impotentiality," persist as a method for all those committed to social change in the integral work of "not knowing what will come of the actions taken at its end and includes the possibility of expanding or dampening momentum" (227). In the end, these insights are clearly not just a feminist and queer contribution but, more so, should be read as a stunningly trans critique.

The writing of the core chapters becomes progressively more captivating throughout, and the chapters read together well, though they each will also draw specific audiences. The author's writing brings even the most recently converted sci-fi and avant-garde neophyte (I wave) up to speed quickly. After a devastatingly delicious theoretical mic drop of an introduction, the first two chapters examine a selection of 1970s feminist experimental and documentary films. This introduction is a must-read regarding how temporality and possibility shape lesbian, queer, trans, and feminist thinking.

The first chapter looks at feminist experimental films, including video newsletters sent from feminists between cities. The next chapter, "Producing Freedom," is on prisoner and ex-prisoner documentaries set in, and just out of, women's prisons. Prison studies scholars get a rare glimpse into post-Attica uprising experiences from women's perspectives. The third chapter, "Raising Fannish Consciousness," provides a riveting account of the ways that 1970s feminist science fiction (SF) fanzines and conferences (featuring the likes of Joanna Russ and Samuel Delany, among others) created new models of feminist communication and self-understanding and collective insight that helped to define (lesbian) feminist correspondence and understandings of the self as (lesbian) feminist.

My favorite chapter comes last. With all the emphasis I can put on a page: "Tip/Alli: Cutting a Transfeminist Genealogy of Siblinghood" belongs as a reading on every Intro to GWS/S, Trans, Feminist, Gender, Sexuality, etc. Studies course out there. Samer relays a new gendered or trans reading of the seemingly well-known outing story of one of 1970s feminist SF's most famous authors, James Tiptree Jr., who was in fact Alice B. Sheldon and who later identified as a Lesbian (*L* intended). In their nuanced exploration of Tip/Alli's multitudinous gender—primarily focusing on their slash signature, which the author used to pair their pseudonym or alternate and birth identities—Samer puts forth a "transfeminist genealogy" that emerges in the embrace of "trans women as sisters," going on to write that "all trans people as siblings is in fact very much in line with 1970s feminism. It does not matter where you cut the lines and how you can join them afterward." In other words, feminists and trans people alike can turn to the past not only for their own well-being or self-knowledge "but for a history of the reimagination of gender and sexual existence, which we might in turn pass along" (184).

I enjoyed when the authors discussed their own experiences in the archives, where we are suddenly witnessing the immeasurable lesbian force through them instead of in the materials alone. So, here I add my own lesbian tale: as one of the still small realm of lesbian queer trans feminist scholars, I want to note that I am colleague and friend to both authors. I review these books because in their texts they both helped me drastically redraw what a lesbian, a trans person, and any gendered being is, was, and could be. As a CUNY Graduate Center student writing a dissertation on lesbian and queer spaces from the 1980s through the 2000s, Chinn invited me to organize a panel on Lesbian Spaces in the 1970s as part of that 2010 conference.[2] Looking back on the long, lively, and packed panel Q&A (with an audience mostly over the age of sixty), my notes make no mention of audience claims of anger about trans presences in lesbian feminist debates (including my own at the table)—and, oh, was I worried—but instead I recorded the range of lesbians in the audience who sought to have their labor and materials accounted for. In *Information Activism* and *Lesbian Potentiality*, the range of lesbian identities and the objects they left behind are increasingly getting their due, as these authors shed light on worlds already, and still, and again not yet imagined.

Jack Jen Gieseking is a research fellow at Five College Women's Studies Research Center. Their first book is *A Queer New York: Geographies of Lesbian, Dykes, and Queers* (NYU Press, 2020). He is presently writing their next book, *Dyke Bars*: Queer Spaces for the End Times*. She can be found at jgieseking.org or jegiesek@mtholyoke.edu.

Notes
1. CLAGS is now the Center for LGBTQ Studies.
2. The panel included Madelyn Davis, Deb Edel, Julie Enszer, and Stina Soderling.

Works Cited

Beins, Agatha. 2017. *Liberation in Print: Feminist Periodicals and Social Movement Identity*. Athens: University of Georgia Press.

Chinn, Sarah. 2011. "In Amerika They Call Us Dykes: Lesbian Lives in the 1970s [Reports from CLAGS]." *CLAGSNews*, Spring, 8–9.

Potter, Clare. 1986. *The Lesbian Periodicals Index*. Tallahassee, FL: Naiad Press.

Roberts, J. R. 1981. *Black Lesbians: An Annotated Bibliography*. Tallahassee, FL: Naiad Press.

Sex and State Are Action Verbs

Paisley Currah's *Sex Is as Sex Does: Governing Transgender Identity*, New York: New York University Press, 2022

Claudia Sofía Garriga-López

In the face of the present moment's relentless culture-war legislation against transgender people, *Sex Is as Sex Does* is a gift to educators who want to teach transgender studies from a political science perspective. This book is accessible and clearly written in a way that makes it especially suitable for undergraduate students as well as people outside of academia who want to deepen their understanding of transgender politics. Paisley Currah's experiences as both an advocate for transgender rights and a social theorist guide readers to look at big-picture questions about the social construction of sex in and through governance practices, without losing sight of the immediate material needs of trans people for political reforms. Currah moves through a series of legal cases, administrative rules, and legislation to demonstrate what sex categorizations do across a wide range of government agencies and institutions. In doing so, he demonstrates the plasticity of sex as a tool of governance, as one of many categories used to distribute resources and exert control over populations. Sex classifications and the requirements for sex reclassification are a function of government, even or especially within agencies that purportedly have nothing to do with sex. Currah points out that institutions that surveil, confer benefits, or incarcerate have different sets of interest when it comes to sex designation. He helps us make sense of the contradictory and uneven distribution of sex reclassification policies by pointing out the different work that sex classification does in a driver's licence, on a marriage certificate, in prison, and so on. Through this narrow yet versatile focus on the regulations surrounding sex reclassification, Currah theorizes state formations. Sex is as sex does, but also, government is as government does. States are not inherently coherent, unified, or rational; they are an amalgamation of practices that often contradict one another.

WSQ: Women's Studies Quarterly 51: 3 & 4 (Fall/Winter 2023) © 2023 by Claudia Sofía Garriga-López.

This book can be thought of as a transfeminist theory of state. Transfeminism offers us a path through which to move beyond the gender essentialism and biological determinism that has plagued feminisms since the sex/gender divide was made a central principle through which to refute women's subordination. Currah's state-based political analysis compliments transgender scholarship's deconstruction of sex as a stable biological category in the fields of medicine and gender studies. Currah sustains that despite their limitations, it is many times necessary to employ talking points about the correct medical and scientific understanding of sex or the need for sex reclassification, even as he proposes that a more just approach would be to do away with sex classification altogether.

Currah traces how sex categorization was founded on the institutionalization of patriarchal norms over landownership, education, employment, inheritance, voting rights, and so on. He argues that while liberal feminism has been rightly critiqued for the ways it reinforces racial capitalism, it has also been effective at removing the formal use of sex categorization for access to rights and resources in ways that has made sex reclassification possible for trans people. Similarly, while queer critics of same-sex marriage have rightly pointed out its homonormative effects, Currah notes that the legal prohibition against same-sex marriage was a major obstacle for trans people being able to change their sex designation on official documents, on account of the speculation that same-sex couples would seek out marriage certificates by changing the sex designation of one of the partners. Currah repeatedly reminds his readers that sex classification has historically been used to limit access to rights and resources to far more than just trans people.

Currah also intervenes to undo the cisgender/transgender binary in relation to a commonly employed narrative within transgender advocacy about trans people's increased risk for policing and incarceration. He argues that this emphasis obscures the function of race and class in determining which trans people are at an increased risk of incarceration. Herein lies an example of the work "transgender" does to link together under one umbrella category a wide range of people differently situated across axes of power in a way that structures this identity as normatively white. As a corrective, he proposes that we contrast trans prisoners not with cis prisoners but to trans people outside the prison system in order to bring questions of race and class back into focus.

Currah's book is reminiscent of Ruth Wilson Gilmore's work on the prison industrial complex and her critique of the tendency of anticarceral

activists and scholars to frame prisons as primarily serving to generate prof-
its through unpaid or underpaid prison labor, and of *The Revolution Will Not
Be Funded*, a collection of essays published by the INCITE! Women, Gender
Non-conforming, and Trans People of Color Against Violence Collective
that provides sharp critiques of the nonprofit industrial complex by people
whose observations are based on their long-standing experience working
within nonprofit organizations. His criticisms of narratives commonly
espoused by transgender advocates is based on his experience of seeing firsthand their immediate gains and long-term limitations. One of the strengths
of *Sex Is as Sex Does* lies in its ability to propose transformative politics like
prison abolition and the eradication of sex classification, alongside practical understandings of why transgender advocates propose reformist policy
approaches. It is clearly written, nuanced, and bold.

Claudia Sofía Garriga-López is an assistant professor of queer and trans Latinx studies
in the Department of Multicultural and Gender Studies of California State University,
Chico. She currently works with the Museum of Contemporary Art of Puerto Rico, where
she serves as a fellow in the Arts Research with Communities of Color program. She can
be reached at cgarriga-lopez@csuchico.edu.

TransArchitecture

Adrians Black Varella

Redefining its objectives based on the current needs for social change (based on freedom, equality, and mutual aid), Adrians Black (they/their/them)'s radical-social art and its approach to the moving contexts of present times can be a political instrument to unveil and struggle for new landscapes. Their interdisciplinary artworks take the shape of urban interventions, performances, photos, happenings, trans-media events, and environmental projects. They operate the mutual contamination of diverse media that is immersive, collaborative, and participatory in nature and intended to stimulate critical thought (articulating art with anarko-feminist-trans-queer and anti-colonial set of positions). Promoting potency space-times for the uprising of subjective identities that give power to the collective, Black created TransArchitecture drawings (2019—). The project supports the Brazilian indigenous struggle for territories, autonomy, identity difference and against the destruction of forests, operating forms of resistance to hegemonic narratives that represent subjects doomed to subalterity and deterritorialize the modern/colonial project of power, knowledge, and being.

TransArchitecture also foresees architectural interference in private and collective homes of LGBTQIA+ people. Starting from the idea that the oppressive logic of rationality shapes, through architectural instrumentation, our bodies and behaviors, marginalizing and submitting bodies that are considered undesirable in a pathologizing and normative perspective of the bipartite female-male condition, TransArchitecture is insurrection. From the different movements of the bodies, it builds new spaces of life and coexistence. It is a flow of contra-position to the structures of these previously marginalized bodies that now vibrate, survivors. It is a dispositive of

WSQ: Women's Studies Quarterly 51: 3 & 4 (Fall/Winter 2023) © 2023 by Adrians Black Varella.

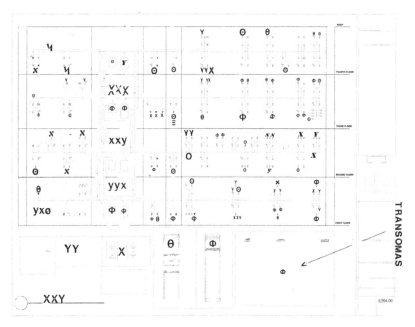

Adrians Black Varella, *TransArchitecture*, 2019–. Paper and ink.

worlds that penetrates the base of the traditional architectural structure to present new ways of being, and living together in the world. To paraphrase the philosopher Didi-Huberman, the artworks involving TransArchitecture "are like fireflies of hope."

Statement by Natasha Marzliak

Adrians Black Varella is a multi-disciplinary artist who makes audio installations, photographs, drawings, performances, video-art experimentations, computer installations, and site-specific/public art works. They create and organize the AnarkoArtLab in New York City, https://www.anarkoartlab.com. Their work can be found at www.adrianavarella.net. They can be reached at adrianavarella@yahoo.com.

The Creative Resistance of Trans of Color Culture, Technology, and Movements

Jian Neo Chen's *Trans Exploits: Trans of Color Cultures and Technologies in Movement,* Durham, NC: Duke University Press, 2019

Natalie Erazo

Trans Exploits: Trans of Color Cultures and Technologies in Movement, Jian Neo Chen's book debut, engages transdisciplinary critique through the examples of trans, gender nonconforming, and disabled artists and activists of color working across film, performance, literature, and digital media, among other cultural practices. Chen locates radical aesthetics and activism that challenge dominant paradigms ordering the world according to racial and colonial binary sex/gender systems (4). Taking as its departure point the 2014 *Time* magazine cover featuring actress Laverne Cox announcing the "transgender tipping point," the book critiques the ways in which racialized trans identity has become minoritized in our neoliberal multiculturalist climate and absorbed within the capitalist free market system, yielding merely symbolic rather than tangible structural change. Instead, the book locates trans of color identity outside the confines of nation-states, and it centers communities that continue to emerge and resist singular definition.

Chen builds on the legacies of foundational trans of color community-builders Marsha P. Johnson, Sylvia Rivera, and Miss Major Griffin-Gracy and activist scholars such as Christopher Lee and Emi Koyama, whose contributions were often eclipsed by the predominantly white leadership of the first wave of transgender organizations in the 1990s. Using *trans* in accordance with the likes of Susan Stryker, Paisley Currah, and Lisa Jean Moore, Chen highlights the adaptive, relational, and liberatory possibilities of opening up *trans* to other meanings and to inclusiveness of gender nonconforming and variant identities and expressions (5). This challenges the pathologized perceptions of transgender identity and embodiment held by white settler-colonial binary and medical systems as well as conventional Western

WSQ: Women's Studies Quarterly 51: 3 & 4 (Fall/Winter 2023) © 2023 by Natalie Erazo. All rights reserved.

notions of family and kinship. Focusing on Asian, Black, Indigenous, and Latinx artists and activists, Chen draws connections between embodied experiences of "racial gender displacement and subjugation" and the inter-related legacies of U.S. imperialism, colonization, and captivity, both within and beyond national borders (4). Nodding to Michel Foucault's "biopoliti-cal genealogies of state and social power," Chen offers crucial considerations about state policies and carceral infrastructures that create power imbal-ances within society, ascribing "affective hierarchies of social value including the criminal and civil, sick and productive, perverse and moral, foreign and native" and justifying systemic policing along these lines (16).

The first chapter, "Cultures," explores performance, the body, and sensa-tion and the ways in which Asian bodies have been constructed by the West. Trans migrant Korean performance artist Yozmit uses performance as a way of expressing trans embodiment and the "body's potential metamorpho-sis through gender" (33). Citing Judith Butler, Chen illustrates the ways in which the subcultural practice of drag performance has been connected to the "imitative structure of gender itself" and a method for deconstructing gender altogether (34). In her 2012 performance, "Sound of New Pussy," which appears on the cover of the book, Yozmit plays with the surface and depth of gender expression through the use of unveiling mesh-screened skirts, thereby challenging the cisheterosexual order of vision. The perfor-mance "gestures toward a different web of sensory relations between outer and inner life and body" (38). Similarly employing the use of veiling, queer nonbinary Indonesian Italian American artist Zavé Martohardjono blends Balinese dance with Black and Latinx ball cultures and challenges Oriental-ist perceptions of the veil as a symbol of traditional feminized domesticity. Whereas the act of unveiling represents a demystification of the invisi-ble within the Western imaginary, Martohardjono's use of unveiling "only reveal[s] more gender shifting and threat" (52).

Throughout the book, Chen offers rich discussions of film and digital media technologies as conduits for aesthetic experimentation and subver-sion. In her 2008 short film *Shape of a Right Statement*, trans Chinese American visual artist and activist Wu Tsang offers tribute to trans autism-rights activist Mel Baggs's 2007 video *In My Language*, in which Baggs calls attention to the ways in which disabled people are pathologized under hierarchies of communication and thought. Chen argues that Tsang's "incongruent" image-making practice mirrors the alienated social histories of racially gendered Asian bodies (47), thereby bridging struggles between people with disabilities, transgender people, and trans people of color (40). Through the example of Taiwanese American filmmaker Shu Lea Cheang's work, Chen looks at the ways in which networked media technologies have been used to deploy dominant racial and binary conceptions of gender, sex, and sexuality (69), examining how this serves to mediate the transnational neoliberal capitalism that bolsters Global North powers. Cheang's 2000 film *I.K.U.*, described as a porn rip-off of Ridley Scott's 1982 film *Blade Runner*, calls out the Hollywood science fiction genre's tendency to depict whiteness as at risk of becoming an underclass amid the "rival threat of Asian-inflected global multicultural economy" (62). The film depicts sexual interactions between human and clone characters that are irreverent to cisheterosexual normativity. Cheang's film is prescient in a time when surveillance technology and AI developments have been questioned on their ability to be free of cultural bias and subjectivity, noting how biotech capitalism penetrates the most intimate spheres of the human body and subjectivity (69). However, amid technologies that have been usurped by dominant powers, Cheang's trans media offers possibilities for pleasure, joy, and play.

Looking at Janet Mock's *Redefining Realness: My Path to Womanhood, Identity, Love and So Much More,* Chen considers the significance of the memoir genre in performing both personal and collective memory work. Recounting Mock's coming-of-age as a Black Native Hawai'ian trans girl, the memoir received wide acclaim and readership within the U.S. Citing scholar Julie Rak, Chen discusses the ways in which memoir democratizes opportunities for marginalized communities and destabilizes the elitist autobiographical genre. Mock's memoir is significant in its "collectively embedded personal memories about the fugitive practices of reconstructing self and kin on the outskirts within and outside the US civil society and national body" (89). Mock's recounted journey of trans self-realization is not reduced to the dominant privatized narrative of state-assisted medical transition from one sex to another. Rather, her memoir reckons with the legacies of U.S. occupation of the kingdom of Hawai'i, the captivity and dispossession of Black women's sense of embodiment, and the white settler imposition on Indigenous sexual and gender sovereignty.

Some of the book's most compelling insights are its considerations of trans activism through examples of social justice movements that employ digital technologies to critique U.S. transnational empire and offer mutual aid solutions. South Africa–based Iranti-Org creates video documentaries highlighting the violence against gender nonconforming Black lesbians in low-income areas of South Africa (110). Analyzing the continuous impact of structural adjustment policies, the World Bank, and the International Monetary Fund that impoverish local economies of Global South nations, Chen illustrates the radical approach Iranti-Org takes in countering the neoliberal human rights frameworks often backed by these entities. Another example is U.S.-based Colombian-American queer trans femme artist and activist micha cárdenas, who posits the framework of "transreality" as a counteraesthetic to dominant social reality (122). In collaboration with the Electronic Disturbance Theater (EDT), cárdenas produced the 2009 video *Transborder Immigrant Tool: Transition,* which connects the Indigenous roots of Mexican migration to contemporary immigration along the U.S.-Mexico border. The video uses an application that connects migrants crossing the border with water sources. In another collaborative project, *Local Autonomy Networks (Autonets),* cárdenas develops a fashion line of electronic cloth-ing that allows users to report their location for safety support. Illustrating what Chen describes as "embodied social mobilization" (128), both proj-ects aim to destabilize state and corporate uses of surveillance and GPS technology by reorienting them towards marginalized communities all too often criminalized by such technologies. The book concludes with a discus-sion of trans Latinx activist Jennicet Gutiérrez and the #EndTransDetention campaign's mobilization against the plight of trans migrants in detention centers. Citing their public disruption of the 2015 White House LGBT Pride event, it attests to the continued cross-cultural embodied resistance for trans liberation around the globe.

While the artists featured in *Trans Exploits* are primarily U.S.-based, they offer a nuanced analysis of the ways U.S. imperialism colludes in transna-tional economies and dispossesses trans and gender nonconforming people around the globe. Chen acknowledges the limitations of their use of "trans" terminology, as it emerges from a Western, U.S. context, while also bridg-ing the multitude of trans and gender nonconforming experiences across social and geopolitical lines. This is notable in their example of Thai *kathoey* filmmaker Tanwarin Sukkhapisit, who navigates the complexities of making "crossover" works amid transnational film industries that profit off remakes of original South and Northeast Asian films and storylines. While *Trans Exploits* offers unvarnished truths of the geopolitical contexts facing trans communities of color around the world, it also reminds us that trans of color embodiment, technologies, and resistance can coexist alongside joy, plea-sure, and play. To borrow from Trinh T. Minh-ha, Chen "speaks nearby" the artists featured in the book, co-creating expressive spaces of critical thought and connection.

Natalie Erazo is a Colombian American film programmer and youth educator based in Brooklyn. Their work focuses on films and moving image works that consider race, gender, labor, and decolonial praxis. Natalie has programmed film series for the Brooklyn Academy of Music (BAM) and region(es), as well as organized screenings for youth audiences through The Repertory Project. Their writing has been published in Hyperallergic and the BAM blog. They are currently pursuing an MA in women's and gender studies at The Graduate Center, CUNY. They can be reached at nerazo@gradcenter. cuny.edu.

"Mic check, one, two, one, two":
Hip Hop Heresies: Queer Aesthetics in New York City

Shanté Paradigm Smalls's *Hip Hop Heresies: Queer Aesthetics in New York City*, New York: New York University Press, 2022

Rocio Rayo

Shanté Paradigm Smalls comes in hot with their recently published *Hip Hop Heresies: Queer Aesthetics in New York City*. In the first few pages, Smalls clearly defines why NYC, why aesthetics, and why queer; then shifts deeper into defining both queer and Black aesthetics—ultimately answering the question of why hip hop. As they remind us that "hip-hop is middle-aged," they very clearly maintain it is a genre housed squarely with young adults and teenagers. Hip hop's mercurial nature is one that constantly changes underfoot—making it solid ground to build a queer, Black, hip hop aesthetic framework. Smalls decided to locate hip hop aesthetic in "disorganized street culture" permitting messiness. This beautiful chaos allows the reader to jump on the beat Smalls produced through their demand to disrupt "and eradicate settled public modalities" of what "authentic" hip hop meant (and means) in NYC. They state, "The book argues that New York City hip-hop artists use queer, Black, and hip-hop aesthetics to queerly—disruptively, generatively, inauthentically—articulate gender, racial, and sexual identitarian performances through specifically New York City based aesthetic and artistic practices and cues" (24). Importantly, Smalls clarifies that this is only possible due to the "creativity and expansiveness of Black genius."

Hip Hop Heresies is broken up into four chapters, with an introduction and conclusion. The first chapter, "Wild Stylin' Martin Wong's Queer Visuality in New York City Graffiti," queers the narrative that there is a "lone wolf" success story in hip hop and instead focuses on the origin point, where different styles, cultures, and people intersect. While the protagonist of this chapter is Martin Wong and his contributions, the undercurrent is the liminal space that focusing on Wong carves out and defines in relationship to Latinidad and Blackness within a hip hop context. Wong's location on the lower east side of Manhattan connects him to "Nuyorico" while simultaneously erasing his connection to Blackness. Smalls does a phenomenal job of locating him within the body of a Black hip hop aesthetic history. In their second chapter, "Ni[99]a Fu: The Last Dragon, Black Masculinity, and Chinese Martial Arts," Smalls "offers an alternative model for Black racial formation, queer heterosexual Black masculinity, and a hybrid cultural identity" (59; spelling changed by me). Focusing on "The Last Dragon" allows Smalls an opportunity to reorient heterosexual Black masculinity as queer by removing it from an embodied experience "in relation to white, patriarchal, hetero norms" to a Black masculine experience that challenged controlling images of what it meant to be both Black and masculine. Leroy's popular performance (and the acceptance of his performance) as both masculine and Black while the actual character was "virginal awkward and ill-fitted for the mean streets of mid-1980s New York City" is itself an exercise in queering the expectations of what Black masculinity meant and means. Smalls's third chapter, "'Casebaskets': Listening for the Uncanny in Jean Grae," steers us away from "Asian American and Afro Asian connectedness and queer masculinity" and positions us within Black womanhood—using methods from Black feminist thought and psychoanalysis. Smalls uses the work of Jean Grae and psychoanalytic theory in order to implore fantasy, the uncanny, invention, intuition, and the psychic. Smalls argues that using Jean Grae's body of work allows for the anatomy of Black femininity and psychic expression to be dissected and studied through the lenses of gender, race, and sexuality. The final chapter, "Queer Hip Hop, Queer Dissonance," takes us on an ethnographic stroll through hip hop cultural history from 1982 to 2005. The question answered in this chapter is as follows: if back in "those days" it was impossible to be part of an NYC club scene without being "among gays, lesbians, trans, and other sexual outlaws," why would hip hop culture be so different? Smalls posits that since white supremacy defined hip hop as only Black, masculine, and poor, it must also be one-dimensional, unsophisticated, and antithetical to queer sexuality and gender. Throughout the book and in this chapter in particular "queer" is invoked as a disruption and destabilizer. That is not to say that queerness is divorced from LGBTQ+ people. Smalls is "not interested in queerness without homosexuality or transsexuality" (123).

Smalls positions the book as the first "to connect Blackness and queerness to hip hop culture and studies" (24). It absolutely does. In doing so, they also codify another layer of the framework that queer methodology is located in. The revolutionary intervention by Smalls in this book is their ability to showcase not only the plot points, places, and spaces, but the soft tissue that connects those formations. Smalls acknowledges, indexes, and defines the intersections, but what was phenomenal is that they did not erase the roads that got them there. The places between the two points. While drawing a clear line between Blackness, queerness, hip hop, and aesthetics in a specific place and at specific times, Smalls defines and indexes these moments, but most effectively Smalls leans into the movement between those moments with delightful syncopation.

Smalls's ability to move between points allows for the connective fibers to act as stand-alone praxis, uncovers a breadth of knowledge, and sets the stage for future scholars to act on. I look forward to the future explorations that will grow out of the morsels to which Smalls alluded. Specifically, their assertion that the designation of Black women being assigned as the shadow of Black men offers a provocative opportunity to destroy the body casting that shadow, and the fear that ensues as well, the "close to the ground" invisibility and hypervisibility of "good" minorities to produce and perform. One question I was left with was, how does Black motherhood fit into the reproduction of hip hop culture? They state, "In the time it takes for a group of kids in the neighborhood to go from wide-eyed young'ns to confident teen arbiters of style, slang, wing and swagger to grown folk moving on and out . . . the culture has turned over again" (6). My sixteen-year-old son's embodied experience as a young Black man in New York City who performs and consumes Black masculinity through hip hop culture agrees with the declaration that southern trap and mumble rap were, as Smalls concluded, the dominant soundtrack for hip hop music. He felt the need to explain to me that for "his generation" it was underground rap that was "on the come up." Hip hop requires constant tillage, it is a culture led and grounded by youth, yet Smalls reminds us that the ground is fertile because of the labor of Black and queer artists in NYC.

Rocio Rayo is currently the director of transfer services at Hostos Community College. She graduated from Hostos Community College in 2011 and completed her BA/MA in history at the City College of New York in 2014. She is currently working on her PhD in anthropology at The Graduate Center and developing a theory of motherhood by investigating the birthplace of women's militancy—comparing Nicaraguan and Irish women's anticolonial revolutionary involvement. She can be seen on most nights and weekends with her wife, cheering the loudest at high school sporting events. She can be reached at RRayo@hostos.cuny.edu.

Writing about Mentorship, and Mentorship through Writing

Nancy K. Miller and Tahneer Oksman (eds.)'s *Feminists Reclaim Mentorship: An Anthology*, Albany: State University of New York Press, 2023

Maya von Ziegesar

My copy of *Feminists Reclaim Mentorship: An Anthology* is thin and pink, floppy almost, with title matter written in modern, lowercase letters. Nancy K. Miller and Tahneer Oksman, both English professors and themselves a mentor-mentee pair, introduce the book humbly and auto-biographically, musing on COVID, the '80s proto-girlboss film *Working Girl*, and their own experiences with mentorship and feminist community. For these and other reasons, including an intrusive, gen-Z cynicism about second-wave feminism that try as I might I can't always suppress, I picked up *Feminists Reclaim Mentorship* expecting reminiscences about boys'-club academia, open-secret sexual harassers, older women hardened by their own ascents to power, commitments to reimagining old and broken systems, communities of peer mentors, and reiterations of the importance of reciprocity and listening. I was *not* expecting such a thoughtful, ambivalent, and sharp book; not expecting to be forced to put it down in order to think deeply about the mentors I've had, the almost-mentors I wish I'd had, my mother mentors and peer mentors; not expecting to end up less sure than ever about the right way forward or even the meaning of the word. In short, I underestimated this book. *Feminists Reclaim Mentorship* has teeth.

Feminists Reclaim Mentorship is broken into three parts, following a familiar arc. First, mentorship as we have received it: hierarchical and implicitly patriarchal. The authors in this section reflect on the powerful people they used to aspire to be, or their own successes and failings once they had transitioned from mentee to mentor. They ask when mentorship ends, whether mentorship can transcend its inherent asymmetry, how to listen to your mentees and become a better mentor. The middle section is a crisis point for the meaning of mentorship. The authors here talk about mentor ghosts and

WSQ: Women's Studies Quarterly 51: 3 & 4 (Fall/Winter 2023)

mentor imaginaries, a radical break from traditional mentorship, a refuge for those of us never meant to find our home in hierarchical patriarchy. Finally, in the last section, mentorship is reimagined and reconfigured. Mentorship becomes a fluid, reciprocal relationship between feminist peers and colleagues, something nonexclusionary and new. In this section, mentorship is reformed by some authors and rejected by others.

When I finished reading, I was left with a longing for a final turn of the narrative that would never come. The pernicious and deeply ingrained problems of our social world are articulately described and diagnosed, while solutions are offered, tentatively, as experiments in half-imagined, living alternatives. The aching of the first section—recollections of being a graduate student in search of a mentor who would never manifest—continued throughout the book's arc, culminating in a crushing ambiguity. The final piece, "A Special Place in Hell: Women Helping Women and the Professionalization of Female Mentorship" by Angela Veronica Wong, was especially biting. Wong explores corporate and neoliberal appropriations of "feminist" mentorship, the extreme burden of unpaid mentoring labor on women of color, and the inability of mentorship to fundamentally transform broken systems. Can or should mentorship be reclaimed? I'm not sure.

Here was my glimmer of hope: throughout the book, one author would mention a writers' collective founded by another. Three more would mention the same feminist author, who mentored them through the pages of her book. CUNYs and SUNYs popped up throughout, both as refuges and as symbols of immovable academe. Slowly, around me, I was seeing a community of feminist mentor-mentees, supporting one another and urging the collective forward. The fact that the editors are a mentor-mentee pair, which my aforementioned gen-Z cynicism had urged me to dismiss as cute or gimmicky, emerged through the book as a real, radical force. The editors model feminist community and a restructuring of the mentorship relation through the book itself, a type of prefigurative politics enacted in text. As the reader, I felt invited into this community and invited to reflect on my own experiences. I thought about my all-male logic class, where the emeritus professor once wrote a family tree on the board, tracing his advisor's advisor's advisor and so on all the way back to some Baroque German mathematician, a lineage that of course I would never be a part of. I thought of my many feeble, desperate attempts to make a woman I admired come to admire me. I thought of my mom, who writes grants, and my dad, who writes books, and how I am always too scared to show them what I write. I thought about the CUNY-affiliated middle school I first enrolled in when I was eleven years old and about how, now that I am a CUNY PhD student, I am in the same union as all of my middle school teachers, and how that school calls all alums "alumnae."

After I had finished a draft of this review, I attended a book reading of *Feminists Reclaim Mentorship* at the CUNY Graduate Center. Unlike any other book reading I had been to, this one was more or less nonhierarchical, with nine of the book's contributors each given four minutes to talk or read or reflect, and Nancy Miller barely speaking at all. That said, without saying much, Miller emerged throughout the event as occupying a special role. One by one, people revealed themselves to be her former research assistants, dissertation advisees, and students. But the mode of relationality in that room was not dominated or controlled by Miller. She was what many of us had in common, an icebreaker until we found out what we all *really* had in common. She cared about the people in that room, and she cared about their relationships with *other* people in that room. She cares so much about this type of relationality that she, quite literally, wrote a book about it. Can mentorship be reclaimed? I still don't know, but at the book reading, I met many wonderful folks who are trying to reclaim it, reconfigure it, and reimagine it. I earnestly wish them luck.

Maya von Ziegesar is a PhD candidate in philosophy at the CUNY Graduate Center. Before coming to CUNY, she completed a Fulbright ETA Fellowship in South Korea and graduated with honors in philosophy and visual art from Princeton University. She works in feminist epistemology, and is especially interested in unjust epistemic structures and local practices of epistemic resistance. She can be reached at mvonziegesar@gradcenter.cuny.edu.

PART IV. **PROSE**

Ben & Brianne @ Home

Brianne Waychoff

Ben &
Brianne

@home

+ jules & luce

Home is where I want to be
Pick me up and turn me round
I feel numb,
born with a weak heart
I guess I must
be having fun

The less we say
about it, the better
We'll make it up
as we go along
Feet on the ground,
Head in the sky
It's ok, I know
nothing's
wrong,
nothing

Brianne Waychoff. *Ben and Brianne @ Home*, 2020. Pen and ink.

WSQ: Women's Studies Quarterly 51: 3 & 4 (Fall/Winter 2023) © 2023 by Brianne Waychoff. All rights reserved.

Brianne Waychoff. *Ben and Brianne @ Home*, 2020. Pen and ink.

"It is as if one were looking through a Reversed opera glass and through a microscope at the same time."

Brianne Waychoff, PhD, was associate professor in the Department of Speech, Communication, and Theatre Arts at Borough of Manhattan Community College. She was the founder of the Gender and Women's Studies AA Program at BMCC, which she coordinated across departments. Brianne's published articles and creative scholarship appear in *Pacific Affairs*, *Text and Performance Quarterly*, *Liminalities: A Journal of Performance Studies*, and *PAJ: Performing Arts Journal*. She has served on the Performance Studies National Review Board, as chair of the National Women's Studies Association Community College Caucus, and on the editorial boards of *Text and Performance Quarterly*, *Liminalities: A Journal of Performance Studies*, and *Women and Language*. Dr. Waychoff's work used performance as a method for investigating issues of gender justice. She danced with the Joffrey Ballet and trained with Anne Bogart and the SITI Company, Augusto Boal, Goat Island Performance Group, and with a range of practitioners in the Japanese Avant-Dance form butoh. She was a former member of the International WOW Company. Her performance work has been presented at professional venues and festivals throughout the United States and abroad. Additionally, with her background in community organizing and activism, she served on the Faculty Advisory Board for the New York City Alliance Against Sexual Assault. In 2016 she was recognized as a "change-maker" at the inaugural United State of Women Summit.*

*Dr. Brianne Waychoff passed away on July 25, 2022, from 9/11-related kidney cancer. She was general editor of *WSQ*, with Dr. Red Washburn, from 2020 until her passing. Dr. Brianne Waychoff was also guest editor of *WSQ*'s *Nonbinary* issue, along with Dr. Red Washburn and Dr. JV Fuqua.

Trans Visibility Cloak

Audacia Ray

One Sunday afternoon, as Aiden walked through the vestibule of their Brooklyn apartment building, they saw a long cape hanging on a coat hook near the mailboxes. They thought this odd. Often there were packages dropped off here on the floor, but they'd never seen a tenant use the coat hooks. It was a remnant of a bygone era when this brownstone was inhabited by one family instead of split into three apartments.

Aiden had been a goth girl in high school, wore a homemade cape then, a thing that shrouded their ever-changing body in mystery. It made the hated curves of their body invisible but made them a target of merciless teasing. In the New Jersey suburbs of the 1990s, it got Aiden the nickname Dracula. Secretly, they were kind of into being called Dracula, because it meant that the girl name they'd been given by their parents wasn't being formed over and over again in the mouths of sneering teens. They felt a pang of nostalgia and kindness toward their teen goth self as they looked at this cape.

What the hell, Aiden thought, and they lifted the cape up and, with a practiced flourish, swung it around their shoulders. They had been heading out to go buy some snacks anyway, might as well do it wearing a cape and play into someone else's story, *I was out getting coffee and I saw someone casually walking around in a cape!*

When they got to the bodega, one of the men who was often sitting outside on a broken milk crate was on his way into the store. "Sup, bro?" the guy asked, holding steady eye contact with Aiden as he held the door open for them.

Aiden tried not to look startled. This guy usually looked offended by Aiden's existence, like Aiden's asymmetrical haircut and gender

WSQ: Women's Studies Quarterly 51: 3 & 4 (Fall/Winter 2023) © 2023 by Audacia Ray. All rights reserved.

nonconformity meant they were a threat to his cis-hetero existence. In the cape, they were no longer a threat, but—what?—a comrade in arms?

Aiden gathered their snacks and continued a slow saunter around the neighborhood. They began to get in the groove of getting head nods and uncomplicated greetings from men. What was this sorcery? Men being nice to them? They stopped briefly in front of a chaotic window display in a hardware store, which depicted a backyard BBQ with plastic flames fluttering in the breeze of a small electric fan, and lawn chairs with red, white, and blue NY football helmets emblazoned on them. "Go Giants!" a passing man said to them cheerfully.

They continued their walk, thoughtfully crunching away on Funyuns. Their feet took them toward their favorite neighborhood plant shop, where there were always tiny succulents in adorable little ceramic pots with faces painted on them. Very hard to resist. They swept into the store, feeling the whoosh of the cape around their ankles. A twenty-something femme with a lip piercing and an undercut with the long part dyed cactus-green gave them a nod of queer acknowledgment. How could it be that on this one walk, they had been treated with kindness by cis men and also given the community nod from a queer femme?

Maybe it was the cape? Was the cape gifting them with the smoothness of a visibility that toggled depending on who was looking?

When they left the plants shop, they took off the cape, draped it over their arm. An experiment. They resisted the urge to wipe their greasy fingers on it and instead used their jean shorts. As they rounded the corner onto an avenue, a group of people in a coupe drove by with the windows down. One of them yelled, "What is *that*?" and threw a partly full cup of ice and soda at them. The cup exploded at their feet, splashing sticky cola onto their legs. They stared straight ahead at the ground, did a practiced override of their flinch reaction, dissociated briefly from their surroundings.

Aiden felt a creeping sense of sadness. They wanted to be the nonbinary gender freak they are and be left alone. They didn't want a safety only made possible by a magic cape. They wanted to be read as a man by straight cis people and as a queer person by other queers and have those assumptions run in parallel tracks. But they knew that the world wasn't ready for their kind of trans visibility. They swung the cape around their shoulders and continued down the block.

Audacia Ray (they/she) is director of community organizing and public advocacy at the New York City Anti-Violence Project and lead author of AVP's report *Under Attack: 2022 LGBTQ+ Safe Spaces National Needs Assessment*. Dacia's short stories have been published in *Necessary Fiction*, *Litro Magazine, NonBinary Review*, and *Stone Canoe*. Their nonfiction work has been widely anthologized, most recently in *We Too: Essays on Sex Work and Survival*. She was an editor of *$pread* magazine and its respective best-of anthology published by Feminist Press. Dacia has a MA in American studies from Columbia University and a BA in cultural studies from the New School. They can be found at audaciaray.com or hey@audaciaray.com.

Another Way to Fly, from *Terry Dactyl*

Mattilda Bernstein Sycamore

The first time I met Sid she was on the dance floor in a silver and gold tube dress pulled over her head except it wasn't just a dress because the fabric went on and on and somehow she knew the exact spot on the dance floor where the light would shine right on her or that's how it felt when she was writhing inside this tube of fabric, pulling it up and down, a hand out and a hand in, and then her face exposed in harsh white makeup and black lipstick with long glittering eyelashes and then she rolled onto the floor, she was crawling or more like bending but also she was completely still in the bouncing lights and all this was somehow happening on a crowded dance floor at the Limelight while I was sipping my cocktail and I didn't know what I was seeing I mean it felt like this went on forever, how many songs, it was like there wasn't even music anymore just my body inside the fabric peeking out and then suddenly she pulled the dress up around her neck like a huge elegant collar, and underneath she was wearing a gold bodysuit with a silver metallic skirt that flared out, with ballet slippers also painted gold and she walked right up to me and said what did you think.

And I had no idea how she even saw me but I must have mumbled something because then she took my hand and said let's go upstairs, honey, and I thought we were going to the balcony but we went up the stairs in the back, and at the top she kissed the door person on both cheeks and then we went inside.

And there was a whole other dance floor there, the club inside a club that I'd heard about, and she guided me over to the bar and said: I can't believe she's gone.

And then she said it again: I can't believe she's gone.

WSQ: Women's Studies Quarterly 51: 3 & 4 (Fall/Winter 2023) © 2023 by Mattilda Bernstein Sycamore. All rights reserved.

And then she looked up at me and started laughing hysterically—oh honey, she said, I totally thought, I totally thought.

And then she just stopped right there. I didn't know if she thought I was someone else, or if she thought—I really just didn't know.

She said what are you drinking, honey, but she didn't wait for my answer she just ordered two vodka sours with grenadine, I loved the color and after I took one sip I knew this would be my drink from then on. She poured some coke out on a coaster and then handed me a straw, and I made sure just to snort half but she motioned her hand like you take the rest, and when I was done she handed me a big flat round pill and I swallowed it with the vodka sour.

I was a little worried because I was already a bit coked up and alcohol messes with ecstasy too, but I definitely knew not to turn down free drugs, I mean wasn't this what was supposed to happen in New York?

Sid, she said. Sid Sidereal.

Terry, I said. Terry Dactyl.

And she touched my back, and said: Where are your wings?

It was the way she touched me. Like she was drawing my wings on. I could feel them right then.

One by one, the others came upstairs, and took their magic pills—I didn't know anyone yet, but when they saw me with Sid it was like we were old friends.

Sid was so high that her eyes would roll back whenever she wasn't speaking, and I was ready to go there. Jaysun Jaysin kept petting her coat like it would take her to heaven or maybe she was already in heaven. Bleached curly hair with dark roots, eyebrows dyed green, and she was wearing a big ratty faux-fur coat and maybe nothing on underneath and she touched my nose and said: twins. I looked at her nose, and noticed her gold septum ring did match my silver one, and everything in her eyes. And then String Bean arrived in clown makeup and ruffles, platforms that made her so tall it looked like she could touch the ceiling. And CleoPatrick, with a giant red Afro and tattered ball gown. And then Tara and Mielle, in matching suits and bleached hair with spit curls like Jazz Age–style dyke twins.

And eventually Sid said: is everyone ready? And we all went downstairs to the coat check and Sid picked up a box with her coat, and then we went outside and jumped in two cabs—I didn't usually take cabs in New York because I was still in love with the subway but here I was with Sid, Jaysun, and Cleo, all of us squished together in the backseat and Sid said

Christopher Street Pier and then soon enough we were there, one cab and then the other like we were in tandem.

And I'll be honest here and say that I hadn't even been to the piers before, I mean I saw *Paris Is Burning* in high school when it played at the Egyptian, and then of course everyone started lip-synching to Madonna and practicing those moves, but that was about all. It was late, and I didn't see anyone voguing, but there was music, and just as we started walking out onto the pier this queen ran up behind us and said Esme!

And Sid turned, and this queen said girl, I thought you were dead.

And Sid said: I thought I was dead too.

And this queen said: Oh honey I've missed you and your messy makeup.

And Sid said: My messy makeup can't compare to you.

And then she put her box down, and opened her arms, and the two of them were jumping up and down and Sid said oh Monique. And right about then I started to feel this pounding inside and I looked around to see if everyone else was feeling it too, and Monique said so are these your children or did someone get lost on the way to the circus.

Monique was ready to read each one of us, and we just stood there in the way it takes a while to react when the X is really kicking in and when Monique got to me she said girl, you're as tall as me and you've got them tranny shoulders and that freakshow makeup, but something does smell fishy here, I don't know what it is—and it felt like I'd been waiting for someone to say tranny shoulders all my life, yes, what was I doing wasting my time with the dead white men of the Core Curriculum when I could be so alive right here with tranny shoulders the air on my skin so much air and that current going through my body my eyes yes my eyes and lips yes lips and tongue, and there it was, language, when I said: Well then don't let the river run dry.

And Monique shrieked at that one, and she held out her hand and I got on my knees and kissed it, and she said oh honey I'm not a lezzbian but I do like the attention. And then when she was done clocking all our outfits, she said: So what's in the box.

And Sid said JoJo.

And Monique gasped, and stepped back, and she was so dramatic about it that at first I didn't realize what was happening, but then she and Sid hugged again, and this time there were tears, and I got a chill up my back even though it wasn't cold, not really, was it, I mean a second ago I was sweating and now I was cold and I knew this X was going to be good but also I felt like this wasn't what I was supposed to be feeling, even if I could tell we were all feeling it, and maybe that was the point.

And Sid said I came here to tell Estella, and Monique said she's with a date. And Sid said JoJo wanted her ashes in the river.

And Monique said that bitch stole $100 from me, twice, and then paused, and said: Not that I hold it against her.

And Sid said could you tell Estella for me. And Monique said what's in it for me?

And Sid pressed something into her hand, and Monique held a baggy of coke up to the light and said oh honey you know me, you know me too well, and then she kissed her on both cheeks and we were off.

And when I say we were off, it wasn't exactly runway it was just the only way to walk, all together now, walk, and at this point my eyes were rolling back and I was licking my lips and holding someone's hand, feeling that clamminess, we were all bodies and wind and the cars going by—me and Jaysun, String Bean and Cleo, Sid and TaraMielle—they went by one name together I didn't get it the first time but I got it now.

We walked down the West Side Highway until we got to another pier, I don't know how long we walked and I don't know which way because I've never found that pier again or maybe I found it but it didn't look the same so all I know is when we got there it was just us, and I knew that was the point, just us in the sky, the sky and the air, the sky in the air in my body inside this coat and we walked out to the middle of the pier, and Sid opened the box, and I'd seen this before, the ashes in a box like this or a big glass bottle or a beautiful urn or sometimes just a bowl so you could touch with your fingers, yes there were chunks of bone but on ecstasy it felt like I was part of this ash, this water, this bone, this air, the sky, this breath, it was all of us.

Sid handed out paper cups and maybe I was thirsty but the cups were for the ashes, each of us filled one up and we walked out to the edge of the pier, the thing about the Hudson is it's always wider than you think and you're looking out at the skyline but it's Jersey. The lights, I said, look at all the lights and everyone nodded their heads, we were there, in the lights, I could feel it.

And Sid said before we get this party started, I want everyone to know one thing, and we all turned to face her, and she said: Don't ever call me Esme, okay? Sid, Siddhartha, Sadie, CeCe my Playmate . . .

And Jaysun said: Come out and play with me.

And Cleo said: Do you know what that bitch said to me? She said . . . No, never mind.

And Jaysun said: What.

And Cleo said: No, no, I don't even want to say it . . . Okay, she said: you look better as a boy.

And we all gasped. And then String Bean hurled her cup of ashes way out into the water just like that, and then she did some kind of om shanti thing, blessed be, she kept saying blessed be blessed be blessed be, and I definitely didn't believe in any kind of blessing but my eyes were open wide. Cleo said JoJo's the bitch who taught me to walk, and she turned to show us, and so we all turned and there it was, New York, New York—New York, New York and JoJo I mean Cleo was walking with New York, she was walking with New York but leaning to each side because New York was heavy in those big platforms that weren't tapered so they looked kind of dangerous and right then I realized I needed to get the ones like String Bean's with the wedding cake effect, and when Cleo turned she almost tripped but what was wrong with falling, we were all falling another way to fly and some of the ashes flew out of her cup and when she got to us she said see, I still don't know how to walk, and we can all blame JoJo. And you could really see the glitter in her eyes—I tried to hear the ashes land but what do ashes sound like, just the water and the cars and the music, I mean it was the sound of the water against the piers or maybe metal slamming a buoy somewhere but it was music now.

TaraMielle sat down on the ground and we sat down with them, and that's when Jaysun started crying and Sid put her arms around her and then we became one big mass of breath and oh and oh and ohhhhhhhhhhhh-hhhhhh and I wanted to say this is the best way to celebrate death. But I couldn't say that, could I? And just as I was thinking how did we even get here, when we were at the Limelight, suddenly it was like we were at the Limelight again because Sid pulled the tube dress over her head and down to the ground, there was so much fabric she was in the tube and I realized that earlier was a rehearsal because here it was again one hand out of the fabric toward heaven, and one foot out of the bottom toward the water beneath the pier and the way she could roll over herself, twisting around I mean everything was fluid and brokenness and this was a dance for death, I knew it now.

And then String Bean started waving her arms and Cleo was twirling around and around and then I threw my ashes into the air and they fell down on us as Sid was pulling one arm in and then pushing one arm through, like each part of her body wasn't connected to anything, just floating on its own, her face peeking out, just one of those gold eyelashes and then back into the fabric, it was like we were all in the fabric we were inside we were inside we were inside we were inside-out.

Mattilda Bernstein Sycamore's new book, *Touching the Art*, about her fraught relationship with her late grandmother, an abstract artist, will be released in November 2023. Sycamore is most recently the author of *The Freezer Door*, a *New York Times* Editors' Choice and a finalist for the PEN/Jean Stein Book Award. Winner of a Lambda Literary Award and an American Library Association Stonewall Honor Book, she is the author of three novels and three nonfiction titles, as well as the editor of six nonfiction anthologies, most recently *Between Certain Death and a Possible Future: Queer Writing on Growing Up with the AIDS Crisis*. "Another Way to Fly" is an advance excerpt from *Terry Dactyl*, a novel Sycamore is currently completing. She can be reached at nobodypasses@gmail.com.

Palmetto, from *Black Girl in Triptych*, Part 1

Dána-Ain Davis

The short man muttered to himself as he limped toward his seat in the fifth car of the Palmetto leaving Charleston, South Carolina . . . the car where Negroes sat. His body was slight, wisp-like, but his mouth sounded like he was swishing seven marbles. He spoke kind of funny because apparently, he never left his Haitian accent back in Acul-du-Nord, even though he arrived in Edgefield County, South Carolina, ten years earlier. The pout of his lips, from which the accent fell, was why they called him Frenchy—a name a lot of South Carolinians called Haitians who first came to Charleston in the 1700s from Saint Dominique.

Frenchy boarded the train in his gray pants and light-blue short-sleeve polo shirt. He had the collar up, and the top two buttons were undone so his gold necklace was visible. His hair was slightly conked and combed back. Such a dapper man might have had a larger suitcase, but his was just a medium-size, tan tweed and cognac-colored leather. His valise was the size of man who had left someplace in a hurry. Yet, his manicured nails—perfectly square with rounded edges—told a tale of living a well-appointed life. Those hands, almost dainty, pulled out a ticket from his pant pocket. It read "15A," which came as a relief because it was the window seat. When Frenchy found the location, a young woman was already getting settled in 15B and was reaching over the aisle to hand the two little girls across from her, orange sections in a napkin.

Frenchy sighed because now he was going to have to navigate another person taking up space in his own small world. The young lady looked up as Frenchy lingered by the arm of the seat before hoisting his suitcase to the overhead bin. The suitcase, the size of which suggested its owner did not

WSQ: Women's Studies Quarterly 51: 3 & 4 (Fall/Winter 2023) © 2023 by Dána-Ain Davis. All rights reserved.

have much or did not plan to stay where he was going for very long, nestled in its place much more easily when Frenchy turned it sideways.

Now came the small talk that would get him to his window seat. *Ma'am that's my seat. Ok, give me a second*, she said. Frenchy waited all of five seconds for the woman to swivel her hips and legs to the right so he could inch his way past her. Frenchy made his wispy body even smaller by holding in his nonexistent stomach and side-shuffled to his seat. When his body arrived, he sat down and was so glad to be doing so. Now he could rest his head on the window instead of taking a chance that when sleep came to get him, his head would drop and lean into the aisle. That could be the job of the lady, he thought. She could create the disturbance in the aisle, not him.

As soon as Frenchy sat down, one of the two little girls said, *Mama, when we gonna get there*? The little girl's mother looked around, checking people's faces against the volume of her daughter's voice. She put a red-painted finger up to her lips and told her daughter, *Gilda-girl, hush, don't nobody wanna hear you*. Gilda-girl whined, *But Mama, I jus' wanna know when we getting' there. I can't wait to see Cousin Do, and Pookie.*

Frenchy leaned over just a bit so he could see this loud child. She was dressed the part of someone leaving one place going to another but not sure about the road leading to where she was headed. Gilda-girl had on a brown coat and Frenchy could see a little pink hem peeking out of the bottom of the coat. When she stood up because she was so excited, Frenchy could see that the coat fit, but it was just "too right." Too right—Frenchy had worn a lot of "too right" clothes over his lifetime. You know, when something fits too right, the arms don't let you hug comfortably. Or, the seat of your pants are too close up on you. Too right means you always run the risk of ripping the garment at the seam and signals hand-me-downs. But, the little girls' black Mary Janes shined, and Frenchy knew right away that someone had rubbed Vaseline with a white terry cloth towel on the shoes to make them shine like mirrors.

Gilda-girl, jus' set. We got a long ride, now settle down. Give your sister some of that orange and be sure she don't mess up anything. Gilda-girl slinked back to her seat and turned toward her sister. *Here Frankie, take this and don't let orange juice drip down—use the napkin.* Frenchy couldn't see the other little girl . . . she was tucked in her seat, but he sure did hear when she said, *I don't want none.* What Frenchy didn't see was that the little girl pushed her sister's hand away. Gilda-girl was annoyed, so in return, she hit her sister's hand—it was a minor little-people's commotion, but one that nonetheless made their

mama get out of her seat. Teeth clenched, the girls' mama spoke slow—
each word followed by a period, becoming its own sentence. *Frankie-Mae.
Gilda-girl. Do. Not. Make. No. Scenes. On. This. Train. Watch yourselves.* She
was so Negro-mama stern, that her voice made Frenchy remember his own
Mamman, who caught him one Sunday when he thought she had gone
visit Tati Roseline, in her blue satin dress, white shoes, and red lipstick.
The memory worked its way through his body with such fear. Mamman
was so mad, telling him she did not raise a *masisi*. His mother's words and
anger collided with the stern words coming from the mouth of the woman
sitting next to him, made Frenchy shudder. The memory of his past transgression, which became one way that lived his present life, made him so
afraid to witness the scene between his train-mates that he stopped leaning forward to see what was happening.

But now that she was standing, Frenchy could see very clearly some
things about the lady sitting next to him. He noticed that the pleats of
Gilda-girl's mama's brown dress had cream piping and fit snuggly against
her shapely body and wondered if it could have come from Julia's dress
shop in Aiken. The lady's back was straight as an arrow—maybe she had
good posture, or maybe she just drew herself up so the girls would be intim-
idated. But whatsinever the reason, the lady sure looked good in the dress
and the lightweight cream-color sweater held together by gold-like clasp.
The sweater was draped over her shoulders to ward off a potential chill,
but guaranteed, Frenchy knew she was gonna have to take that sweater off
herself and the brown coat off Gilda-girl at some point on this trip, because
it was as hot as July, even though it was May.

Yeah, Gilda-girl and Frankie Mae's mama looked good. Frenchy continued his assessment. She had straight bangs resting across her forehead, a
slight bouffant with flipped curls at the back. The slight bouffant gave it
away . . . she must have gotten her hair done by Nickie Mae Corley, who
had one of the best beauty shops in Aiken. Frenchy knew of Miss Nickie
and had sought her out to learn about doing hair. She was kind to him when
he arrived in 1954. In fact, sometimes she let him run the shop when she
went to Atlanta to meet the likes of Dr. Martin Luther King. She was a good
woman, quietly working behind the scenes of the Civil Rights Movement.

Anyway, although the young woman's hair looked done right, it was the
brown shoes that gave away all that she wasn't—her heels were worn down
on the outside, scuffed and old. They looked like Frenchy felt, tired. Frenchy
just wanted the Pullman Porter to come take his ticket so as he could settle

in for the fourteen-hour trip. The train pulled out slow and stunted, crawling on the tracks like a turtle crawls over rocks. He just wanted to get to Harlem, but it was going to be a long ride.

Dána-Ain Davis is professor of urban studies at Queens College and director of the Center for the Study of Women and Society at The Graduate Center, CUNY. Davis can be reached at dana.davis@qc.cuny.edu.

Trans CUNY Zine

Elvis Bakaitis

Elvis Bakaitis. *Trans CUNY Zine*, 2023. Pen and ink.

WSQ: Women's Studies Quarterly 51: 3 & 4 (Fall/Winter 2023) © 2023 by Elvis Bakaitis. All rights reserved.

Elvis Bakaitis. *Trans CUNY Zine*, 2023. Pen and ink.

Elvis Bakaitis. *Trans CUNY Zine*, 2023. Pen and ink.

Elvis Bakaitis is the Head of Reference at the CUNY Graduate Center. They are proud to serve on the University LGBTQ Council, where they engage in activism around queer/ trans visibility issues across 25 campuses in New York City. Elvis is the author of many zines, is a queer herstory educator, and served as the PI for a 2020 Mellon Foundation grant awarded to the Lesbian Herstory Archives.

QPOC Conference Keynote: UCSB
Originally written for May 15, 2015

Kay Ulanday Barrett

I would like to thank QPOC Conference here at UCSB, the organizers, the students, the late nights and missing meals, the gas money and the delusion it takes to create social justice and critical and party space all in one dreamy QTBIPOClandia is a feat. If you get new ideas, get new crushes, have new protest chants, it's because of those who've brought you here. Thank you to everyone who brought us here, the people who clean and care for this building, the earth that feeds us, the native and indigenous, Two-Spirit communities whose land we are occupying, specifically the Chumash community. Gratitude to those who, like my mama, a motel worker, are globally exploited, forced migration, for this clean air, and my own witty remarks uninterrupted by military or police. #americandream?

To honor those who brought me here, politically and spiritually:

I want to uplift the femmes of color whose labor is deemed invisible. Y'all feed us, critique, protest, create this world, and you deserve the most high. I want to hold the trans femme women of color who raised me, whose politics are true salve but aren't booked to many conferences unless they are super fancy and look a kind of way that makes us comfortable on real-ness or womanhood. For Bamby Salcedo and for my Tita Alby who did my makeup and made sure I was fed, made me do my homework as she got ready for beauty pageants and flagrant cop searches. I am thankful to my Sick and Disabled Trans and Queer People of Color who lead movements even when they are abandoned or have to be kept in secret to be considered "functional," who cannot afford travel, aren't given the space to travel, you deserve to be here. I do this work for you and for this universe we build to believe that all bodies are valid. All bodies are intrinsic to building a future.

WSQ: Women's Studies Quarterly 51: 3 & 4 (Fall/Winter 2023) © 2023 by Kay Ulanday Barrett.
All rights reserved.

Let's begin with this:

Being exceptional isn't revolutionary, it's lonely. It separates you from your
community. Who are you, really, without community?

—Janet Mock

Fifteen Plus Things I Wish I Knew in College as a Poor-Ass QTPOC from an Immigrant Household (the REMIX)
Originally performed at University of California, Santa Barbara, for the Queer
People of Color Conference

15.
fuck the word "uppity." you do not have to choose any community over
the other, academic, of color, queer, chronically ill, political, mixed, poor,
refugee, transgender, from the hood. if possible, embrace and let them all
live, inform, and complicate one another. You are beyond formula or stan-
dardized confines.

14.
odds are you will be forced to study mostly white, straight, skinny, cisgender, european/anglo, possibly rich people's discourse. read it to read it, to
unlearn it. I know it is so boring. find the work that really calls your skill
and passions. As Calloutqueen, trans femme of color mark aguhar said:
"LOL Reverse Racism."

14.5
when a friend of privilege calls you or intros you as their _____ [insert
race, ethnicity, sexuality, identity here], back fist them. no wait, don't.
hmmm, well maybe. no, don't. talk it out and if that doesn't work out, dump
them.

13.
take advantage of the fancy gym membership if you can. P.S. you are brilliant. You deserve to be here. Don't let anyone question that.

12.

all the "free" food in the cafeteria isn't really free. it's actually money you are going to owe well beyond your diploma plus interest and by then, you'll actually need real free food.

11.

you may wake up late to your classes because you've shacked up with a new lover. don't forget the diploma. studying before sex. hey are you listening to me? STUDYING BEFORE SEX. Yes, yes, examine polyamory, precolonial relationships before monogamy, but seriously?

11.99

we know that queer sex is the shit. always practice safer sex: communication, consent, gloves, dams, condoms, etc. sexy and kinky times is our liberation song from our marrow. Let your bones rattle and tremble with this goodness as long as possible!

11.5

Let's decolonize the cool. Let's not homogenize the hip. What is desirable for you? Who is considered valuable to you? Who gets to be beautiful? Who gets the most likes? I want Black brown fat trans femme disabled wobbly migrant and multilingual justice. As Lourdes Hunter from Trans Women of Color Collective states: "Assimilation was never the goal." What have you bought into that tells you what is hot? Who gets to make it to the party? Who gets to dress all the patterns but never talk about their wealth or class status, but OMG white peopleamiright? Now let that formula carve out who gets resources, who isn't incarcerated/psychiatrized, who can get hormones, who's not a terrorist? who can pay rent, who can gentrify and buy land not their own? who has parents paying their rent? who comes from wealth and elite but tries to represent everybody? who gets to live past thirty?

10.

as professors look to you to speak for your entire people (queer, nonbinary, people of color, asian, disabled people, etc.), and likely, not be able to pronounce your name or misgender you. clench your jaw the way you do to a fist. anything you say here will be misinterpreted. any response you have is genuine.

9.

when you feel uncomfortable/unsafe in either bathroom option, "mens" or "womens," find your nearest queer org or supportive faculty and peers. let them listen to you. do what you can to make the campus more transgender-empowered. This, however, is not your responsibility. Cis people must show up for you. Cis people have power that needs to be not only swayed but arced in your favor. If they are not at your service, they are withholding your autonomy and dreams.

8.5

The call-out, the tweet, the sound bite is only a beginning. Be interested in the relationships, the unsaid, after the conference badges and the protest slogans, ask yourself what is your practice? We can all say "down with the colonial cis straight white heteropatriachy!!!" (or can we?) How do you explain that to your mama? How do you explain that to the Medic- aid worker? To the people who do the actual work of who grows the food, cleans the buildings, holds you when you rock back and forth with the trauma? The sharpest analysis isn't just the Foucault of it. Liberation is a process where no one is left behind, where we show up for one another and if you can't get into the event, can't get access to a safe place to live, if they don't have a ramp for that entrance then we must create something new for each other. Invest in not the gossip or the next big thing, but the time, the source of heartbreak, the pulse that you are missing. In the quiet, lost, miss- ing, and slow places, liberation needs us there.

8.

when your dorm roommate shops at bloomingdales, barney's & co, and gets upset when their dad gets her the hunter green range rover instead of black (like he requested). don't show that you add up the total they've spent on how that would pay your family's food, mortgage, gender affirmation surgery, migration lawyer, how your family/friends don't make that much in annual salary—don't workshop them, you aren't paid for it and you both will just end up staring blankly at one another which will prove awkward when you will both be sharing the same closet, sleeping, and eating space.

7.5

if a classmate in your composition and rhetoric class says, *they shouldn't live in the u.s. if they don't speak english.* run to your homeland tongue(s), read poetry only in this language for an hour, appreciate its curve and girth. Laugh in that language. Cry in that language. Curse in that language. Fuck in that language. fall back into the joyful (even if few) memories before your family were forced or fled. go back to your neighborhood if you can and hear the languages that you grew up with—in the market, at church, over a table of dominoes or mahjong.

7.
chances are that you will be a purveyor of exotic tastes, religion, language, and geography. exotic = ostracized. exotic = scapegoated. exotic = isolated.

6.32
there is a possibility that a classmate or roommate may confuse you as *the help* or as a foreign exchange student. kindly move away and do your homework. tell them off only if you won't let it rot you.

6.18
you are brilliant and you deserve to be here. let no one question that.

6.
your final transcript will not say:
grandpa died your freshman year, hence the incomplete; your girlfriend is abusive and hits you bloodied but enough to hide it, hence the tardiness; you will be considered a hero and a traitor to your family for being educated and for being educated.

5.75
likely, someone will use the words "retard" "slow" or "lame" like a daily uppercut on your existence. likely the elevator will be broken, likely you will be blamed for being late to class for being with limited mobility or can't attend events. Likely, they'll be like, *come run jump hike and have programs only in English, let's stand for four hours!* And that means they don't think of bodies like yours or haven't considered their own ablebodied privilege. They will call on Frida or Harriet as a rally to defy the odds of the POC and women, but ignore their disabled fabulousness. likely being anxious, being a QTPOC surviving in a system that harvests madness without any love for the blooming won't be considered enough. likely people will think your body is broken, your mind is broken, needs to be cured or ignored,

and likely the disability resources center is still stuck in 1967 serving only white people. You are gorgeous. Bless every crack in the bones that makes the music of you. Eat protein. Drink water. Google: disability justice. sick and disabled queers. we are waiting for you.

5.60
take crying breaks. they help, honest.

5.
don't sign up for any credit cards without a good workshop and community awareness on finances.

4.75
take care of yourself financially, holistically, emotionally, and spiritually. take care of your people just the same. There is no competition. There is no epic hero. Nobody can do this life alone. All of us deserve value. ALL are critical for your moving beyond survival, but joyous action.

4.
when the cis liberal gay white people considerately tell you to *just come out* to your family, understand they have no idea what the F*** is going on in your life or how your race/ethnicity/cultures are so different. You know better, your life is not a one-time event! You are an embrace of your cultures and a reimagining. find other queer people of color, elders, and allies (if they even exist where you are) to support you.

3.76
there may be a moment when white people, abled people, american people, straight people will exotify you under the guise of being "radical." You will be their "only," their checkbox to appease their guilt. At night they will say, but we had that one migrant, disabled, transgender person—#diversity. Don't let their delicious potlucks fool you. don't let their small morsels of affirmations confuse you for ongoing tangible change and systemic shifts of power. ignore them at all costs but be civil. they are dangerous. Sometimes they do not know they are dangerous.

3.
you are brilliant and you deserve to be here. let no one question that.

298 QPOC Conference Keynote: UCSB

2.5

reminded of transcestors, here is my alternative next to the above reality:

We have to do it because we can no longer stay invisible. We should not be
ashamed of who we are. We have to show the world that we are numerous.
There are many of us out there.

—Sylvia Rivera

2.29

somewhere there is a mentor, an organization, a department, a club that
thinks you are amazing. That YOU poop gold! That YOU are the next revolutionary, better than your grandma's steamed rice. keep them in your life
for as long as you can. But also make sure they critique you too. Remember
you need someone when the storm is coming and not just when you radi-
ate like the sun. trust: those people will have your back.

2.

grades are the paper of it and you need the grades to play the game. get
good grades, but seek communities committed to work that you are curious about or committed to.

1.

this is a system meant to destroy you. you may lose some of yourself in the
process. understand that is the sacrifice and that you will rebuild some of
yourself too. promise.

Named one of "9 Transgender and Gender Nonconforming Writers You Should Know" by *Vogue*, **Kay Ulanday Barrett** is a poet, essayist, cultural strategist, and A+ napper. They are the winner of the 2022 Cy Twombly Award for Poetry by Foundation for Contemporary Arts, winner of a 2022 Tin House Next Book Residency, and a recipient of a 2020 James Baldwin Fellowship at MacDowell. Their second book, *More Than Organs* (Sibling Rivalry Press, 2020), received a 2021 Stonewall Honor Book Award from the American Library Association and is a 2021 Lambda Literary Award Finalist. They can be reached at info@kaybarrett.net.

PART V. **POETRY**

O Loveland

Ximena Keogh Serrano

Attachments
Such wild, precious, unruly things

Say, for example, this form of attachment—
to   a person
         a country
         a piece of paper

               I laugh at the thought, then note how we just want a place
                                            to be held
                           or a place to be possible

Because humans, like countries, share the principle of naming
as a constituent for being born,
paper participates in the theatre of emergence—
where my body equals letters, spaces, words
which is not to say that the letters, spaces, and words equal my body,
                                        No.

Countries, bodies, paper—all such tragic scenes, ripe
with illusions, texts & pretexts, discipline(d), so ripe
with possibility

No wonder we get attached
We just want a place to be held

Why else would I enter
                       this page?
Having already given up on the others
I am seeking a place
to be possible

WSQ: _Women's Studies Quarterly_ 51: 3 & 4 (Fall/Winter 2023) © 2023 by Ximena Keogh Serrano.
All rights reserved.

Hybridity

Ximena Keogh Serrano

In the 19th century,
the term *Hybrid* becomes the noun used to connote a person of mixed race;
rooted in the botanical and zoological conception of cross-breeding,
Hybrid   does what it says
shifts habitat

Like European colonizers, settling over the Americas
centuries before,
the linguistic sign daggers into dictionaries—
keen to address the biological and cultural spheres of human contact

Contact   such a beautiful word
        that sense of *with-ness*
        so lovely
and yet, how its underside shrivels
perverse

Like when *Contact*
came to denote what emerged
from the arrival of *shitface* to today's so-called America
                [& here, as always, I mean the continent]
Where other names include:
Discovery   Invasion   Creation   Encounter   Disaster

DICED is what we are

                :   :

WSQ: *Women's Studies Quarterly* 51: 3 & 4 (Fall/Winter 2023) © 2023 by Ximena Keogh Serrano.
All rights reserved.

In hybridity
there is always a winning race
through embodiment, the winner surfaces via codes
ascribed to levels of pigmentation

In a family, the possibilities of color are infinitesimal
Hues, like reproductive history, mount across the genealogical pool
& so, symbolic wins and losses shape our so-called human form

   Even as you strive to renounce it
to shame its contemptable construct
Hybridity clings to our skins, to our mouths, to our speech acts
Just as the fabricated scale of *the Great Chain of Being* told us white was
above all,
we believed it
& so our complicity with harm

Mine, came in tiny explosions
barbarous acts

Before I could even name it—
as in that wish for wholeness, that wanting to be that which I was not
I, impure   mix
       For impurity is an element of hybridity
The want drilled a hunter in me

In the fold of an in-between carnal coat
I could be a question
while keeping my mouth closed

In the observation field, I would learn just how
to renounce my Andean lines, cut them cold
so as to ennoble the European switchblade in me

We all become half-experts in the duties of the colonial enterprise
We are so very well trained

I for one have killed so many parts of me,
I can't even remember where I left her

                                                                                                                her

her

Reptile Moves

Ximena Keogh Serrano

I climb outside my body
the way I did when I was fifteen
                              climbing outside our house window
the way I did when I was born
                              climbing out of mamá's belly-home
Now
            again, a fire-y invocation

                              How to return?

This flesh never belonged to me

only echoed outside
life-ruins

            Malleability of skin like test

Witness here
how a soul escapes

To learn from the scenes of a gushing—
what bleeds
from square glass
blade-view

A self,
            budding
into soars
of confetti

WSQ: Women's Studies Quarterly 51: 3 & 4 (Fall/Winter 2023) © 2023 by Ximena Keogh Serrano.
All rights reserved.

Ximena Keogh Serrano is a poet and scholar of Latin American and U.S. Latinx literary and cultural studies. Her research and writing move across genres of literary criticism, visual culture, and studies in gender and sexuality. She is an assistant professor at Pacific University, and lives in Portland, Oregon. She can be reached at xkserrano@ pacificu.edu.

Nocturne with hysterectomy

Kay Ulanday Barrett

how you paused when the nurse said your name, not
your real name, but the one lodged onto your government ID.
where you correct her, slurred and fevered, claim your pain level

is a seven, and she tells you you'll slide into the white cove for
a CT scan. the drip in your veins allot enough energy not to wince.
you hold your breath. they record your pelvis, tell you that everything

will be hot, your toes spark star fire. *don't worry it's temporary*
is a saying you have heard & squint at. are you peeing on yourself?
did the nurse use the wrong pronouns again? you laugh at this new

privilege—how your white nurse will have to pick up after brown piss.
how the rust you make is homegrown, how you can't tell who
is the butcher anymore. your own uterus after all asked to be bent,

did you sling the slaughter? you imagine warmth, the fish roasted by your
mother's hands, how seafood is the joke metaphor between our legs.
after the scalpel, what will you smell like now? never mind this pandemic

how your partner is informed she cannot go any further, she cannot sit
with you in re-wiring, your dizziness lacquered by less organs.
Two weeks before: *emergent.* The report dictated, the field of

your abdomen appeared a rorschach of cells, *both my parents died
of cancer.* You confess this inheritance of blooms. *Ovaries can stay,*
the surgeon repeated. To not cry at the cephalopod shaped clots,

shells of who you once were. To peel back sheets as they contort
colors you didn't know you had in you. To not have the face of anyone
on the pamphlets. To know you are again, your own manual.

WSQ: Women's Studies Quarterly 51: 3 & 4 (Fall/Winter 2023) © 2023 by Kay Ulanday Barrett. All rights reserved.

Mid-day subway: there are no icebreakers or pronouns for this

Kay Ulanday Barrett

For a long time I wanted there to be no barrier between pelvis and the
tectonic plate of my chest. Just open. It's impossible though. My beloved
swoons at my nipples, re-stitched, body a tell-all, body terror. Strangers cull
me on train, even in afternoon, spit out my looks like cherry pits even though
I fold page in some book,

secretly recounting how many steps it takes to get to the exit. I think
about how to make a man's loud slander silence on the prism of my heel. I
breathe in shapes I don't want, my exhale puffed to the circumference of fist
if any one's too close. Three ways I can synthesize jugular, make husk of an
eye. I muster

courage. Proud uncles called me "Black belter" didn't know eventually I
was ready to spar with men who mirrored their drunken haze. I'm familiar
with the sequence of bruised rib turned
cinder dust. Not again. There, I said it. In the name of this
labor let me smile at the sun, finally. In the name of all of us,

no set of teeth sharpened every time we have to cross the street. By the
look of your terse pupils, you woke up sweat drenched
under the starlight thinking it could be sheath too.

You, wishing streetlamp were baton. You were hoping
to dream something buttery soft slick, hoping without
nightmares of pummel, hoping to give the moon a break.

WSQ: Women's Studies Quarterly 51: 3 & 4 (Fall/Winter 2023) © 2023 by Kay Ulanday Barrett. All rights reserved.

A postmortem story or how archaeologists might fail me

after Lourival Bezerra de Sá
after Lady Cao

Kay Ulanday Barrett

More than my femurs will be found sprouting below a lilac bush,
my left front tooth a wavy millimeter, my pelvic bone an avenue
in U turn. Archaeologists might find body a like mine, one like
burnt clay pots, cheekbones compressed by loam. My tibia
long as a brittle bow that once kicked up to the wind.
To argue about my bone-dust before I'm actually dead.

To plot silhouette of my afterlife like video game. Do you think
a schematic of a human is only calcium? Did you know trans
people recognize more than marrow? Did you know this state
or documents could never jot down my plot twists?

Eighty policies introduced in law say trans children can't
play sports, can't mouth truths to doctors. Congress wants
badly to get between our legs, to dictate a child how to run and
what indicates triumph. So obsessed by wonder bread lives
to harangue young and forecast the dead.

Sacrum and tailbone are not some confetti. Trans people on
Reddit make psalm on keyboards, obliterate possible pencils
from our bones. One said he'd *rather swallow flames,*
his sinew turned soot so archaeologists don't fumble pronouns
even after we've become our own blossoms full of blood.

I do not blame them. When I'm dead, maybe I'll drift to
the sea. My shoulder blade blushed with anemone, my
collarbone filaments swerved on rising tide by some bashful
lovers at sunset. A constellation of quiet carrion nestled in
the blushing shimmer of a wave.

One will say to the other: *Hey, do you see that sky?*
I made that for you and by then we will all know that trans
is in everything, so continuous.

It's silly to wage our wakes at top speed. Trans people
have always been interstellar, becoming upturned comets
when banished in outpatient psych wards, family
reunions, a junior high history book.

Of course this is all speculation; lament for a future
only maybe habitable. As this hot hot earth is turned into
a corporation, fahrenheit slaughters bird lungs at border
walls, deer droughts next to your patrol brick, but the
concern, hundreds of years after I'm long gone—
if I'm only male or female?

Let's be honest you aren't ready for the future. Won't
have energy to dream up my bones. You can hardly
even pronounce the piss of me in the next stall.

Named one of "9 Transgender and Gender Nonconforming Writers You Should Know" by *Vogue*, **Kay Ulanday Barrett** is a poet, essayist, cultural strategist, and A+ napper. They are the winner of the 2022 Cy Twombly Award for Poetry by Foundation for Contemporary Arts, winner of a 2022 Tin House Next Book Residency, and a recipient of a 2020 James Baldwin Fellowship at MacDowell. Their second book, *More Than Organs* (Sibling Rivalry Press, 2020), received a 2021 Stonewall Honor Book Award from the American Library Association and is a 2021 Lambda Literary Award Finalist. They can be reached at info@kaybarrett.net.

PART VI. **ALERTS AND PROVOCATIONS**

NB-ous: On the Coalitional Drive of the Nonbinary

Marquis Bey

The aim here is not to give an incessantly clear definition of nonbinariness, such that we would then have an "accurate" or "correct" definition. Indeed, this impulse—to clarify pristinely, to excavate etymological roots in order for a term to be illuminated once and for all, obviating misuse—is one I have long had, and I feel its tugs now. But that will not save nonbinariness from misuse or misunderstanding. There is in fact something in nonbinariness that refuses this impulse, it seems—something that has long asserted that *even if* this or that meant X (or shall we say "Q" or whatever other non-X/Y letter so as not to imply gender- and sex-laden allusions) in its supposed origins, in its etymological DNA, as it were, it does not mean that it must be that now, true-bluely. Because what is nonbinariness if not to say, to demand, that yeah, *maybe* I *was* Q when I was young, and even when I started to get older, but I am not that now. And do not have to be. And do not wish to be.

Like Beans Velocci, who I have met briefly, on a brisk evening in Philadelphia (my hometown) in a heated restaurant tent enjoying food and company and intellectuality, I was made trans. Not, as with Velocci, by Foucault—although he is a supplemental culprit, just not the primary actor—but by other things. In my case, by suggestions and experiences and drives and, too, cartoons. I speak to this in my book *Cistem Failure: Essays on Blackness and Cisgender*, where I detail across multiple essays the ways that *Dragonball Z* or *The Powerpuff Girls* were sites of imaginative inhabitation, where what was extant in my world did not have to be all of the possibilities for myself; the ways this movement of a hand or rejection of a space or unfitness within a community were sites of exquisite rebellion and testament to how we could move differently, think differently, en- and ungender differently in proximity to unsanctioned imaginaries. I came to my nonbinariness

WSQ: Women's Studies Quarterly 51: 3 & 4 (Fall/Winter 2023)

by way of a double refusal: I was refused entry into this or that space, this or that modality, expected as it was and predicated on criteria far less attractive to me than most; but, too, I refused those spaces in tiny, muted ways. They did not want me, at least as I wished to be and become, and I did not want them—there was, in short, "a throwing up of hands and an embrace of the refusal that was the term nonbinary" (Velocci 2022, 476). I love this refusal, a term I have returned to over and over, to the point of exhaustion now, it feels to me, but a term that continues to emerge for its utility, its depth, its feeling of *Yes, that's it.* Because it is in that refusal, or whatever one wishes to call it—I hope it is clear that I am not too hung up on the words one uses, as long as they allow you, us, to do and be and reach for the thing we are working toward—that something is going on. That is, very often it seems that much of the scholarship or the activism out there tries to explain the extant categorizations, making them seem softer, more natural, more workable, kinder, but nevertheless, still there. Always such an equalizing of "men" and "women," or making more palatable masculinity ("Men are allowed to cry! That will solve everything," or some such quip), or if only we found instances of homosexuality "in nature" then all the homophobes would realize they were wrong, or just be comfortable with your gender expression. The list elaborates ad infinitum. In all of this, "The focus ... [i]s not, for the most part, liberation *from* sex and gender so much as an effort to explain these categories' construction," Velocci goes on to say (477). This is frustrating, not so much because of the violence an insistence on the gender binary might cause, though that is nothing at which to scoff, but because of the stubbornness in not wishing to push, to take another step, to say it is not simply about making these orders a little easier on us but *refusing the system* tout court. I need us to go there.

Coalitional is a term given to, in my view, a more mature, robust togetherness than something like community. Surely this is not to malign community, only to think alongside this term to see what is more and less possible when moving through it. For the purposes of this meditation, the coalitional indexes a kind of pulsing being-and-becoming-with without presumption, beautifully monstrously open to any and every being, without criteria, only desiring and knowing that being-with will do something, move something, allow for the coalition to emerge and expand. In this is that which the nonbinary, or nonbinariness, might texturize: rather than an individualistic me-ness concerned with how I don't fit gender, nonbinariness can be figured, possibly, in this instance, as precisely a way to decline the very imposition of gender as a requisite for sociality. Insofar as the nonbinary indexes not a "new" type of gender but a refusal of its imposition, it expands the ambit through which the term and its effects are understood: if it is not about getting exactly correct what my gender is and how I am uniquely (not) gendered and is instead about how gender itself is a bad scene that misnames us all, we come to a different understanding of not just ourselves but all of us, which then permits another way of considering how we wish to be together. Indeed, there are so many ways that gender's circulation and imposition *dis*allow our being-together in certain ways, in ways unsanctioned—which is to say, being in coalition—so to decline gender as an organizing apparatus, which is further to say to understand the nonbinary as a *dis*organizing nega-apparatus, is what is meant by its coalitional drive.

It is because, and I have long timidly thought this, gender is not the thing we think we want it to be. We want gender to be, and very often think gender is, the thing that will free us or make us whole. If only I can spin and fluff gender in this new precise way, then I'll be seen by it and, thus, seen by others. For sure, that is sensible. That feels so real, and it is, I know. There are so many that feel, of course, seen by binary gender, such that it never even occurs to them as a thought to have. Gender feels so central to many of our transgender kinfolk who go through hellish medico-juridical, not to mention interpersonal and social, terrains to feel affirmed in their departures from perinatal assignations of gender. Gender *feels* like the thing. It does, it really does.

But, I promise you, it is not the thing.[1] It is never the case that I "am" nonbinary, though the pronouns I currently use are "they/them" and I talk about "my" nonbinariness. The aim has never really been to be or achieve nonbinariness, of course. Though I wonder, even if I feel such a statement's sensibility, if many would flinch at or view critically others who say that they "are" nonbinary. I fear many would not, making the sensibility with which my remarks here are received slightly suspect. I "am" not nonbinary; for me, and for how I conceptualize nonbinariness—where the suffixive "-ness," as a marker of a state of being, a nounifier, as it were, might belie precisely the mobility and unfixedness I wish to imbue in it—nonbinariness is a matter of how I seek to emerge onto, and even away from, the scene of sociality. It is not a state of being; it is a radicalization of the terms under which subjectivity can express and unexpress, be read and unread, be done and undone.

Curious, then, it is that between "cis" and "nonbinary" I, personally, underwent few, if any, corporeal interventions. It is an open question, interestingly interrogative *because* of its openness, if I ever "was" "cis"—we have reams of pages, some of which I have written, devoted to the ways that blackness uproots the constitutive ligaments of coherent cisness, for example—but nevertheless, one wonders about nonbinariness's legitimacy when there seems to be no set external, corporeal criteria for it. In other words, what even is nonbinariness when a purportedly previously cis dude can now, with the mere designation from "his" lips, be nonbinary? It is this seeming paradox in which I nestle this meditation on nonbinariness precisely in the immeasurability of criteria. Depriving the corporeal surface of legitimate finality on one's validity as a certain gender is a substantive node of what is driven at here; another node is the call nonbinariness inflects: that gender is to be discontented with, thus leading to a decided unobsession with the presumption that a certain body can ever be a metric for assessing the extent to which someone "is" a certain gender, that nonbinariness is, effectively, a "noping" out of gender proper *as well as gender as a vector through which one is to be read.* I have on a variety of occasions known to me, and I'm sure many more occasions not known to me, been viewed askance because I did not "look" nonbinary. There have been a few (well, a couple) occasions in which I was either disallowed nonbinariness or, if allowed it as a self-identification (how generous), which is not quite the correct way to pose the relationship, was made to concede the "fact" of my male privilege, which is in effect to bring gender, forcefully and without recourse to criticality, to the very subject who sees gender itself as a violence and attempts, radically, to depart from gender's violence. (And no, I don't really care about the "material consequences" of privilege. Believe me, I know this discourse and I have been asked about this many, many times. I know those who ask rarely mean harm. But honestly, I'm a little tired of talking about it, so hopefully this[2] suffices.)

A friend of mine, so very dear to me, shared a marvelously interesting characterization of how they came to their agender. We sat in a restaurant in New Orleans, where the doors were floor to ceiling and the waitstaff called us *baby* in that New Orleanian accent that gives the word the francophonic air of *bebé.* There were three of us, in intimate, radical conversation. This friend never quite got all the way to "nonbinary." Only maybe 75 percent, something not lining up in the end. And then, agender, as a nongender nondescription, resolved the missing 25 percent. As I listened, gleefully and enraptured, I found myself knowing that other enbies might say, "No, you misunderstand," attempting to mutedly proselytize about the salvation that is nonbinary *identification*. But that's the thing, my friend was not looking, it seems, for a "correct" identification per se, not some way to "fit" neatly. What was being yearned for was a way to not fit, to float—not needing to be any particular thing yet being able to be any and every thing and any and every nothing. I felt no defensiveness, blessedly, because we were not in different camps, not on different teams vying for validity and recognition. Right now, for these reasons, where you (dis)locate yourself with *dis*respect to gender is in the orbit of agender. Right now, for these reasons, I am in the orbit of nonbinary. But how incredible it is that even as I write this, the "you" and "I" begin to dissolve; your agender which is not yours and my nonbinariness which is not mine are dancing right now, entwined in a beautiful entanglement. They are not their own but given to one another, lovingly. Sure, there is something in nonbinary that does not get all the way there for you, and there is something in agender that does not get all the way there for me, but how glorious, yes, that they move because the other moves, are there because they have another with whom to dance.

Because it is not about the term. It is about that dance, that entanglement. These words, as serious as they are—and I know how important words are, as one trained in literature—are also, perhaps more fundamentally, playful. They are, we might say, generatively, toys:

> With my kids, most of what they do with toys is turn them into props. They are constantly involved in this massive project of pretending. And the toys that they have are props for their pretending. They don't play with them the right way—a sword is what you hit a ball with and a bat is what you make music with. I feel that way about these terms. In the end what's most important is that the thing is put in play. What's most important about play is the interaction. One time we were driving in the car and my kids were playing this game called "family," and it's basically that they've created an alternative family and they just talk about what the alternative family is doing. This time, when they had really started enjoying the game, my eldest son looked at me, I could see him through the rearview mirror, and he said, "dad, we have a box, and we're going to let you open this box, and if you open the box, you can enter into our world." That's kind of what it feels like: there are these props, these toys, and if you pick them up you can move into some new thinking and into a new set of relations, a new way of being together, thinking together. In the end, it's the new way of being together and thinking together that's important, and not the tool, not the prop. Or, the prop is important only insofar as it allows you to enter; but once you're there,

it's the relation and the activity that's really what you want to emphasize. (Harney and Moten, 105–6)

Maybe I'm using "nonbinary" in improper ways, and maybe my friend is using "agender" in improper ways. Or maybe there was a misuse of the term *nonbinary*. But that's of no matter. Why care about the toy any of us are playing with, as long as we like the noise it makes, the joy it brings; indeed, why care about the toy itself, as a toy, when what is happening is something that far exceeds the toy? The toy is not the thing.

The toy you used, dear friend, was agender, and I used nonbinary. We played and continue to play with these toys. But we are here, and we got here, wherever that is, with these different toys. The toys themselves are not the important thing; it is that we are here. Together. Because of the toys, sure, but now—what toys? We are already here, together.

Marquis Bey is professor of black studies and gender and sexuality studies, as well as affiliate faculty in English and critical theory, at Northwestern University. They are the author, most recently, of *Black Trans Feminism* and *Cistem Failure: Essays on Blackness and Cisgender* (both Duke University Press, 2022). Currently, they are working on a three-volume collection of essays concerning "jailbreaking" gender, race, and class. Contact them at marquis.bey@northwestern.edu.

Notes

1. I absolutely must shout-out two wonderful, wonderful thinkers—Madeleine and Mustafa, M and M—for introducing me to this formulation, albeit in a slightly different context (the context of the "body"). Thank you both for gifting me language for this mode of thinking. I find myself using it often now—gender is not the thing, the body is not the thing. Few things, here and now, are ever the thing.

2. Okay, here we go. I'll reproduce what I've said before, on two occasions. First, in a conversation with a friend and fellow philosophically trans thinker, who happens to be absolutely brilliant and one of the kindest people I've met. In that conversation, I say:

   I have also, however, encountered many—even in purportedly radical and social justice spaces—who tell me that I have "male" privilege. So when I show up to the meeting for social justice doers with the ways my body presents itself, despite my nonbinariness and refusal of gender normativity's hold over me, there is a discourse present that demands I not only reckon with but *accept* and *reiterate*

male-masculine privilege as an ethical gesture. They say that someone who looks like I do must acknowledge the reality of how my
body accrues benefits bestowed by patriarchy. And if I do not acknowledge this, I wrongly try to rebuke the privileges I undoubtedly,
unceasingly, always and forever, have. I fail to check my privilege. I
know, I think, what they mean, and I know the kinds of politics and
discourses from which they draw. It seems too often, though, that the
requisite to acknowledge and check is in fact a requisite to content
myself with the existing order as if it is natural, as if nothing can—nor
should—be done about it. It seems often that they want me to *be* a
man. And how cruel is that, how violent, to me and others. In a sly
undermining of the political valence and intention of nonbinariness
(e.g., to subvert, interrogate, and displace the assumption that a body
means something a priori and that gender can be assumed by making recourse to the corporeal surface), I am called to deem and make
myself, over and over, a legible man in a perverse commitment to
gendered ethics.

This is me living on another terrain, fiercely and committedly, yet
others demanding that I live on their terrain. I just want to live elsewhere, right here. (Desloover and Bey, forthcoming)

Secondly, I've written this in a chapter on nonbinariness:

I am concerned with how the assertion of a legible gender at times
acts as a coerced capitulation that forecloses a radical alternative possibility in favor of requisites that one must "fess up"—to their privileges, to their physicality—as an ethical gesture. What becomes the
primary point of interest for the occasion of this chapter is the radical
assertion of gender's refusal as one's (non)gender and the effects that
inhere therein. (Bey, forthcoming)

Apologies for the long self-quotations, but as I've said, I've encountered
this and written about and talked about this before, and I'm a little tired. I
hope that's okay. It's just exhausting, you know? To have to constantly talk
about privilege and material realities and the like when you're actually over
here unconcerned with "reality" and trying to float around wholly outside
of such regimes. Like, can we imagine vaster, grander things instead of, yet
again, making recourse to privilege privilege privilege? How does that ever
get us to imagine and live something else? Spoiler alert: it doesn't.

Works Cited

Bey, Marquis. Forthcoming. "Faceless: Non-confessions of a Gender." In
Feminism against Cisness. Durham, NC: Duke University Press.

Desloover, Elyx, and Marquis Bey. Forthcoming. "Playing and Hiding Joyfully in the Rubble: Thinking with Marquis Bey on Black Trans Feminism." *Social Text.*

Harney, Stefano, and Fred Moten. 2013. *The Undercommons: Fugitive Planning and Black Study.* Wivenhoe: Minor Compositions.

Velocci, Beans. 2022. "Wrenching Torque: On Being Professionally Nonbinary." *Historical Studies in the Natural Sciences* 52 (3): 476–84.